New Series Edited by Eric Blom

BIZET

Carjat

GEORGES BIZET, AGED ABOUT THIRTY-FIVE

BIZET

by

WINTON DEAN

Illustrated

London   J. M. Dent and Sons Ltd.

J. M. DENT & SONS LTD.
Aldine House · Bedford St. · London

Made in Great Britain
by
The Temple Press · Letchworth · Herts.
First published 1948

PREFACE

THOSE who have written books on Bizet, especially in France, have usually found themselves generating moral indignation on a large scale, either against the treatment the composer received in his life-time, or against the height of his posthumous reputation. To such an extent has he become a battle-ground that it is still difficult to approach him with the level tread of a historian; for both parties have suppressed or distorted the facts that did not suit their case. In fact no biography of Bizet has yet been written that is reasonably full, reasonably fair and reasonably accurate; and no biographer has carried his research so far as to establish such elementary facts as the Christian name of his mother and the address where he was born, or to give a full catalogue of even his published works, and still less to list or comment on the vast pile of unpublished material in the Paris Conservatoire Library. Pigot's life, the first and still the fullest, is vitiated by its adoring and uncritical tone; there is much too much of *le jeune maître*. Gauthier-Villars's acid study, hitherto accepted as the standard for modern purposes, is not only so biased as to be valueless as criticism, but by its manipulation and omission of important facts almost qualifies as a masterpiece of misrepresentation. Landormy, making no attempt to relate Bizet to his period, gives a totally false impression of the man, his music and his times. Nor has much been done to right this picture. By far the most sensitive study is Edgar Istel's *Bizet und Carmen*, but that is largely devoted to a close examination of a single work. Adolf Weissmann's book is fair and accurate, but too slight—an exceptional fault in a German critic. France still owes Bizet the compliment of a critical study. Her best is still that of Camille Bellaigue written in the eighties, though Combarieu's acute chapter in his *Histoire de la Musique* deserves notice.

Hence more inaccurate statements are in circulation about Bizet than about any composer of equal standing. It is too much to hope that all errors have been eradicated in the present book, but I have attempted to trace and check the source of every statement of fact. I must plead the complete absence of a reliable authority to which reference can be made as an excuse for the apparently excessive detail of the biographical chapters. But it seemed worth while to collect as much as possible of the evidence bearing on such matters as the projected and unfinished operas, and at the same time to look into the background against which Bizet worked, neither of these fields having received anything but the most perfunctory treatment. Most of the fresh biographical matter is the result of searching printed sources, some of which (e.g. the important Bizet number of the *Revue de Musicologie* of November 1938) have become available only in the last ten years; but I have consulted a number of unpublished letters in the libraries of the Opéra and Conservatoire in Paris and found a great deal of biographical as well as critical interest in the musical manuscripts at the Conservatoire. Some of these were roughly summarized by Jean Chantavoine in *Le Ménestrel* in 1933, but a great deal is virgin ground. In addition it has often been possible to base new conclusions on information that has been available for many years (e.g. on the reason for Bizet's withdrawal of *La Guzla de l'Émir* and the breaking of his engagement to Geneviève Halévy). The vocal score of *Noé* reveals that much more of this opera than has ever been supposed is Bizet's work; while I have been able to throw light on the vexed question of Bizet's intentions with regard to the timing of Carmen's murder (as well as on various other matters) by examining the original manuscript of the opera.

In the course of my work I have received generous help from many people. Those to whom I am most indebted are the librarian and staff of the Paris Conservatoire Library for their patience and helpfulness; Mr. Paul Hirsch, who allowed me to borrow many volumes from his library, now happily the property of the nation; Dr. Alfred Loewenberg; Professor J. B. Trend; Mr. Ellis Gummer; Dr. R. S. Thatcher, who gave me access to the operatic full scores in the Angelina Goetz collection at the Royal Academy of Music; M. Jean Cordey of the Opéra Library in Paris, who allowed me to reproduce three illustrations from the catalogue of the 1938 Bizet Exhibition (facing pages 55, 185, and 212); Mme Élie Halévy, who allowed me to reproduce the portrait of Bizet by Giacometti (facing page 20); and particularly Mr. Philip Radcliffe for a seemingly inexhaustible flow of criticism and suggestion. I also thank the editors of *The Music Review* and *Music & Letters* for permission to use matter that has already appeared in their pages.

W. D.

June 1947.

CONTENTS

ILLUSTRATIONS

CHAPTER I

CHILDHOOD AND TRAINING (1838–57)

ON 25th October 1838, at 26 Rue de la Tour d'Auvergne, Paris, a son was born to the wife of one Adolphe Armand Bizet, a worthy but humble musician, and registered under the formidable designation Alexandre César Léopold. It seems that the operative name was intended to be César, for one of his Conservatoire compositions is signed 'César Georges Bizet, known as Potin' (Gossip). But the imperial *praenomen* was too much for the child's godfather, who at once called him Georges; as Georges he was baptized on 16th March 1840 at the church of Notre-Dame-de-Lorette; and as Georges he was always known, first to his family and friends and later to the world. His godparents were Philippe Louis Brulley de la Brunière and Hippolyte Sidonie Daspres. The Rue de la Tour d'Auvergne runs almost due east and west about half way between the Gares de l'Est and Saint-Lazare on the southern slopes of Montmartre. By 1840 the family had moved two doors along to No. 22, and Bizet continued to live in the district for the whole of his Paris life.

Adolphe Bizet (born 10th August 1810, died 19th December 1886), who like Schubert's father survived his famous son by some years, was a teacher of singing. According to Louis Gallet he was of lowly working-class origin and had begun to study music only at the age of twenty-five. He seems to have been an industrious man without any notable talent. His favourite pupil, Hector Gruyer, was cast to create the part of Faust in Gounod's opera, but, as Gounod tells us, 'despite a charming voice and a very agreeable presence he could not sustain the burden of this important role,' and had to be replaced.[1] This was a great blow to the Bizets, and caused a temporary estrangement between Georges and Gounod. Adolphe Bizet also composed on a small scale: a bundle of his

[1] He sang the part only four times in the middle of the run, having missed the earlier performances through illness. He subsequently sang in Italian opera-houses under the name of Guardi and died at an advanced age, a chevalier of the Legion of Honour, in January 1908.

manuscripts, mostly dedicated to his son and Gruyer, is preserved at the Conservatoire. They include a cantata *Imogine*, a string Quartet (dated 1st February 1853), songs, fugues, piano works and two fantasies for military band on themes from Halévy's *La Reine de Chypre*. At least one of his songs was published in 1854. In his later years he developed a passion for gardening, and meal-time conversation at his house at Le Vésinet was divided between music and vegetables. A photograph shows him as a sturdy old man with a white spade-shaped beard.

Of Bizet's mother (1814–61) we know less. She was Aimée Léopoldine Joséphine Delsarte (the name is sometimes spelt del Sarte, and even Delzart, in which form it appears in the church register at Georges's baptism), and came of a musical family. Her elder brother,[1] François Alexandre Nicolas Chéri Delsarte (1811–1871), was a well-known teacher of singing with many successful and fashionable pupils, one of whom in 1859 published a treatise on his method. He seems to have been both gifted and eccentric. He studied physiology, anatomy and psychology, and applied their principles to his work. He abandoned a job at the Théâtre des Variétés to become a Saint-Simonian and later studied for the Church. At his concerts he was instrumental in reviving the works of Lully, Rameau and Gluck, and he edited a volume, *Les Archives du chant*, in so scrupulous a manner that he not only refused to put a personal gloss on this old music but even reproduced misprints (or what the nineteenth century took to be misprints) in the original editions. He finally abjured the world and gave himself up to speculation on philosophy and aesthetics. Aimée Bizet was herself a talented pianist, and according to Ludovic Halévy a woman of the highest intelligence. From her son's letters she emerges as a homely affectionate person, troubled by chronic ill-health and a great capacity for worrying over the welfare of her nearest and dearest. She had continually to be reassured that her son was running no needless risk in Italy. There is no truth in the statement, sometimes heard, that Bizet had Jewish blood, but a member of the Delsarte

[1] Not her brother-in-law, as is often stated. Many of these facts are here collected for the first time. Only one of Bizet's biographers gives the Christian name of his mother—and he gives it wrongly.

family has claimed [1] that there was a Spanish strain, deriving from a surgeon in the army of Charles V who settled in Flanders.

Georges had the advantage of growing up in a musical home. He seems to have been an only child, though one of his father's manuscripts is dedicated 'à ma petite fille.' Who this 'grand-daughter' was is not known; Georges himself had only a son. At the age of four he learned his notes from his mother at the same time as his letters. He early formed the habit of listening to his father's lessons through the door. Thus when at the age of eight he was called in and given a piece to sing at sight, he astonished his father by singing it correctly without looking at the music. Thus early did he show signs of that prodigious musical memory which served him so well in later years, but in one sense served the world so ill: for he took to the grave at least one opera which he had completely composed but not bothered to write out in full. From the first Adolphe Bizet intended his son to be a composer. Perhaps through having made a late start himself, he was determined to lose no time, and now set about teaching him the piano and the rudiments of harmony. This enthusiasm for long-term planning nearly miscarried, for Georges was at first more strongly attracted to literature than to music, and his parents even had to hide his books to prevent his reading when he should have been working at his music. Bizet never lost his love of literature and at his death left a large and varied library. The notion sedulously fostered by certain French critics that he had no general culture outside music is quite ludicrously wide of the mark. He was one of the liveliest letter-writers among the leading composers.

At the age of nine he had learned all his father could impart, which was doubtless little enough. Steps were then taken to send him to the Conservatoire. He was not yet old enough to enter, but, hoping for a special dispensation in view of his precocity, Adolphe Bizet enlisted the support of a friend at the Opéra, and together they went to see Meifred, a famous horn virtuoso and a member of the Committee of Studies at the Conservatoire. An interview was arranged and began inauspiciously. Meifred was contemptuous:

[1] *Revue de Musicologie*, November 1938.

'Your child is very young.' 'True,' replied the proud father calmly, 'but if he is small in stature he is big in knowledge.' 'Really? And what can he do?' 'Sit down at the piano, strike some chords, and he will name them without a mistake.' Meifred did as suggested, and the boy, with his back to the piano, not only named the most recondite chords that Meifred could play, but elaborated in detail all their functions. Meifred was enthusiastic: 'You, my boy—you're going straight to the Institut!' In fact, however, the Conservatoire classes were already full; so, until a regular place was available, he was sent to Marmontel's piano class on the introduction of his uncle Delsarte. At this time he was able to play Mozart's piano sonatas with taste and without affectation. On 9th October 1848, just before the completion of his tenth year, he was officially admitted to the Conservatoire in the splendour of his full Christian names.

Something must be said here on the question of his precocity. The Meifred anecdote, of course, proves nothing beyond a good memory and a quick ear; it implies no artistic ability (who but a fool would look for this in a boy of nine?). Adolphe Bizet's not unnatural pride, together with the over-adulatory tone of Bizet's first biographer, Charles Pigot, provoked a certain school of criticism, led by H. Gauthier-Villars, to deny in withering terms the legend of Bizet's precocity as a young man and to allow him nothing but a mere text-book competence. These critics pointed to the lack of evidence behind the legend; they failed to observe the equal lack of evidence against it, and they were duly confounded by the recent discovery of the Symphony in C major, written at the age of barely seventeen, which reveals not only sure technical ability but signs of a natural genius perhaps never exceeded by a composer of Bizet's years, Mozart, Schubert and Mendelssohn not excepted. There can be no doubt that Bizet as a child showed quite exceptional gifts, both of assimilation and, as time went on, of creation also. His teachers were perfectly aware of this: when he was sixteen Halévy said of him: 'There is a great musician.' Marmontel was struck by the individuality of his views and preferences, which he sensibly encouraged, as well as by his steady perseverance. He described him in youth as fair and pink, with a rather plump but very alert face. As he grew up his features strengthened and took on that appearance

4

of energy and sincerity, not untouched by irony, that can be seen in his portraits. He was very short-sighted and habitually wore spectacles. His most prominent feature was a mass of fair curly hair, later supplemented by an ample beard.

Six months after his admission Bizet won the first prize for solfeggio. He was then introduced to Zimmerman, at the latter's request, and joined his fugue and counterpoint class. Pierre Joseph Guillaume Zimmerman was an old man and on the point of retiring; but he had a real love of teaching, and although he had already given up his regular fugue and counterpoint class he still kept a few special pupils. He had been a pupil of Cherubini, who was regarded as the leading contrapuntist of his period and, by Beethoven among others, as one of its greatest composers. It was this tradition that young Bizet imbibed. When Zimmerman was ill, which was often, his place was taken by his son-in-law Charles Gounod, whose first opera, *Sapho*, had recently been produced. Gounod took an immediate liking to the boy, who in return conceived an admiration for Gounod, both as man and artist, which, though modified in later years, left a permanent mark on his style. In 1856 he arranged Gounod's Symphony in D major for piano duet.

In 1851, the first time he competed, Bizet won the second prize in Marmontel's piano class; in the following year he shared the first prize with one Savary. Of his skill as a pianist there were no two opinions. Marmontel, himself a brilliant performer and a very successful trainer of others, paid ample tribute to his gifts; so did Berlioz, Liszt and indeed every one who heard him. In his Conservatoire days he had not developed that delicacy and mellow touch that characterized his playing later, but he was already a brilliant virtuoso. At all times he showed extraordinary skill at playing from full scores. From Marmontel he passed to Benoist's organ class. Benoist,[1] according to Saint-Saëns, was a very ordinary organist but an admirable teacher and was much loved by his pupils. He was employed by the Opéra for writing ballets, which he used to score in his class while his pupils played the organ (it is said that this in no way interfered with his teaching) and for putting life into the

[1] He was organ professor at the Conservatoire for more than half a century. Both he and Marmontel outlived Bizet.

scoring of other people's works: his clarinet parts to Sacchini's *Œedipe à Colone* earned warm praise from Berlioz for the Italian composer. Again Bizet was quick to learn: in 1854 he won second prizes for organ and fugue, in the following year first prizes for both. Meanwhile on Zimmerman's death in 1853 he had entered Halévy's composition class. Jacques François Fromental Élie Halévy was an important figure both in French music and in Bizet's life. A Jew (his real name was Lévy, but like Meyerbeer and Reyer he preferred to take the fashionable course of lengthening it), he was a prolific composer of operas in various styles. As a composer he had (like his master Cherubini) little lyrical gift, but on occasion a powerful sense of the stage, and it is not surprising that in his serious operas he fell more and more under the influence of Meyerbeer. As a teacher he seems to have been indulgent to a fault. He was often so absorbed in his work that he forgot to turn up for his classes, when his pupils took it upon themselves to give each other instruction far less indulgent than their master's. As a man he was indolent, good-natured and charming; consequently he was continually bothered by self-seekers, impossible tenors and would-be artists of every description. Bizet had a high respect for his character and talents, and was on intimate terms with his family. His brother, Léon Halévy, archaeologist and dramatist, and Léon's better-known son Ludovic, were both among Bizet's librettists, and in later years he was to enter still closer into the family circle by marrying Fromental Halévy's daughter. His father-in-law's influence on his musical style cannot be compared with that of Gounod, a much more individual composer. Halévy's style, like Meyerbeer's, was eclectic; his music often sounds like Weber without the tunes; but it is possible that the marked eclecticism of Bizet's early works owes something to this source.

A number of Bizet's student compositions are preserved in manuscript at the Conservatoire library. These consist mostly of piano works and fragments of cantatas that had been set as exercises for earlier Prix de Rome competitions. The earliest, two Songs without Words for soprano voices, date from the boy's twelfth year. Rather more ambitious efforts followed: *Grande Valse de Concert* (Op. 1), a brilliant piece in the superficial style of contemporary salon music with one theme that very remotely anticipates the trio of the Minuet in *L'Arlésienne*, and *Premier Nocturne en fa majeur* (Op. 2), both for piano, and dating from September 1854; *Première Ouverture pour orchestre*, a lively piece showing strong Italian influence; and, in 1855, *Première Symphonie*. This last is the delightful work in C major, first performed under Weingartner in 1935. We know nothing of the circumstances of its composition, except that it was begun on 29th October 1855, four days after his seventeenth birthday, and finished before the end of the following month: Bizet was already an expeditious worker. With the exception of two songs published in 1854, it is the only work written before Bizet's sojourn in Rome that has been either published or publicly performed within living memory.[1] There is no truth in the statement made by Octave Séré, repeated in the third edition of Grove's *Dictionary*, that a one-act operetta by Bizet called *La Prêtresse* was produced at Baden in 1854.

Exactly a month before Bizet began his Symphony, Halévy recommended him to the director of the Opéra-Comique as 'a young composer, pianist and accompanist.' Perhaps he served the Opéra-Comique in some humble capacity at this time (if so, it is his first known connection with the theatre). At any rate, he was already marked out for future success. As early as 1853 Halévy had declared him fit to compete for the Prix de Rome, the highest honour that France could confer on her young artists. But Bizet prudently abstained till 1856. The set piece for the Prix de Rome was always a cantata on some edifying subject drawn from the Bible, ancient history or the age of chivalry. The text for 1856 was *David*, by Mlle de Montréal, who wrote under the pseudonym of Gaston d'Albano. Gounod, taking a very fatherly tone, advised Bizet not to be in too much of a hurry, not to seize the first idea that came into his head under the impression that it would be the only one, to be self-critical and not to work at night, since night work usually had to be done over again in the morning. The judges deliberated for a long time. Eventually they decided to give no first prize, but

[1] Some of these early unpublished works, and others of later date, were performed at a meeting of the Société Française de Musicologie on 27th October 1938, in honour of the centenary of Bizet's birth.

Bizet was awarded a second prize, which did not entitle him to the Rome subsidy. He may possibly have been kept back because of his youth (the same fate would have befallen Paladilhe a few years later, had not Berlioz pointed out with tart logic that the prize was given for talent, not age).

Between his first and second attempts at the Prix de Rome Bizet wrote his first stage work.[1] Offenbach, in whom the fashionable Paris of the Second Empire already liked to see its glittering reflection, now offered a prize for a one-act operetta, the winning work to be produced at the Bouffes-Parisiens theatre. Hoping to see operetta admitted to musical respectability, he acquired a formidable jury headed by Auber, Halévy, Thomas and Gounod. The libretto was *Le Docteur Miracle* by Léon Battu and Ludovic Halévy, the latter of whom was one day to collaborate with Bizet in a work of very different calibre. Bizet, perhaps glad of a change from fugues and cantatas, wrote his score very rapidly, and the prize (for which there were seventy-eight candidates) was divided between him and Charles Lecocq, his colleague in Halévy's class but his senior by several years. Lecocq continued in the same vein, and spent the rest of a long life turning out a stream of operettas, of which only one, *La Fille de Madame Angot*, achieved lasting popularity. It was considered impossible or inadvisable to mount both operettas in the same programme, and so they were produced on succeeding nights; Lecocq's on 8th April 1857, Bizet's on the 9th. The work received little attention, which is not surprising: serious musicians regarded operetta as a very debased form, much as they regard musical comedy to-day. Bizet's 'omelette quartet,' however, was praised, and other promises of talent were detected here and there.

Two prizes were offered by the Prix de Rome committee for 1857. The winner, the laureate of the year, would get the full five-years' pension; the runner-up, to whom would go the previous year's prize, would have only the four years' pension that remained, a nice economy being thus exercised in favour of the State. The cantata set was *Clovis et Clotilde* by one Amédée Burion; the text so charmed

[1] Not counting the very early one-act *opéra-comique, La Maison du docteur*, probably written for private performance among his colleagues at the Conservatoire.

Gounod that he told Bizet he would like to have entered himself. Again the judges found difficulty in making their award. In the first announcement the musical section of the Académie des Beaux Arts gave the first prize to Charles Colin (later oboe professor at the Conservatoire; died 1881), the second to Bizet. On the following day the full Academy confirmed the names of the winners, but reversed the order. Bizet had reached his first major goal, having experienced scarcely a check. After a brilliant Conservatoire career he had won the highest academic honour open to a young musician. But it was no more than the first step. It entitled him to few advantages after his five years' pension was over; it was of little help, as many former winners had found to their cost, in getting his works performed; still less did it guarantee a favourable reception from the public. As Gounod wrote in his letter of congratulation (5th July 1857): 'Now your real artistic life is going to begin—a serious and severe life.' No doubt at the time Bizet enjoyed his triumph to the full and thought little of future obstacles. His cantata was performed (for the first and last time) at the Institut on the third Saturday in October, in accordance with long-hallowed tradition. It was a festive occasion, with a specially invited audience of garlanded academicians, relatives and friends. The work had a great success and was long and loudly applauded. The auguries for the future were good.

CHAPTER II

ROME (1857–60)

THE winners of the various Prix de Rome (there were prizes for painting, sculpture, architecture and engraving as well as music) received a pension from the State for five years. In return for this they had to submit a work or works every year, on which the relevant section of the Académie des Beaux-Arts in Paris made a report—or rather two reports, one for publication and another, of a more confidential nature, that was sent to the artist personally. These works submitted were known as *envois*. There were certain regulations as to their nature: the first *envoi* of a musician, for instance, had to be a mass or other sacred work on a large scale. Other regulations, which differed at various periods, governed the residence of the pensioners. In Bizet's time the painters, sculptors and engravers spent the full five years in Rome, the architects three years in Rome and two in Athens, and the musicians two in Rome, one in Germany and two in Paris. In most respects these stipulations seem reasonable enough; but during the middle and later years of the last century there was great debate about the value to a musician of two years in Rome. When the prize was opened to musicians in 1805 the rule could be justified: French music was in a backward state and Italy still retained some of her ascendancy of the previous centuries. But by 1850 French musicians regarded Italy (not without some reason) as musically decadent and calculated to debase rather than enhance an artist. At that time it was scarcely possible to hear the German classics without going to Germany, and there was something to be said for spending more than a year in that country. Gounod, who won the prize in 1839, spent well over a year there. On the other hand Italy did offer opportunities, by no means negligible to provincial young Frenchmen, of coming in contact with a wider culture. If Rome's present was artistically inglorious, there was still her past, and even to a musician art should mean something more than minims and crotchets. This point was strongly argued by

10

Gounod in an article written in 1882 replying to the detractors of the French Academy at Rome; and Bizet, with his temperamental love (both physical and spiritual) of the Mediterranean sun, and his insistence on the need of literary and wide artistic culture in a musician, wholeheartedly agreed with him.[1] But perhaps the greatest value of all to a young artist lay in the opportunities it gave him to find himself in beautiful and congenial surroundings and free from the preoccupation of earning his daily bread. To all too many of them, Bizet included, it was the first and last such opportunity that life afforded.

The French Academy in Rome was housed in the Villa Medici. This noble building, built in 1540 for Cardinal Ricci and reconstructed with the assistance of Michelangelo by Cardinal Alessandro de' Medici (later Pope Leo XI), had been acquired by France in 1803. Standing amid its own gardens on Monte Pincio, it commands a magnificent view over Rome, with the Sabine mountains in the distance. Here the pensioners lived a communal life under a director, usually a distinguished artist, appointed for a six-year period by the French State. When Gounod went out the director had been the painter Ingres, who was succeeded after a year by another painter, Victor Schnetz. Schnetz was again in office when Bizet arrived, and no doubt was able to smooth his path. A gruffly humorous, genial and conspicuously hirsute man, he was deservedly popular with the students. He held the post for three periods, eighteen years in all (1840–6, 1852–64).

Bizet and his four fellow-pensioners left Paris on 21st December 1857 and travelled by Lyons, Vienne, Valence, Orange, Avignon, Nîmes, Arles, Marseilles, Toulon, Nice, Genoa, Leghorn, Pisa, Lucca and Florence. This was probably his first journey of more than a few miles, and his letters are full of delighted comments. In view of later circumstances his impressions of the Rhône valley are interesting (except for a hurried and anxious return journey he never visited it again). It was 'magnificent country,' the weather was like spring, as hot and sunny as Paris in July. The ancient buildings, the

---

[1] 'I sincerely pity those who have not won the prize, or those who get it before attaining the necessary maturity.'—Letter of 17th August 1860.

mountain scenery, above all the sea, made a tremendous impression: 'the spectacle of nature is something so unknown to me that I find it impossible to analyse my impressions. . . . An artist ought to profit by it, be he painter or musician, sculptor or architect.' Bizet and his companions were indefatigable tourists: no climb was too rough for them if it promised a fine view or interesting ruins. Within a week he had grown noticeably thinner and had worn out two pairs of shoes: he is careful to point out to his parents that the mountains are made of rock, not of clay 'like our bourgeois Montmartre.' At Toulon they went round the harbour in a boat and looked over two battleships.

Early in the New Year they reached Italy, and Bizet was thankful for the Italian lessons he had taken in Paris; he was the only one who had a smattering of the language. This was fortunate, for he had from the first been appointed treasurer of the party, and some care had to be taken if the treasure was not to disappear. Despite the joy of picking roses and oranges at the roadside, his first impressions of Italy, like Gounod's eighteen years before, were not very favourable. He admired the scenery, especially the *corniche* road between Nice and Genoa, but was disgusted with much of the architecture— 'churches painted like monuments in cardboard'—and with the people, who seemed to be all priests and beggars (and Bizet found himself making less and less distinction between the two). 'The Piedmontese have several ways of begging—humbly by day, and with a blunderbuss by night.' The travellers were in Florence by 12th January, and Bizet at once went to see Verdi's *I Lombardi*, but found the performance very bad. The Tuscans also showed a remarkable propensity for extracting money from travellers, and this is one of his constant complaints all over Italy. They stayed eight days at Florence, where Bizet's enthusiasm for the art treasures knew no bounds. He was particularly impressed by Raphael and Andrea del Sarto, a painter then apparently unknown in Paris. Yet paradise as it was (*féerique* is Bizet's word), Florence had no living art whatever, not a single musician, poet or painter of talent. This again he was to find all over Italy, and he put it down to the fact that political decadence is always followed by decadence in art.

On 28th January, three days before the latest date allowed by the regulations, the party arrived in Rome, which apart from occasional journeys was to be Bizet's home for the best part of three years. He settled down at once. Within a month he was a social success: he had a triumph as a pianist at Schnetz's house, went to a masked ball dressed as a baby, dined often with the Russian ambassador and was up to the ears in invitations. But, he is quick to point out, he accepts few of them: 'I am not here to amuse myself.' And he set to work composing a *Te Deum* for the Rodrigues prize, worth 1,500 francs and open only to the Rome pensioners. Here already we see two characteristic sides of the man, an easy assurance in personal relations and an intense capacity for hard work. He was not spoiled by social success; impetuous as he was, he could soon take a detached view of his actions. After mentioning his ovation as a pianist, he adds: 'It is only fair to say that there are no pianists in Italy, and if you can only play the scale of C with both hands you pass for a great artist.'

Bizet's years in Rome were probably the happiest of his life. He embraced Gounod's good advice to open his heart like a child to all that Rome offered 'in her incomparable and inexhaustible abundance' and to admire as much as possible, for 'admiration broadens the soul.' Despite his contempt for the Italians, both as a nation and as individuals, he soon came to love the city—and not its more obvious beauties alone. Every street, even the dirtiest, had its character, and he would not have it different: 'I should cry murder if a single pile of dirt were removed.' He loved the museums and art galleries, the second-hand bookshops and in particular the climate and the surrounding countryside. Living in the Villa Medici with fellow-countrymen and fellow-artists, at the expense of the French Government, he was having the best of two worlds. At that time the French, owing to the imperialistic tendencies of Napoleon III, were not trusted in Italy, being hailed alternately as liberators and traitors in proportion as they saved the Italians the trouble of fighting for their own independence. They did not mix in society (with the exception of Schnetz, who according to Bizet was Italian at heart and had 'espoused Italian interests and customs to the extent of never washing his hands'), but they were both feared and courted. The students at the Villa Medici consequently made themselves free of the country, untroubled by political considerations and treating the Italians as an inferior race. Bizet enjoyed the communal life, found it so easy to work that he dreamed of one day returning to Rome to compose, revelled in the sunrises and sunsets, and made periodic excursions into the country. In the early summer of 1858 he spent a fortnight in the Alban Hills, playing on various organs and finding them all barbarous. On his return he visited the chief organ-builder in Rome, who looked surprised at his inquiries and told him that he had no organs, nor even a case or the wood to make one; but if Bizet wanted one built, let him pay in advance, and he would go and buy the necessary tools. The man had taken over his father's business ten years before, and never had occasion to build an organ; he lived by his other professions, which were those of flautist, tobacconist, cab-hirer and national guard.

Bizet was on good terms with his fellow-pensioners. At one stage he was giving a course of musical instruction to a painter and a sculptor, making them sing portions of Mozart operas; but, he told Marmontel, he was too much of an egoist to be a good teacher. Among his friends at this time was the writer Edmond About, whose witty satirical tongue gave more pleasure to Bizet than to the French Government. He was writing bitter articles on the priesthood for a Paris paper, and was presently recalled for imperilling international relations. Bizet had a real gift for friendship. He demanded, and gave, complete frankness and loyalty. Though his temper was quick, he was equally swift to withdraw a harsh remark or unfair judgment. The one thing he could not tolerate was deception or intrigue. Samuel David, Prix de Rome winner of 1858, whom at first he liked, earned his permanent hostility because he ran with the hare and hunted with the hounds.

In the summer of 1859 Bizet went for a prolonged holiday. Leaving Rome on 11th May with two companions and a dog (of whom he liked the latter not least), he spent some days at Anzio, where there was a convict settlement. He described the 250 convicts as the happiest and most esteemed part of the population, without a thief among them. He paid a visit to Cape Circe, went on to Terracina and then turned inland through magnificent mountain scenery, visiting among other places Frosinone, Anagni and Rieti, and returning to Rome on 14th July. He sent Marmontel an amusing account of the tour:

What a country, and what travelling companions—Cicero at Astura, at Cape Circe Homer and his Ulysses, at Terracina Fra Diavolo. This is pure Scribe, and it amuses me to think that only three leagues divide Scribe from Homer. I leave to-morrow for Naples and am going to pass some hours with Tiberius and Nero. That is rather a come-down, as you see, but Virgil and Horace will console me for the tyrants.

Despite the discomforts of travel, including bugs and lack of sleep, he enjoyed every moment. He rose at four in the morning, made progress with riding and Italian, and proposed to learn Latin. The travellers had not been at all incommoded by the war in northern Italy, culminating in the Battle of Magenta. In fact Bizet found the Italians on the whole little interested in fighting for their national unity: 'They know how to shout and form provisional governments, and that's all.' He was kept at Rome by a touch of rheumatism resulting from a cold bath, but on 4th August left for Naples, where (and at Pompeii) he remained till late in October. Although the bay was wonderful, and Pompeii set his imagination on fire, he was greatly disappointed with the town of Naples. Soon one of his companions was threatened with typhoid. At the first alarm five of the eight who composed the party rapidly decamped, leaving Bizet and one other—a friend of a fortnight's standing, himself badly afflicted with boils—to nurse the sick. Before returning to Rome Bizet too was stricken with illness, a heavy cold bringing on an attack of the throat complaint from which he suffered all his life and which was eventually to kill him.

An amusing incident happened about this time. Before leaving Paris, Bizet had been given a letter of introduction to Mercadante from one of the professors at the Conservatoire, an ancient Neapolitan nonentity named Carafa.[1] He had intended to use this on his visit

[1] Michele Enrico Francesco Vincente Paolo Carafa di Colobrano (1787–1872) was one of those curious figures thrown up by the Napoleonic wars. Originally a rich man and a soldier (he fought both for and against Napoleon, and was decorated for his part in the Moscow expedition), he

to Naples, where Mercadante lived, but whether through neglect or preoccupation with the sick-bed, he had not done so. On his return to Rome, overcome by curiosity, he opened the letter. It read as follows: 'The young man who will bring you this letter has had great success with his studies. He has won the chief prizes at our Conservatoire. But, in my humble opinion, he will never be a dramatic composer as he has not a groat's worth of enthusiasm.' Bizet was much amused. 'You old scoundrel!' he broke out in a letter to his mother. 'One day, father Carafa, I promise to write your biography and give this letter in facsimile.' On his return to Paris he met Carafa, who asked him if he had used the letter. Bizet's reply was characteristic: 'Monsieur Carafa, when one has the good luck to possess the autograph of a man like you, one keeps it.'

In November, with the approval of Schnetz, Bizet applied for permission to spend the third year of his pension in Italy instead of Germany.[1] He gave as reason that he had begun an important work, which he would be unable to finish before July. 'In leaving Italy without having finished my work, I should be afraid of finding myself unready by the time the *envois* are due and, on the other hand, of not being able to profit as I desire by my stay in Germany.' Schnetz in his letter of recommendation said that the 'beautiful Italian climate' should have a happy influence on Bizet's work, and we may well agree. The 'important work' can only have been the abortive Symphony (mentioned below) which was very soon destroyed. But on 9th December the authorities granted the request. Another source of encouragement was the arrival early in 1860 of Ernest Guiraud, winner of the 1859 prize, whom Bizet knew well

---

was compelled in 1814 to take up music for a living, wrote innumerable operas and piano pieces after the manner of Rossini and died a member of the French Academy. Among his operas, very popular in their day, were *La Fiancée de Lammermoor* and *Masaniello* (produced two months before Auber's work on the same theme).

[1] This seems to have worried Gounod, who a year later was still advising him to go to Germany: he must work hard in order to fertilize the germs he had brought from Rome, which would otherwise remain absolutely sterile. But Bizet never stayed long in Germany, though he paid at least one visit to Baden.

in Paris and who was to be his close friend for life. In June 1860 he made another short tour in the mountains. In July his portrait (which he describes as 'ravishing') was painted by his friend Giacometti.[1] In the same month, his mind already full of plans for his future life in Paris, he said farewell to Rome.

Of the many compositions projected by Bizet in Italy few reached completion. The *Te Deum* which he submitted for the Rodrigues prize was begun in February 1858 and the scoring finished in May. It has never been performed, though the manuscript survives. Bizet, who had no feeling for sacred music and very little for established religion, found it an effort and wanted it out of the way so that he could tackle an Italian opera libretto which greatly pleased him. This was *Parisina*, already set by Donizetti; Bizet intended it as his first *envoi*. But he seems never to have begun it, nor did an *opéra-comique* in one act with words by Edmond About progress much farther. Bizet, who treated it less seriously than About, found the libretto 'charming, but a little too comic for the Opéra-Comique.' His comments on the *Te Deum* are those he nearly always passed on a recently completed work:

> I don't know what to think of it. Sometimes I find it good, sometimes detestable. What is certain is that I'm not cut out to write religious music. So I shall refrain from writing a mass. I shall send an Italian opera in three acts, I like that better.

Here common sense and his artistic conscience spoke together; but, as we shall see, there was another voice as well.

In June he found that his chosen poem, presumably *Parisina*, was no good; but after a long search, during which he went through 'all the libraries of Rome and read two hundred pieces,' he found what he wanted in a second-hand bookstall in a back street. It was 'an Italian farce after the manner of *Don Pasquale*. . . . I am decidedly built for *la musique bouffe,* and I lose myself in it completely.' This libretto, accurately described by Bizet, was *Don Procopio* by one Carlo Cambiaggio. It was not a new work: it had been set by

[1] There is also an unfinished portrait painted during his first year in Rome by a fellow-pensioner, Sellier. This shows Bizet without beard or spectacles.

Vincenzo Fioravanti and others in 1844, and was even then only a reduced version of Prividali's *I pretendenti delusi*, set by Mosca [1] and produced at Milan in 1811. Bizet set happily to work, well aware that the authorities would censure his choice of subject, but hoping for a good report on the music.

In September he heard that the only other competitor had won the Rodrigues prize. His immediate reaction was: 'That's most up-setting!!! But still, I shan't die of it.' A few days later he gave three reasons for not being downhearted: he was not in Paris whereas Barthe, the winner, was; he had neither the ability nor the knowledge to compose church music; and Barthe was in the fifth year of his pension and, being thus unable to compete again, was probably, and not unjustly, rewarded by the judges for a good string of *envois*. 'For all these reasons I have not had to console myself for a defeat which is no defeat and which has had no publicity.' Whatever may be thought of Bizet's reasons (and the second at least was right on the mark), the significant thing is that he should have had to give them at all: this is one of the first signs of that inner lack of confidence that so long dogged this apparently spontaneous and ebullient composer. It was this, and no mere love of money or flattery, that made some measure of worldly success so important to him. In the misfortune that deprived him of this success in his lifetime, rather than in the mere fact of early death, lay his tragedy.

Meanwhile *Don Procopio* continued to go well. He was aware that his music was Italian (he likened it to Cimarosa rejuvenated): 'On Italian words one must write Italian music; I have not tried to cast off this influence.' [2] But he intended to aim higher. 'I feel

---

[1] In this work Mosca claimed, somewhat barrenly, to have anticipated Rossini in the use of the orchestral *crescendo*.—Alfred Loewenberg, *Annals of Opera*.

[2] These words were printed at the head of the vocal score when *Don Procopio* was published in 1905. The manuscript was lost for many years and only came to light in 1894, among some posthumous papers of Auber's. The first performance took place at Monte Carlo in 1906. Gauthier-Villars states that two airs from *Clarissa Harlowe* were then inserted; but he gives no authority, and no airs from *Clarissa Harlowe* are known to have survived.

certain dramatic tendencies developing in me, as a result of which next year I shall try a grand opera.' His second *envoi* was to be an opera on Victor Hugo, *Esmeralda*, his third a Symphony: for if he was drawn more and more to the stage, he never lost the ambition to shine in absolute music. At this period we see manifest for the first time that division of aim which is discussed in Chapter X. To which of the two types of genius—natural genius or rational genius—did his own talent conform? Should he interpret by instinct, or hunt for an 'idea' and cudgel his brains working it into shape? Should he follow Mozart and Rossini on the one hand, or Beethoven and Meyerbeer on the other? If pressed too hard the distinction becomes unreal, for both processes obviously co-exist; but that it represented a parting of the ways for Bizet there can be no doubt. So far, in the Symphony and *Don Procopio*, he had followed the instinctive way, composing fluently and with little revision, allowing his creative imagination to work without much conscious interference. Now he began to have grave doubts. He became self-conscious. In a letter to Gounod in September he compared himself to a bad swimmer in deep water: 'I flounder a lot and progress little. . . . I have always been very much the student; it is not easy to become one's *self*.' His letters in the winter of 1858–9 are full of confessions like this:

I mistrust my facility: I have around me ten intelligent fellows who will never be more than mediocre artists, and all because of the fatal confidence with which they abandon themselves to their great cleverness. Cleverness in art is almost indispensable, but it only ceases to be dangerous the moment the man and the artist find themselves. I want to do nothing *chic*, I want to have *ideas* before beginning a piece, and that is not how I worked in Paris. It results in a certain paralysis which I shall only completely surmount in a year or two.

Bizet seems to have been confusing cleverness with spontaneity; at any rate, a kind of paralysis did set in, and its effects are apparent for a good deal longer than two years.

The immediate result of the struggle was a determination to com-pose 'German music.' This term must not be taken too literally. In the years that followed Bizet did fall under the influence of German composers, particularly Schumann, Weber and Mendelssohn, but by German music he clearly meant the other type of genius, the rational as opposed to the natural. And (strange as it seems to-day) this included the music of Gounod, in which the Schumann influence was strong and which sounded positively Teutonic to ears attuned to the Italian vivacity of Rossini, much of Meyerbeer and the reigning school of Auber. It is ironical that Bizet was particularly pleased to find *Don Procopio* completely free from the influence of Gounod; for he was about to abandon the method of *Don Procopio*. 'Next year I shall write something tragic and purely German. I shall finish perhaps by pleasing every one or, rather, by pleasing no one.' As if to emphasize the irony in the last words, his next letter contains this comment on the early death of a fellow-composer: 'Worry yourself sick to get the Prix de Rome, struggle to make a good position on your return, and it will all end perhaps in death at thirty-eight.' We can hardly help thinking of the card scene in *Carmen* and Bizet's own death at thirty-six: he almost literally finished by pleasing no one.

The summer of 1859 saw many projects taken up and rapidly abandoned. No progress was made with *Esmeralda* (years later he gave it to Galabert to set as an exercise and improvised a couple of scenes at the piano). The visit to Cape Circe and its grotto suggested an ode-symphony [1] to be entitled *Ulysse et Circé*.

There are some charming things to be done on this subject—the chorus of Ulysses' companions, the scene of Circe's spells, the drunkenness scene. There will be four purely symphonic pieces and five or six with voices and chorus.

Nor was this all.

Convinced that an intelligent musician should find the idea for his poems for himself, I am very busy. Get the *Tales of Hoffmann* from the library and read *Le Tonnelier de Nuremberg*. I want to do three acts on this delicious poem. Tell me what you think of it in your next letter. The singing contest will be a very original and undoubtedly effective scene. There are also some things in Voltaire's tales which please me very much.

---

[1] This form achieved a brief popularity in France about the middle of the century; its prototype was Félicien David's *Le Désert*.

Chevojon

PORTRAIT OF BIZET BY GIACOMETTI, 1860

He urged his mother on no account to mention the *Tonnelier* idea, or he would find it already on the stage when he returned to Paris. But his mother's reaction was cool. In July he wrote:

I am annoyed that the success of this story seems less sure to you than to me. The scenes of the portrait, the singing contest, the games and the workshop are nevertheless certain in their effect; and then it's so attractive, so German! Read it again and you'll discover that touch of sentiment that only Germans can find, and that is so popular with us.

(France was just falling under the spell of Schumann.) Here, probably because of his mother's attitude, Bizet dropped the idea. Perhaps it was as well. For the three acts on this delicious poem were to be the work of a very different composer: the seed of *Die Meistersinger* had already lodged in Wagner's brain, although neither poem nor music was yet begun.

At the same time *Ulysse et Circé* was discarded. 'Old Homer is obstinate about being arranged or rather disarranged. I should like to do something new. I'm looking for it. Shall I find it?' In August his ideas were still more ambitious. 'I have my head full of Shakespeare: Hamlet! Macbeth! But a librettist?' This search for that operatic rarity, a satisfactory libretto, was to bother Bizet all his life. About the end of September he put his second *envoi* aside (deciding to wait for the report on his first) and began a Symphony. Yet he wrote in October:

For some time I have been cherishing the idea of a tragi-comic-heroic *Don Quixote*, and I read in a paper that Gounod is working at it. It seems that my ideas are not too bad. One of these days someone will do my *Tonnelier*.

It is significant of his lack of self-confidence that, while one promising plan was dropped probably on account of his mother's coolness, the prospect of rivalry with Gounod killed another.

Meanwhile the first (public) report on *Don Procopio* had arrived. Bizet had been awaiting it in mingled confidence and defiance. ('Whatever they say won't change my opinion in the least, for good or ill.') The report was entirely favourable and made no mention of his breaking the regulations. The judges found a notable advance on his earlier work and, after commending nearly every item in the score, especially the first finale, the serenade and the trio for three basses, summed up as follows:

> In short, this work is distinguished by an easy and brilliant touch, a youthful and bold style, precious qualities for the *genre* of comedy, towards which the composer shows a marked propensity. These qualities open the way to novel effects, and M. Bizet will not forget the obligation he has undertaken as much towards himself as towards us.

Bizet was much encouraged: 'I feel more confident than ever, though I don't conceal from myself the immense progress that remains to be achieved before I get anywhere, but I have good hopes.'

The Symphony was now to be his second *envoi*, but early in December, after two months' work on it, he found he had taken a wrong turning and began again afresh. He noted that he had become very hard to please; *Don Procopio* he now found 'extremely feeble.' Yet he was still sufficiently in the mood to dream of beginning his Paris career at the Théâtre Italien—a new idea, as he said, but, considering the low repute of that theatre, a very questionable tactic. Towards the end of the month the second Symphony went the way of the first—into the fire; but Bizet had found a librettist, one Louis Delâtre, whom he described with justifiable irony as 'a very learned man, who knows and speaks twenty-five languages but writes his own in a not very intelligent manner.'[1] To him Bizet entrusted a scenario of his own, based on the *Lusiad* of Camoens. *Vasco de Gama*, which became his second *envoi*, was an ode-symphony avowedly after the manner of David's *Le Désert* and *Christophe Colomb*. The music came easily enough, but Bizet had considerable trouble with Delâtre's verses, some of which he had to rewrite. He was still pursued by ideas for a symphony: by the middle of January 1860 he had 'almost got as far as putting a finale on its feet,' and he hoped to get his third *envoi* well ahead while writing his second. He was pleased with his progress. 'I revise very easily and I know the value of what I am writing: two good symptoms. . . . The very good is so difficult that a whole lifetime is not enough to approach it.'

---

[1] This did not prevent him from publishing a treatise on the conjugation of French verbs (1851), besides poetry and books on classical antiquities in both French and Italian. He was much older than Bizet.

Other projects still crowded his brain. Disgusted with Delâtre, he decided to be his own librettist. 'I have an enormous longing to write something in the comic vein, such a longing that I am rhyming for myself an *opéra-comique* on a piece by Molière, *L'Amour peintre*.' For some time he worked on this and *Vasco de Gama* together. But the second report on *Don Procopio* arrived in the middle of March and instantly put a stop to *L'Amour peintre*. This document, signed by Ambroise Thomas, the austerity of whose principles conflicts comically with the mild quaverings of his muse, duly censured Bizet for writing a comic opera instead of a mass, and proceeded: 'We will recall to him that the liveliest natures find in meditation and the interpretation of the sublime a style that is indispensable even in light compositions and without which a work will have no lasting qualities.' This egregious nonsense (might it be held to justify the sacred works of Sir Arthur Sullivan?) could not have surprised Bizet, and certainly should not have dismayed him; yet his self-reliance was so weak that he instantly succumbed.

The most simple thing would be to complete my *envoi* with a Credo. This portion of the Mass includes drama and action besides religious sentiment. The Resurrexit, Et ascendit, etc., would allow me to abandon Christian sentiment a little and substitute action, drama. But that would be repugnant to my ideas: I don't want to write a mass before being in a state to do it well, that is a Christian state. I have therefore taken a singular course to reconcile my ideas with the exigences of Academy rules. They ask for something religious: very well, I shall do something religious, but of the pagan religion. Horace's *Carmen saeculare* has been tempting me for a long time. . . . It is more beautiful than the Mass from a literary and poetic point of view; it is Latin poetry instead of prose, and so much more measured, more rhythmical, and as a consequence more musical. Then, to tell the truth, I am more pagan than Christian. I have always read the ancients with infinite pleasure, while in the Christians I have found only system, egoism, intolerance and a complete absence of artistic taste. It goes without saying that I except the works of St. Paul and St. John.

He considered writing to Thomas, developing these ideas, but seems to have thought better of it. Instead he indulged in an outburst of petulance (to his mother) on the musical section of the Academy and the slapdash manner in which they judged the *envois*.

The work is played as it comes, and only once, then the areopagus sits in judgment on a young man who is the equal, if not the superior, of most of his judges (this applies not only to me but to every one). . . . What can one expect from those animals? Reber is dumb, Berlioz absent, Auber asleep, Carafa and Clapisson listen (alas!). There remains only Thomas, but he is so lazy!

Perhaps provoked by this state of affairs, he thought of trying his hand at musical criticism. 'I'm not much more of an ass than many others who don't write too badly: why shouldn't I also try to say what I think of our art and our artists?' He could hardly have found a less adequate reason for embarking on a critic's career.

The *Carmen saeculare* was never finished; Thomas and his committee never received from Bizet a religious *envoi* of any sort. The sole result of the incident was the abandonment of a promising light opera. But Bizet's mood of self-distrust was followed, as if in compensation, by a bout of extreme assurance. Looking through *Vasco de Gama*[1] before sending it to Paris, he found it much better than he expected.

Whatever the gentlemen of the Academy say, my opinion is formed, and it is good, very good even. I tell you this in secret, altogether confidentially: if I compare my *Vasco de Gama* with the great things of art I remain well below them, that goes without saying, but if I want to compete with our good contemporary work I believe I have, if not the advantage, at least the right to dispute it.

He goes on to assess the position he believes he has reached.

I can declare at last that I am a musician, a thing I have long doubted. Whether I arrive in two, four or ten years does not matter. I am young enough not to lose the hope of enjoying my successes. Then hope, hope —that means certainty. For the rest, the moment is propitious: Gounod alone is a man; behind him is nothing. Verdi they say will write no more, and even if he does I doubt if he will often recapture those flashes of genius that appear in *Trovatore*, *Traviata* and the fourth act of *Rigoletto*. His is a fine artistic nature ruined by negligence and cheap success. . . . Ah! one needs a lot of strength to create art. It is hard, very hard, especially at Rome. The sirocco has a terrible effect on my nerves. You know me,

[1] It was intended to have a sequel: at the bottom of the manuscript score Bizet wrote the words 'Fin de la Iière Partie.'

and you know that I am not of a very nervous disposition: well, in the days of the sirocco I can't touch *Don Giovanni* or *Figaro* or *Così fan tutte*; Mozart's music has too strong an effect on me, and that makes me really very ill. Certain things of Rossini's, too, produce the same result. It's surprising, but Beethoven and Meyerbeer never go as far as that. As for Haydn, he has long sent me to sleep, likewise old Grétry. I don't mention Boieldieu, Nicolo,[1] etc., who no longer exist for me.

This confession reveals very clearly where his true affinities lay.

Bizet held the lowest opinion of the musical state of Italy. Within a month of his arrival in Rome he was writing: 'Italy is poisoned by bad taste. It is a country completely lost to art. Rossini, Mozart, Weber, Paer, Cimarosa are here unknown, misunderstood or forgotten.' He told Gounod in September 1858 that nine months without hearing a note of good music had left him unable to judge his own work. The great religious ceremonies he described as unworthy farces from the musical point of view; this had also been Gounod's opinion twenty years earlier. The one composer whom he found it difficult to place—and this held good all his life—was Verdi. He was susceptible to his genius, but, perhaps because of the Gounod element in him, refused to surrender to it. 'Verdi is a man of great talent,' he wrote in February 1859,

who lacks the one quality that is essential for making great masters—style. But he has wonderful bursts of passion. His passion is brutal, it is true, but that is better than having no passion at all. His music exasperates sometimes, but it never bores. In short, I don't understand the enthusiasts or the detractors he has roused; he deserves, it seems to me, neither the one nor the other.

Like many others, Bizet did not understand the development then taking place in Verdi's style that was to lead to the two great operas composed years after his own death. He found *Un ballo in maschera* 'noisome,' contrasting it with Gluck's *Orfeo*, in which certain people affected to find no melody. His great hero among the living, of course, was Gounod. The letters are full of his praises—despite a temporary coolness caused by the rejection of Hector Gruyer from the cast of *Faust*; Bizet, ever impetuous in such matters, wrote a hasty letter, but the breach was later healed. 'What a sympathetic nature!

[1] Isouard.

How willingly one submits to the influence of that warm imagination! For him art is a priesthood: he has said so himself. I add that he is the only man among our modern musicians who truly loves his art.' And Bizet waited anxiously for news of the reception of Gounod's operas, especially *Faust*, which he proclaimed a masterpiece (no doubt Gounod had shown him the unfinished manuscript before he left Paris).

Bizet was a devoted son, taking continual pains to reassure his parents of his safety and good behaviour, and always wishing them at hand so that he could profit by their advice. He made elaborate plans for his future in Paris. He preferred to have separate lodgings in the same house as his parents (then living in the Rue de Laval), but if he lived at home he must have his own key.

I do not want you to have to open the door to people whom I'm going to put out five minutes later—that's for directors, singers, etc. Besides, I'm very capricious in my way of life: sometimes I go for walks by moonlight till impossible hours. My liberty of action would be cramped by the fear of displeasing you: that is what we must avoid.

Like Verdi, but unlike an artist of the popular conception, he had a vein of shrewd common sense, especially in money matters. He declared that living within one's means was 'the motto of every honest man and every philosopher,' and proceeded, as a young man will, to count his future chickens at the Opéra and Opéra-Comique. When he has made 100,000 francs

papa will give no more lessons, nor I either. We shall begin the life of a *rentier* . . . 100,000 francs is nothing—two little successes with *opéra-comique*. A success like *Le Prophète* brings in almost a million. So this is not a castle in Spain.

At times he seems to know a little too well on which side his bread is buttered. There is something self-righteous in his comment on a colleague aged twenty-eight who had little experience of the seductions of Paris life. He adds coolly: 'I know that disease, but I will have none of it. I will take my share of the cake like any one else, and it is sometimes a little bitter; I will take it without gluttony and in such a manner as not to have indigestion.' On another occasion he says he has become very severe in regard to the passions.

As regards the fair sex I am less and less the French cavalier. I see nothing in that beyond the satisfaction of self-esteem. I would willingly risk my life for a friend, but would think myself an idiot if I lost a hair of my head on account of a woman. I say such things only to you, for if they became known they would prejudice my future success. . . . I dine every week with Kisseleff,[1] which pleasantly flatters what remains of my sensual greed. I say 'what remains.' For there also I've changed. I no longer love cakes or ices or sweets (except *marrons glacés*). I have become a little perfection. Only my natural quarrelsomeness remains: an elbowing in the street, a gaze too long fixed on me, and brrrrr—off I go! I do all I can to improve myself, but it's difficult, very difficult. . . . Time is a great teacher, he'll manage to perfect me—if it's possible.

There was certainly a vein of shallow thinking and egotism in the young Bizet. Abjuring the need for settled principles, he set out to conquer the world under the delusive guidance of his own star.[2] His judgments of men and politics were superficial and erratic (he went through a phase of jingoistic chauvinism when Napoleon III was trying to win military glory in Italy). He sent a message to Gruyer, the nervous young singer preparing to create the part of Faust: 'If I could give him a little of my assurance [*aplomb*], how things would go! . . . Assurance—in a word, character—and he is certain of success.' But, as he soon found, assurance is not enough. Beneath his apparent detachment and self-confidence there grew up a profound and gnawing self-distrust, rooted in fear. He had not thought out the deeper things in life. 'The older I grow,' he wrote on hearing of the death of a child, 'the more the idea of death terrifies me. That does little credit to my philosophy, but it is a feeling of which I am not master.' He had a superstitious belief, which he was half ashamed to confess to his father, that his friendship brought bad luck. His extreme hatred of priests and organized religion is also symptomatic.[3] As early as 1859 he viewed certain aspects of his future career with alarm: 'I already detest that whole breed of directors and performers whom I am going to have the

---

[1] The Russian ambassador.

[2] See the repeated references in his letters to 'ma chance.'

[3] 'It is odd that the more I am strengthened in my Christian beliefs, the more I detest those who are charged with teaching them to us. Happily one can love God without loving the priests.' It is often easier for the egotist to square his conscience than his vicar.

pleasure of frequenting. Failure is a thing those people never forgive.' Whatever truth there might be in that last sentence, Bizet did not yet know it from personal experience. He had to learn that ability is not an infallible or immediate passport to worldly success, and like other men of genius he had to learn it the painful way, by failure. Needing some tangible encouragement, he was to fix his eyes a little too much on the world's applause; he longed for it, expected it, and was all the more resentful when it was withheld.

But it is essential to remember that we are dealing with a very young man. A number of passages in the Rome letters have been used by unscrupulous critics and biographers, especially in France, to denigrate Bizet's character throughout life. It is not very difficult, and not very creditable, to select sentences from the naïve letters of an ambitious and impetuous young man, written rapidly [1] and in confidence to his parents, rearrange them, treat them as considered judgments and so present a wholly false picture. Some of these passages have been misunderstood. For instance, when Bizet wrote, immediately after the failure of Gounod's opera *Le Médecin malgré lui*: 'I shall probably have much less talent and less settled convictions than Gounod: as things are, this is a chance of success,' the irony in the last words is scarcely veiled. Gauthier-Villars goes so far as to state that it would have been better for Bizet had these letters never been published. But it is obvious that the conception of Bizet as an unattractive money-loving bourgeois, coldly calculating his chances of success in terms of hard cash and only making artistic progress by mistake and when aiming at something quite different, is wholly unfair. He had not, indeed, the reckless abandonment of Berlioz, the inward concentration of Beethoven or the dogged capacity for long-term planning of Wagner. But that is not to say that he loved his art any less than they did. The trouble springs largely from the romantic nineteenth-century view of the ideal artist as a starving visionary in a garret, indifferent to daily bread and common sense, his mind suffused with the rosy haze of infinite aspiration. Bizet, like Mozart and most other eighteenth-century composers (not to mention Verdi), did not forget that music was his livelihood as well as his

[1] Bizet asked his mother to forgive the confusion in his letters, as he never re-read them.

art; and if he occasionally sinned in offering the public what he thought they liked instead of what his inner nature knew to be good, it was certainly not through prostituting his art to serve his purse. There is absolutely no evidence that money at any time held an excessive place in his ambitions; in fact in later life he more than once refused all payment from pupils over whom he took endless trouble. He was a man in some degree divided against himself, and the attitude of his better (and predominant) half towards the artist who consciously abuses his heritage is stated clearly in a letter he wrote to Marmontel just before leaving Rome:

To the devil with all those who have seen in our sublime art nothing but an innocent tickling of the ear. Silliness will always have numerous admirers; but still I don't complain, and I assure you I shall always take pleasure in being appreciated only by men of genuine understanding. I have little use for this popularity to which people nowadays sacrifice honour, genius and fortune.

At the end of July 1860 Bizet finally left Rome, intending to reach Paris in December after a leisurely tour of northern Italy with Guiraud. They were a nicely contrasted pair, Bizet with his quick temper and abounding vitality, Guiraud already notorious for the good-humoured indolence which later caused him to postpone the task of recording his reminiscences of his friend, till one day he fell asleep in his office chair at the Conservatoire and omitted to wake up. Bizet had a wonderful send-off from the Academy. People he never much cared about shook his hand with tears in their eyes, and he himself, like Gounod on a similar occasion years before, was overcome with emotion. 'I had a frightful attack of nerves; I wept for six hours straight off. I realized I was liked at the Academy, and that was very moving.'

They travelled by Viterbo, Rimini and Ravenna to Venice. At Rimini Bizet found his usual delight in sea-bathing and tried without much success to teach Guiraud to swim. He also conceived the plan for a work which was to occupy him on and off for most of his life.

I have in mind a symphony which I should like to call *Rome, Venice, Florence and Naples*. That works out wonderfully: Venice will be **my** andante, Rome my first movement, Florence my scherzo and Naples my finale. It's a new idea, I think.

This was the germ of *Roma*. He told his mother that he was following Auber's advice and had already taken down a lot of music in a note-book.

He found Guiraud's company very congenial, despite the difficulty of waking him up in the mornings, and they sang Mozart all day long. But Bizet himself felt a renewed restlessness.

I have become excitable [*nerveux*] beyond measure, that is to say the opposite of what I was in Paris. I cannot stay where I am; after seven hours of sleep bed becomes intolerable to me, and I notice that for some time I have been growing insensible to the pleasures of the table. I feel a kind of continual irritation, a need, a desire that I cannot define.

It was in this condition that he reached Venice, to find a letter from his mother written from hospital. He had for some time been worried by reports of her health, and the sight of the word 'hospital' produced an extreme neurotic reaction. After a quarter of an hour of dumb fury he picked a quarrel with a gondolier and rushed at him with the firm intention of strangling him. Guiraud pulled him back, mildly observing that he had better read the rest of the letter first. This revealed that things were not quite as bad as he had feared, but he decided to leave for Paris at once (September). As he passed anxiously through Provence one of his fellow-travellers, Gaston Planté, made a sketch of him in the coach. His mother seems to have rallied about the time of his arrival, but early in 1861 she had a relapse and died during the summer. Thus just at the outset of his career, when his mercurial nature most needed guidance, he was deprived of that being whom he believed most fitted to give it.

CHAPTER III

THE YEARS OF STRUGGLE (1860–70)

In order to follow the vicissitudes of Bizet's career after his return to Paris, it is of first importance to understand the rather peculiar background to French musical life under the Second Empire. Virtually the only road open to the young composer of serious ambitions and without private means was the stage. In 1860 there seemed to be no future for a French composer of symphonies and no market for his wares. The only organization that gave regular orchestral concerts was the Société des Concerts du Conservatoire, founded by Habeneck in 1828. But it had only a small hall, with a limited audience who mostly took tickets by the season, and it concentrated entirely on the accepted classics, making no attempt to cultivate native talent. Not till 1868 were its doors opened to Gouvy, who for twenty years had been regarded as France's most promising symphonist. The Société Sainte-Cécile, founded by Reber and the violinist Seghers in 1848, had introduced Mendelssohn's 'Italian' Symphony and some works of Gounod's early symphonic period, but its career had closed in financial failure in 1854. The composer who wanted to hear his orchestral works performed had to hire an orchestra and a hall for himself, a procedure which, as Berlioz and others found, was both uncomfortable and unprofitable. The first sign of advance was the foundation in 1861 of Pasdeloup's Concerts Populaires de Musique Classique, which while mainly devoted to Beethoven and other classics did give many young native composers, including Bizet, their first chance; but it was not till after the Franco-Prussian war that the way was cleared for the flourishing French school of orchestral music of the last years of the century. With the foundation of the Société Nationale (1871) and Colonne's concert organization (1873) the one-sidedness of French musical life came to an end; but by then Bizet's days were numbered.

Chamber music was in no better case. There were the fashionable salons, where pianist-composers like Thalberg and Stephen Heller (and occasionally Liszt) amazed their impressionable listeners with cascades of virtuosity, and titled ladies accompanied themselves on the harp in a succession of banal romances. But, failing another genius like Chopin, this was hardly the nursery of a virile and enduring art. The more serious works of chamber music, such as Beethoven's quartets, were played only in select circles, and would probably have been incomprehensible both to the general public and to the bevies of dilettanti that made up a large part of musical Paris. There was no hope for ambitious young Frenchmen, and composers like Lalo and Franck, who were both years older than Bizet, had to wait for the Société Nationale to give French chamber music a new lease of life.

With church music in full decadence, there remained only the stage. Here at first glance the situation seems more promising. Opera and ballet (which the French liked to combine in a single spectacle) had originally been aristocratic forms, and at the premier national theatre, the Opéra [1] in the Rue Lepelletier, they continued to be so regarded; but the musical heirs of the French Revolution and First Empire, in particular Auber, Boieldieu and Hérold, had brought them down within the comprehension of the middle classes. Thus the old Opéra-Comique, which had originated over a century earlier as a parody of the tragic stage, now took up residence in the Salle Favart as a kind of bourgeois younger brother of the Opéra. But though there were two permanent opera-houses in Paris, they were not in a healthy state of growth. Each had its own rigidly narrow conventions and its own rigidly narrow public, and the latter made sure that the former were never relaxed. The Opéra was the more hidebound of the two. By the middle of the century it had become little more than a salon for snobs, to a greater extent even than the Covent Garden of pre-war seasons. The audiences were more interested in themselves than in the performances, which combined the lowest degree of dramatic and artistic distinction with the highest rate of public expenditure. The repertory consisted mostly of old music revived, and music by foreigners at that; for France was going through a period of intense snobbery towards her own composers of serious music. It is a curious fact that the leaders of the French stage have so often been foreigners: Lully triumphed

[1] Its full title was (and is) Académie Nationale de Musique.

in the seventeenth century, Gluck and Piccinni in the eighteenth, and in the forty years following 1825 the twin stars were Rossini and Meyerbeer, whose rivalry entertained the fashionable world and effectively barred the way to native talent.[1] Even with the death of these two champions the position did not improve: between 1852 and 1870 the only new French work of the smallest merit (and it had little enough) produced at the Opéra was Ambroise Thomas's *Hamlet*, and during the whole of Bizet's working life in Paris (1861–75) less than a dozen new operas were introduced.

The Opéra-Comique, though it produced more native work, was in little better case. Under the guidance of Auber it had evolved a form of its own, of which the epithet 'comique' gives a misleading impression. The term is not synonymous with our 'comic opera'; it did (until *Carmen*) imply a happy ending, but its most distinctive characteristic was that recitative was replaced by spoken dialogue, as in the German *Singspiel*. The Paris bourgeoisie liked its music broken up into small watertight compartments set in a framework of ordinary speech, and the leading *opéra-comique* composers—Auber, Adam, Boieldieu and the rest—having found an idiom that satisfied the public of 1830, ossified it and reproduced it for the next forty years. They avoided all complications, whether psychological or technical ('learned music' was a term of reproach more feared than 'highbrow' is to-day), all profundity, all enthusiasm and all experiment. Their music was clear, elegant, polished, often charming, essentially middle-class and sometimes dreadfully vulgar. Some of their earlier operas have a glitter that has still not worn off; but they never advanced, and consequently never widened the range of their audiences' appreciation. Auber was still writing for the Opéra-Comique in 1869 at the age of nearly ninety, and works like Boieldieu's

---

[1] Meyerbeer is said to have paid people to go to sleep ostentatiously during his rival's operas. Rossini, who knew which side his bread was buttered, retired from operatic composition in 1830, but his figure continued to loom large at the Opéra and throughout French musical life. Many other foreigners also set up business in Paris, including Spontini, Donizetti and Bellini; and even Wagner and Verdi came to try their fortunes. But the Opéra audience's stomach for foreign music proved notoriously unable to digest *Tannhäuser.*

LaDame Blanche and Hérold's *Le Pré aux Clercs* remained popular favour-ites till the end of the century. In the sixties the great new success at the Opéra-Comique, as at the Opéra, was a work by Thomas—*Mignon*; and this at the time when Wagner was just finishing *Die Meistersinger*.

Outside the two State theatres there were the Théâtre-Italien, a decadent and peripatetic institution that satisfied the craze for Italian opera of the second rank, and the operetta theatres, where from the middle fifties Offenbach was king. His easy, tuneful, well-turned but essentially trivial muse proved wholly suited to the tastes of the Second Empire, and he actually worked under ducal patronage. Yet interesting efforts were made to fill the lacuna in French operatic life. 'Between the Conservatoire, which is a school,' said a Minister of Public Instruction, 'and the Opéra, which is a museum, a single intermediary—the Opéra-Comique—is not enough.' From time to time between 1847 and 1870 there were attempts to operate a second intermediary, known rather vaguely as the Théâtre-Lyrique (this was the name of the enterprise, not of the building, which was more than once changed). The directors, who were enterprising men, avoided the cliques and the conventions (including obligatory spoken dialogue and the passion for foreigners) that beset one or other of the regular theatres, and made a genuine attempt to give enterprising programmes and build up an enterprising public. Unfortunately, though re-ceiving a certain amount of support from the State and from wealthy private patrons, the scheme was hardly ever solvent and several times had to close down before the war of 1870 gave it its death-blow. Yet it was the Théâtre-Lyrique that produced Berlioz's *Les Troyens à Carthage* (1863), most of Gounod's best work, including *Faust* (which the Opéra refused to touch till it had ten years' success behind it), and the early works of Reyer, Guiraud, Bizet and Delibes.

There were other difficulties under which a young composer or original leanings had to labour. This was still the age of the prima donna, whose passions and predilections exercised a strong control over composers and directors alike (the wife of Carvalho, director of the Théâtre-Lyrique, was one of the leading singers of the day). Thus not only was the voice exalted at the expense of the orchestra, and the individual vocal number at the expense of dramatic unity and psychological consistency, but the composer was expected to make special concessions to particular singers (Meyerbeer's scores are full of details which appear only because such and such a soprano or bass could outreach his or her colleagues). It is easy for critics of another age with different standards to reproach Bizet for his concessions to Christine Nilsson in *La Jolie Fille de Perth*; but it should be realized that this was the general practice of the time, and the composer who refused to conform was apt to find himself in the gutter. The attitude of most directors was frankly financial. They regarded an operatic score not as an artistic whole, but as so much material that could be chopped about and presented in the most appetizing manner. Meyerbeer with his board-room attitude to opera did not create a fashion; he merely fitted the supply to the general demand, and the young composer was expected to do the same without receiving the deference due to an established reputation. He was regarded as very small fry indeed: he was the servant, not only of the director, but of the stage-manager, the ballet-master and even the librettist. Cuts were frequently made against his wishes, and if he wanted anything extra, such as musicians in the wings, he had to pay for it out of his own pocket. Bizet was subjected to most of these restrictions even as late as the production of *Carmen*.

Another handicap was the deplorable level of musical criticism. With a few notable exceptions, such as Berlioz and Reyer, the prejudice and conservatism of the regular critics was exceeded only by their unbelievable ignorance of both the technique and the history of music.[1] This fact may be connected with the ill-disguised contempt with which leading French literary circles of the middle of the century regarded the art of music and its practitioners.[2] It is

[1] Musical history and aesthetics were not taught at the Conservatoire (or anywhere else in France) until 1871.

[2] One result of this divorce, of course, was that few good writers condescended to collaborate with a musician (*L'Arlésienne* was a striking exception). Consequently a race of hacks arose whose job was to turn out libretti to order. It is not surprising that French libretti of the middle of the century are almost incredibly bad. Even Scribe, with his seventy-six volumes of published libretti, all conforming more or less exactly to one of two types (the *opéra* and the *opéra-comique*), was a sizable artist compared with his successors, Barbier, Carré, Saint-Georges, etc.

therefore not surprising to find that Théophile Gautier, who confessed that he preferred silence to music, was among other things a music critic. Saint-Saëns in his memoirs quotes 'one of the most brilliant of the reviews' of 1864:

Our real duty—and it is a true kindness—is not to encourage them [young composers] but to discourage them. In art vocation is everything, and a vocation needs no one, for God aids. What use is it to encourage them and their efforts when the public obstinately refuses to pay any attention to them? If an act is ordered from one of them, it fails to go. Two or three years later the same thing is tried again with the same result.

So the theatres are justified in falling back on established favourites. That is a mild presentation of the method used by the bulk of the French musical press during Bizet's lifetime; and it is interesting to see how Gounod, the one composer before Bizet who attempted to develop French opera, fared at their hands. He was commonly denied the gift of melody; he was variously called the disciple of Handel, Gluck, Spontini, Schumann and Wagner, acclaimed as the reviver of the style of Palestrina and reproached (by the pontifical Scudo in 1862) with his taste for the late Beethoven quartets, 'the polluted source from which have sprung the evil musicians of modern Germany, the Liszts, Wagners, Schumanns, not to mention Men-delssohn in certain equivocal details of his style.' His first opera, *Sapho* (1851), was too modern even for Berlioz, who considered that its attempts to achieve dramatic realism transcended what was per-missible in music. If Berlioz thought this of *Sapho*, is it surprising that every music critic in Paris should have burnt his fingers over *Carmen*?

Such was the musical background of Paris when Bizet returned from Rome. He seems at first to have thought of applying for a teaching-post at the Conservatoire. This was the comfortable course, and that taken by Guiraud and the majority of Prix de Rome winners; but though it provided financial security, it also imposed fetters, and the composer was apt to become submerged in the pedagogue. Whether for this reason or another, Bizet did not pursue the matter. He still had nearly two years of his Rome pension to run and could afford to look about him, though fully aware that a hard struggle lay ahead. He was exceedingly ambitious and at the same time deeply afraid; he already classed the tribes of directors, singers and critics as his potential enemies. He was labouring under a recent bereavement, and was throughout his life the victim of constant ill-health. Before going to Rome he had suffered from angina [1]; he continued to have periodic attacks of pain in the throat and chest. At Rome during March 1858 he had difficulty in swallowing and lost a great deal of weight; every one advised him to have his tonsils out. On several other occasions his letters report ulceration of the throat and similar complaints. Yet there is not a trace of self-pity. He more than once declares that illness has done him a world of good: 'This monotony of good fortune and health was growing tedious.' It is difficult to estimate the seriousness of these attacks; but there is no doubt that they must have impaired his resistance, both physical and mental, and made both the hackwork which he subsequently had to perform for a living and his constant failure to win worldly success peculiarly hard to bear.

Bizet's third *envoi* [2] was finished in the late summer or autumn of 1861, and was thus a year late. There has been some confusion over this, but the following facts are clear. Bizet informed the authorities that he intended to submit a symphony, almost certainly the one entitled *Rome, Venice, Florence and Naples*, which he had projected in the previous summer. However, the illness and death of his mother interrupted his work, and he sent in only two movements, a scherzo and a funeral march, supplementing them with an overture, *La Chasse d'Ossian*. The scherzo, which subsequently found a place in *Roma*, may well have been the movement originally intended to depict Florence, but it seems unlikely that he would have chosen a funeral march for Venice. The inference is that this piece was written on the death of his mother and tacked on to the scherzo because it was the only thing he had ready for submission. [3] He thus

---

[1] This was Bizet's name for it, but the medical evidence is not entirely clear.

[2] A letter of Gounod's (19th August 1861) mentioning a symphony and an overture on which Bizet was then working must refer to this.

[3] The fact that he used its main theme in *Les Pêcheurs de perles* a year or two later tends to confirm that it was not a part of the Italian symphony, a project which he never abandoned. It has no connection with the published Funeral March for orchestra, written in 1868 as the prelude to the unfinished opera *La Coupe du Roi de Thule*.

abandoned his plan for an Italian symphony, only to return to it some years later in a different form. Of *La Chasse d'Ossian* we know nothing except its mention in the Academy's report, though Bizet's habit of using up the material of discarded works may later have laid it under contribution.

The reports of the Academy were reasonably encouraging. In *Vasco de Gama* authority (in the person of Halévy) had discovered 'elevation of style, spaciousness of form, fine harmonic effects, and rich and colourful orchestration.' They predicted a brilliant future for the composer, but warned him 'to beware of certain harmonic audacities which can sometimes be qualified as harshness.' The third *envoi* met with nothing but praise. The Academy noted, as well it might, the grace and skill with which the chief motive of the scherzo was handled and praised the overture in much the same terms as *Vasco de Gama*. It found the talent shown in his earlier exercises amply fulfilled, and this time took no exception to his harmony.

Bizet's fourth and last *envoi* was a setting of a one-act *opéra-comique* by two of the leading purveyors (they usually hunted in couples), Jules Barbier and Michel Carré, entitled *La Guzla de l'Émir*. This was written probably in the winter of 1861 and put into rehearsal at the Opéra-Comique early the following year. This fact does not imply any success on Bizet's part or an enlightened attitude on that of the theatre. The Opéra-Comique received certain funds from the State on condition that it produced the one-act piece which the pensioners were obliged to submit. Only too often the production was long delayed [1] and confined to a single performance; often it was the only one of his works that the prize-winner saw on the stage. But Bizet's opera was never produced. For once in his career he had a slice of luck. It happened that the retiring Minister of Fine Arts, Count Walewski, had just given the Théâtre-Lyrique a subvention of 100,000 francs on condition that the management should produce every year a three-act opera by a young winner of the Prix de Rome. Bizet was the first to benefit under this scheme. The director of the theatre, Léon Carvalho,[2] was one of the few men of his position

[1] For Bizet's own comment on the practice see Appendix E.

[2] His real name was Carvaille (1825–97). He had begun as a singer of small parts, married a celebrated soprano and was director in turn of the

who were not wedded to reaction. He had met Bizet soon after his return from Rome and been struck both by his talents and his personal charm. He at once offered him the libretto of *Les Pêcheurs de perles*, by Carré and E. Cormon (pseudonym of Pierre Étienne Piestre). Bizet thereupon withdrew *La Guzla de l'Émir* from rehearsal at the Opéra-Comique and returned the libretto to its authors, an action that some writers have thought a fine example of artistic sincerity and others have damned as contemptible timeserving. The real explanation, a very simple one, has never been given: one of the conditions attached to the subvention was that the composer should never have had a work staged, and the prior production of *La Guzla de l'Émir* would have invalidated *Les Pêcheurs de perles*. The music of *La Guzla de l'Émir*[1] disappeared without trace (it may have perished in a conflagration of his discarded works which he held shortly before his death, but it is not improbable that parts of it survived in later operas). All we know of it is the opinion of the Academy judges. They picked out for special mention 'a prelude, serving the purpose of an overture, happy in form and very neatly scored' and 'a duet in which is inserted an elegant serenade accompanied by a harp and a pretty design for flute' (possibly an earlier version of the famous duet in Act I of *Les Pêcheurs de perles*); and wound up as follows:

If this work still displays a little too much of the recondite and a certain tendency to sacrifice vocal interest to richness of accompaniment, we are happy again to recognize that loftiness of sentiment, vivacity of style and certainty of execution—in a word, those serious qualities of which M. Bizet

---

Théâtre-Lyrique, Vaudeville (where he produced *L'Arlésienne*) and (after Bizet's death) the Opéra-Comique, where he was responsible for the revival of *Carmen*. He held the latter post for twenty-one years, broken by a spell in prison after the disastrous fire of 1887, which was adjudged to have been due to managerial carelessness. Saint-Saëns quotes some amusing instances of his passion for leaving his personal mark on every new production: during the rehearsals of *Le Timbre d'Argent* he wanted one day to introduce wild animals, the next to cut out all the music except ballet and choruses, and play the rest as straight drama.

[1] The libretto was afterwards set by Dubois, whose version was produced in 1873.

had already given proof and which are to-day the assured guarantee of a brilliant future.

The qualification here is significant: Bizet's reaction against the supremacy of the voice was already causing that uneasiness which was to culminate in the condemnation of his later operas as Wagnerian and anti-lyrical.

There are no published letters dating from this period, but one or two incidents throw light on Bizet's powers and temperament. On 26th May 1861, after a dinner-party at Halévy's, Liszt favoured the company by playing one of his latest works. It was full of appalling (and no doubt spectacular) difficulties, and at the end all crowded round to congratulate the master on the work and its apparently effortless performance. 'Yes,' replied Liszt, 'it is a difficult piece, horribly difficult, and I only know two pianists in Europe capable of playing it as it is written and at the speed I desire: Hans von Bülow and myself.' Halévy, standing by the piano, suddenly remembered Bizet and his memory. 'Did you notice this passage?' he said, striking a few chords in approximation to what Liszt had played. Bizet sat down and played the passage from memory. Liszt, much impressed, thereupon produced the manuscript, and Bizet astonished the company by playing the piece right through without mistake or hesitation. Liszt seized him enthusiastically by the hand and declared: 'My young friend, I thought there were only two men able to surmount the difficulties with which it was my pleasure to adorn this piece. I was wrong: there are three, and in justice I should add that the youngest of the three is perhaps the boldest and most brilliant.' The story may perhaps have been touched up (a young man who was present wrote of Bizet's 'ordinary talent which contrasts so markedly with Liszt's and is much more agreeable'), but it certainly does not exaggerate Bizet's skill, to which there are many testimonies. Berlioz ranked him with Liszt and Mendelssohn for his playing from a full score, and others paid tribute to his beautiful touch, subtle gradation of tone and ability to suggest each individual instrument of the orchestra. His performances of original keyboard music, especially Bach's Preludes and Fugues, Beethoven's 32 Variations in C minor and various works by Mendelssohn and Chopin were equally admired. There is no doubt that had he wished he could have become one of the leading concert pianists of that virtuoso-ridden age. According to Pigot he did receive many tempting offers, but always refused to play in public, though he often appeared at musical parties and occasionally at charity concerts which were sometimes reported in the press. The reason for this is clear enough: he did not wish to compromise his career as a composer. The French public liked to keep musicians in separate compartments: if a performer composed a piece it was instantly given the damning label 'musique de pianiste.' Bizet went so far to avoid this danger that he composed regrettably little for the instrument of which he was such a master; it is matter for regret that he never wrote the piano Concerto which he planned.

Another anecdote, dating from an earlier period, shows his powers put at the service of parody. Among the most successful operatic composers of the day was one Clapisson, a pretentious nonentity, who after a great success at the Opéra-Comique with a work called *La Fanchonnette* was in 1854 elected to the Academy in preference to Berlioz. This impelled Bizet to improvise at the piano, with a vivid imitation of Clapisson's voice, manner and musical style, a piece entitled *L'Enterrement de Clapisson*. It began with a funeral march on the master's most banal theme: first the procession of mourners with the members of the Academy in solemn state at their head, then the funeral oration delivered by Ambroise Thomas, then the cheerful departure of the company, glad to have the tiresome ceremony over. The second part was called 'Apothéose.' Clapisson's soul, clad in full Academy robes with a sword at its side, finding itself alone, flies from the cemetery up to heaven. God, surrounded by the most celebrated composers, receives him with honour among the immortals (here the ceremony of admission to the Academy was parodied). Beethoven in his capacity of president greets him with the opening bars of his fifth Symphony, which Clapisson interrupts with a theme from *La Fanchonnette*. Beethoven, only momentarily disconcerted, resumes his Symphony (left hand), but Clapisson is not to be outdone and pours forth a stream of his choicest melody (right hand). So for some time the contrapuntal battle continues, till Beethoven as the wiser of the two gives in and *La Fanchonnette* is carried to a swelling apotheosis. This piece, which unfortunately has not survived, was in great demand at musical gatherings till Clapisson's death (1866), after which Bizet refused to play it. But he continued to amuse his friends with improvised fantasies on themes from Offenbach and outrageous parodies of the Boieldieu school, adorned with every manner of embroidery and obsolete *fioriture*.

As a young man Bizet was known for his fiery temper. If provoked he would plunge into excited argument, often tilting at imaginary windmills. In August 1862 Berlioz and Reyer went to Baden to inaugurate a new theatre in which operas of theirs were to be the first works performed. They were accompanied by Gounod and Bizet. Gounod's *La Reine de Saba* had just failed at the Opéra, a misfortune which the composer bore stoically enough, but which Bizet, then at the height of his admiration for Gounod, could not forget (he had been helping Gounod with the production). Among the party was one Paccini, a third-rate librettist whom the others were in the habit of using as a butt to sharpen their wits. One day at dinner Paccini, perhaps under provocation, declared that *La Reine de Saba* had deserved its fate. The effect on Bizet was electric: he grew red in the face, waved his arms about and called the librettist every name under the sun. They all but came to blows before Gounod intervened and pointed out tactfully that it was he, not Bizet, who had been insulted. On the same visit Bizet is said to have set the cat among the pigeons by maintaining, in conversation with the critic Jouvin, that 'Wagner is Verdi with the addition of style.' Probably he knew little Wagner at this time and was pulling the ponderous Jouvin's leg; but his habit of uttering outrageous and paradoxical opinions (and this statement would have been regarded as both in 1862), while no doubt it made his conversation stimulating, may have done him much harm. For the story and others to the same effect [1] soon got about, and they were used by the Paris critics as a stick with which to beat nearly all his work from *Les Pêcheurs de perles* to *Carmen*. In fact Jouvin gave the story wide publicity

[1] He was supposed to have challenged Scudo, the Wagnerophobe critic of the *Revue des Deux Mondes,* with the words 'You're an idiot—here is my card' at the Wagner concert of 25th January 1860—at which time he was still in Rome.

immediately after the production of *Les Pêcheurs de perles*, adding that the captious remark ought to have scalded Bizet's tongue. His known views of Wagner, which were well balanced, are recorded later.

In the course of this year and the following winter Bizet composed the music of *Les Pêcheurs de perles*. Fatherly advice was again forth-coming from Gounod. After urging him to be very much himself ('that is the way to be all alone to-day, but to have the world round you to-morrow') he continued in reply to some query of Bizet's:

You regret that the laws do not permit the assassination of certain musicians? But they certainly do permit it, and the divine laws *order* it. Only you must agree over the means. We are all killing: the butchers kill meat; the lazy kill time or flies; journalists kill the dead; and good works kill bad ones. In twenty years from now Wagner, Berlioz, Schumann will reckon plenty of victims. Haven't we already seen some, and famous names at that, half slain by the last blows of Beethoven? There was a grand assassin! Try to be in the camp of the assassins; there is no middle way between that and the camp of the victims.

These were wise words well directed: Gounod's precept was better for Bizet than his example. The opera was finished by March 1863, when Berlioz was in correspondence with Marmontel, Bizet's old piano teacher, on the subject. Marmontel had sent him the score, doubtless hoping for a preliminary puff. But Berlioz, who was still the music critic of the *Journal des Débats*, tactfully pointed out that he was hardly the man to approach, as he was both a com-poser and a critic and therefore full of prejudice. Meanwhile, on 11th January 1863, Pasdeloup had performed the scherzo from Bizet's third *envoi* at the Cirque Napoléon. Both scherzo and funeral march had been played privately at the Institut in November 1861, but this was probably the first occasion (with the exception of the little operetta *Le Docteur Miracle*) that a work by Bizet had come before the general public. The fact of the performance was significant, for Pasdeloup, who in his day played the part of a French Henry Wood, had only just begun to include contemporary works within the classical programmes he was trying to popularize. Un-fortunately most accounts agree that he was a very indifferent con-ductor. Saint-Saëns, who was present, says that Bizet's scherzo was 'badly performed and badly listened to, falling upon general inattention and indifference.' According to Pigot it was received with hisses; and although the rest of the programme, which included Mozart's E flat Symphony and Beethoven's *Egmont* music, was eminently respectable, Pasdeloup was deluged with correspondence from angry subscribers threatening to withdraw their subscriptions. The press was silent or hostile, with the sole exception of J. Lovy in *Le Ménestrel,* the organ of the music-publishing firm of Heugel, who described the scherzo as 'a very pleasing piece, written with a certain verve but with something lacking in the peroration.' On the following Sunday (the 18th) it was repeated in a concert given by the Société Nationale des Beaux-Arts,[1] an institution (apparently short-lived) whose aim was to cater for young composers. Also included in the programme were parts of a Symphony by Saint-Saëns and Félicien David's symphonic ode *Le Désert.* This time, though *Le Ménestrel* in the person of Paul Bernard now found it prolix and lacking in melodic inspiration, the scherzo was warmly received and the press much more favourable. During this same year the Société Nationale des Beaux-Arts gave what appears to have been the only public performance of *Vasco de Gama.*

The first performance of *Les Pêcheurs de perles* was fixed for 14th September 1863, but was postponed till the 30th owing to the indispostion of the Leila, Léontine de Maësen (who was still not quite fit on the first night). The part of Nadir was sung by Morini, Zurga by Ismaël and Nourabad by Guyot. The opera was moderately well received, though the audience seems to have been more surprised than pleased by the vividness of the scoring and the boldness of certain harmonic effects. Bizet was called on at the end and greeted with enthusiastic applause (there is no evidence whatever for Landormy's suggestion that the ovation was due only to a careful dissemination of his friends in the audience). Louis Gallet, who was seeing Bizet for the first time, described him as

a little dazed; his head was lowered and revealed only a forest of thick curly fair hair above a round, still rather childish face, enlivened however by the quick bright eyes which took in the whole hall with glances at once delighted and confused.

[1] To be distinguished from the more famous Société Nationale founded in 1871.

The press, however, with one notable exception, was frigid and patronizing. Bizet was taken severely to task for imitating Wagner, Félicien David and the 'violent effects' of the new Italian school (i.e. Verdi); he was accused of 'harmonic bizarreries born of a misdirected search for originality' and of the unspeakable sin of 'enthusiasm'; he was told that his talent approximated to that of Grisar, one of the most trivial of the *opéra-comique* composers, and should never attempt the pathetic. Jouvin in *Le Figaro* found the opera an orgy of noise and Gustave Bertrand in *Le Ménestrel* ended with a pompous rebuke to Bizet for appearing at the end: if he had to appear, he ought to have been dragged on—or at least have made a pretence of being dragged on. The one exception—and he was an exception to almost everything in France at that time—was Berlioz, who devoted his last critical article in the *Journal des Débats* to *Les Pêcheurs de perles*. His appraisal was remarkably discriminating. He picked out for warm approval some of the most original items, such as the opening chorus and dance and the delightful chorus behind the scenes at the beginning of Act II, and greatly praised the subtlety and novelty of the scoring, while condemning the chorus 'Ah, chante, chante encore,' 'whose rhythm is one of the things one doesn't dare write nowadays.' He observed with typical irony that Bizet had come back from Rome without having forgotten music, and summed up:

The score of *Les Pêcheurs de perles* does M. Bizet the greatest honour, so that we shall be forced to accept him as a composer despite his rare talent as a sight-reader.

But Berlioz, as usual, was playing a lone game, and the opera, though it had a certain *succès d'estime* with artists, was a failure with the paying public. For a time it was played alternately with *The Marriage of Figaro*, but after attaining a total of eighteen performances (the last on 23rd November) it dropped out of the repertory till 1886, when Bizet was both dead and world-famous. Thus, though he had achieved something in having a three-act opera put on the stage, he found himself at the age of twenty-five both financially and artistically insecure. He had advanced only a very little way on the road to success, and now that his Rome pension had run out he had to make a living. His father could not have been in serious straits, for on 3rd October 1863, three days after the production of

Les Pêcheurs de perles, he bought a small piece of land at Le Vésinet,[1] a few miles down the Seine from Paris. Here he built two small bungalows, known as Nos. 8 and 10, Route des Cultures, which served as summer residences for himself and his son (in the winter they continued to live in Paris where their address was now 32 Rue Fontaine-Saint-Georges). The bungalows were small and very simply furnished, and father and son did their own cooking, helped by an ample kitchen garden. Galabert describes the pleasure Bizet took in this place and in walking along the wooded banks of the Seine, accompanied by his great black-and-white watchdog Zurga, called after a character in *Les Pêcheurs de perles.* Yet he must have felt it irksome (even if it were possible) to live at his father's expense. At any rate the next few years tell a sad story of continual overwork in order to make ends meet. Nor was it by any means congenial work. His pupils, who seem to have consisted largely of the talent-less children of the upper classes who wished to acquire the social grace of playing a pretty piece on the piano, merely bored him. He was employed by Perrin and Carvalho to play through the scores submitted to the Opéra and Théâtre-Lyrique. In addition he under-took an enormous amount of hackwork for the publishers Heugel and Choudens. This consisted of piano transcriptions of all kinds, for two and four hands, vocal scores of operas, orchestrations of song-hits of the day and even the composition of third-rate dance music. The transcriptions are models of their kind, far above the general level of the period, which they did much to raise; but Bizet had no illusions about the dance music. In a letter to Galabert (September 1866) he gives an amusing account of his scoring of a certain 'ignoble waltz':

It is maddening to interrupt the work I love for two days in order to write cornet solos. One must live! I had my revenge. I have treated this orchestra more scurvily than nature intended. The cornet utters yells worthy of a low public house, the ophicleide and big drum pleasantly mark the first beat of the bar with bass trombone and cellos and basses, while the second and third beats are pounded out by the horns, violas, second violins, the two first trombones and the drum! Yes, the drum!

The list of works arranged by Bizet that poured from the presses

---

[1] He paid 3,800 francs for an area of 4,697 square metres. Land was cheap in the district owing to the building of a railway.

during the sixties is astonishing: it includes *Le Pianiste Chanteur* (6 series; 150 pieces from all schools), arrangements for piano solo or duet (or both) of *Faust, Hamlet, Don Giovanni, Mignon, L'oca del Cairo* [1] and other operas, and a vast number of lesser pieces. It is perhaps arguable whether labours of this kind impaired his musical style and sense of artistic direction; there is no doubt whatever that they damaged his health. He speaks of working sixteen hours a day and even more, of periods of exhaustion and of frequent recurrences of his throat trouble; the effect of this on a constitution never robust is not difficult to estimate.

No original composition can be assigned with certainty to 1864, though some of the songs and piano pieces published in 1865-7 may date from that year. For the greater part of 1865 he was busy with the five-act opera *Ivan le Terrible* on a libretto by Arthur Leroy and Henri Trianon. [2] This had already been offered to Gounod, who was working on it in 1858 immediately after completing *Faust*, but soon abandoned it. Certain things in *Mireille*, including the air 'Le jour se lève,' were originally intended for *Ivan le Terrible*. Bizet's score, long supposed to have been destroyed by the composer, was recently discovered almost complete, and the opera received its maiden performance at Mühringen (Württemberg) in 1946. It was to have been staged at the Théâtre-Lyrique early in 1866, but for some reason that has not been convincingly explained Bizet withdrew it in December 1865. The traditional explanation is that he suddenly became aware that he had fallen completely under the influence of Verdi and did not wish to be judged on such a work. This is certainly not the whole story. In a letter to Galabert (December 1865) he wrote: 'Ivan is still held up! The Théâtre-Lyrique hasn't a penny!' And later in the same month: 'I have finished with the Lyrique. *Ivan* withdrawn. I am in negotiation with the Grand Opéra.' It seems likely that some action or suggestion of Carvalho's —possibly a restriction on grounds of economy—annoyed the temperamental Bizet. But an unpublished letter in the Opéra library

[1] Victor Wilder's version of Mozart's unfinished opera, produced in 1867.

[2] Wrongly attributed by Pigot in his first edition (followed by most later writers) to Louis Gallet and Édouard Blau, the librettists of *La Coupe du Roi de Thule* and *Don Rodrigue*.

reveals that he then submitted the score to Perrin, director of the Opéra, accompanied by some sour reflections on the lot of a composer. Its subsequent fate is uncertain; Bizet may have withdrawn it for the reason stated (though the peril was quite as much Gounod as Verdi), but it is possible that it was rejected by Perrin. The fact that Bizet never mentioned the opera in conversation with Galabert suggests that it was a sore subject. Galabert mentions another abortive opera of this period, called *Nicolas Flamel*, for which Bizet sketched a scene at the piano in the presence of himself and the librettist, Ernest Dubreuil. He dates this 'before he had begun *La Jolie Fille de Perth* . . . probably in May 1865'; but as Bizet did not begin *La Jolie Fille de Perth* until July 1866 and was working on *Ivan le Terrible* for most of 1865, the date is more likely to be 1866. About this time he wrote his first published piano works, the six 'Lieder sans Paroles' [*sic*] on poems by Méry entitled *Chants du Rhin,* the three *Esquisses musicales* for piano or harmonium, and *Chasse fantastique,* which reads like a transcription from an orchestral score and may conceivably be a rehash of the overture *La Chasse d'Ossian.* All three were brought out by Heugel in 1865–6.

From 1865 date two friendships of which interesting records survive. Early in the year he met Edmond Galabert, a young musical amateur, who became his pupil in June and with whom he conducted a correspondence course lasting several years. Galabert, who later published a much-edited version [1] of the letters he received from Bizet, gives an illuminating account of his methods as a teacher. Before taking him on, Bizet examined him closely, not only in music but in literature, asking him particularly what books he had read in French and foreign languages. When Galabert gave him a list, including Goethe and Schiller, Bizet replied: 'That settles it. People think you don't need any education to be a musician. They are wrong; you have to know a great deal.' [2] After the lessons had

[1] Or rather two versions, one in 1877 and another, somewhat fuller, in 1909.

[2] This alone should dispose of Landormy's preposterous charge, repeated by others, that Bizet was merely a good workman with no cultural or outside interests and only financial ambitions. In fact he had an ample library, was exceptionally well read, loved pictures and kept abreast of the times not only in literature, but in science, philosophy and politics.

been going on for a year Galabert broached the question of fees, on which nothing had been arranged. Bizet cut him short:

Don't ever mention that again. I give lessons for money because they bore me. . . . With you, we are simply talking of things that interest us, things that we love. We are swimming in the same waters. I have been at it longer than you. I know the bad places, and I say to you only: Don't go there, it's dangerous.

He was a conscientious and modest teacher. After giving Galabert the text of a Prix de Rome cantata to set, he called in Guiraud to hear it played, telling Galabert afterwards that he wanted a second opinion in case his teaching was on the wrong lines. He urged Galabert to study Mozart's and Weber's operas and to aim at emotional expressiveness, sacrificing the strict principles of harmony and counterpoint if necessary. 'Let yourself go, aim at the emotions, avoid dryness, don't turn up your nose at the sensuous, you austere philosopher. . . . Let us have fantasy, boldness, unexpectedness, enchantment—above all, tenderness, *morbidezza*!' He particularly emphasized the double profit, spiritual and technical, to be derived from a study of Bach's preludes and fugues and remarked how modern some of them were in feeling, instancing the B flat minor from the first book. Orchestration in his opinion gained by not being too thick. When Galabert played something that had impressed him as effective, Bizet replied: 'No, that lacks air, and in the orchestra you must have air.' To another pupil he wrote: 'Let each part have around it sufficient room to move.' His somewhat cautious advice on the use of wind instruments has been held against him, with little reason; he preferred and recommended the old natural brass instruments, and sought (very successfully) to obtain new effects from original grouping rather than by extending the technical possibilities of each instrument.

In 1868 he gave Galabert the libretto of *La Coupe du Roi de Thule,* which had been set for a competition by the Opéra and which he later tackled himself. His remarks on this subject are of great interest. He laid emphasis on the practical requirements of the theatre, such as giving the characters time to get on and off, and still more on the frame of mind in which a dramatic composer

49

should work. He must get inside the skin of each character and interpret his or her feelings at each moment of the action; he should never set two stanzas in differing moods to the same music; and he can greatly heighten the dramatic tension by bringing back motives associated with a particular person or incident. Bizet at once seized on the character of Myrrha as the centre of the action—'this feline and terrible character . . . no heart, but a head and something else.' He upbraided Galabert for failing to make the most of her, and went on:

She is an old-style courtesan, sensual as Sappho, ambitious as Aspasia; she is beautiful, quick-witted, alluring. . . . In her eyes must be that greenish look, the sure sign of sensuality and egoism pushed to the length of cruelty. . . . Yorick by himself is free; he sings his love with passion and frenzy; he tells it to the clouds and the stars. With Myrrha present he is extinguished. . . . She comes in (for the first time) slowly, dreamily, absent-mindedly; she turns her glance on all around her, and fixes it almost disdainfully on Yorick.

What is this but the Carmen-José situation, throwing its shadow years before the event? The still more interesting musical parallels are discussed in Chapter VII.

Bizet's second new friend of 1865 was a very different person. In September of that year a cottage at Le Vésinet together with a wooded park was bought by Mme la Comtesse Moreton de Cha-brillan, who soon came to know Bizet. This was no common countess. Born in 1824, Céleste Vénard, the daughter of a loose mother and an unknown soldier, had fled from home in her teens in order to escape the attentions of her mother's lover, and in the course of a remarkable career had been by turns prostitute, actress (her stage name was Céleste Mogador), circus rider, novelist, dramatist and author of a volume of memoirs (though she had no idea of spelling and could hardly hold a pen). In 1854, after a varied assortment of dukes, musicians and authors, including Alfred de Musset, had reposed at her feet, she made a romantic and scandalous marriage with Comte Lionel de Moreton de Chabrillan, scion of an old aristocratic family. After his death she was forced to return to the stage in order to pay his debts, and in 1864 had enjoyed a great triumph in one of her own plays. A second and recently discovered volume of memoirs, written in phonetic French, gives a portrait of Bizet from an unexpected angle. It is not certain, though probable enough, that the obvious explanation of their relationship is the correct one (in some respects the memoirs are more remarkable for what they omit than for what they include). She can hardly have helped him on the artistic plane; her cultural level seems to have been that of the drawing-room waltzes which he had to score for publishers. He did not get on well with her friends, a bohemian crew including a pianist who 'thumped like a beast,' or with her mother, who hated both the piano and Bizet's habit of knocking on Céleste's window as he went home from the station at night (for which, on one occasion, she took a medieval revenge with a well-aimed receptacle from an upper room). Yet he spent much time in her company, often working for hours on end in a room, complete with piano and music-paper, which she put at his disposal. According to her account, she was the only woman he invited to the small musical gatherings in his bungalow, at one of which he played through the whole score of *La Jolie Fille de Perth*. Her picture of him does not suggest a contented man; though she calls him in a happy phrase 'the aristocratic savage,' she also says 'I never saw him laugh freely' and more than once remarks that he 'was not very cheerful at this time.' She adds a delightful glimpse of Bizet senior, that '*saint homme*' uniquely careful of his son's independence and as reverent towards him 'as the Holy Virgin must have been towards her son conceived through the operation of the Holy Ghost.' This portrait of an unsmiling Bizet, taken when off his guard, is very revealing of the character behind the ironical mask which he presented even to his friends.

The contract for the production of *La Jolie Fille de Perth* was signed with Carvalho in July 1866, and Bizet at once set about composing the music. The librettists were J. H. Vernoy de Saint-Georges, one of the most fashionable of Scribe's successors and as tiresome as he was incompetent, and Jules Adenis; the libretto was quite the worst Bizet was ever called upon to set. He himself had no illusions about this; he quoted some of the choicest verses to Galabert, remarking that he did not use the words for composing or he would never find a single note (this may account for the bad prosody, a persistent but venial fault in all his operas). His method was to seize the general sense of each section and concentrate on the emotions rather than the utterances of the characters—a method that might have been fatal if applied to a work of art, such as Boito's libretti, but could hardly be said to constitute an injustice to Saint-Georges. He set himself deliberately to repair the faint characterization of the latter's creatures, and certain alterations in Act I (the suppression of a romance for Smith following the opening chorus and the substitution of Mab's couplets, one of the best numbers, for a duet between Mab and Smith) were probably due to his insistence. But it is unfair to condemn Bizet for not rejecting a libretto which he despised; he was bound by contract with Carvalho, and the result of a young composer's rejection of a fashionable librettist's work (however inept) might have been no libretto at all. The music of Act I was finished by September, Bizet declaring himself satisfied with it; he said, in mitigation of Saint-Georges's treatment of Scott, that the original was a detestable novel but an excellent book. His industry at this time was astonishing. The opera was not by any means the only work he had on hand. He was up to his neck in correcting proofs for publishers (which, he said, multiplied by spontaneous generation), scoring waltzes and composing songs.[1] Not only were the six songs published by Heugel under the title *Feuilles d'album* composed this September, but several others, including the admirable *Adieux de l'hôtesse arabe*, date from about the same period. In June he had also resumed a project dear to his heart, the Italian symphony subsequently known as *Roma*; but though he told Galabert a month later that it was finished, this was by no means the end of its history. Two other works probably dating from the spring of 1866 are a two-part fugue, written for Galabert, which has disappeared, and a setting for male voices of Victor Hugo's 'Écoutez. Je suis Jean,' written for a Belgian choral festival. By October Act II of *La Jolie Fille de Perth* was ready, and the complete work was scored and dispatched to Carvalho on 29th December. No wonder Bizet complained of insufficient sleep. But his worries over this opera were not at an end. For one reason or another its production was delayed for a full year, although

[1] Apparently to commission: see the ninth letter to Galabert (July 1866).

Carvalho put on five other new operas (including Gounod's *Roméo et Juliette*) during that period. Bizet, overworked, seething with impatience and quick-tempered at the best of times, may have been unjust to Carvalho. His letters of the early part of the year, with their cries of 'rehearsal or the law-courts,' are cantankerous in the extreme.[1] The truth seems to be, however, that the Théâtre-Lyrique was in very low water (Carvalho had to give up the directorship early in 1868, to be succeeded by Pasdeloup, who was even less successful), and Carvalho evidently thought that *La Jolie Fille de Perth* would be less of a draw than some of the other operas. In January 1867 he prevailed upon Bizet to revise the contract, though Christine Nilsson, for whom the part of Catherine had been written, was re-engaged. In March Bizet went to Bordeaux to hear a new tenor, Massy, whom he promptly engaged for the part of Smith. But then Nilsson, preferring to create Ophelia in Ambroise Thomas's *Hamlet* at the Opéra, threw over her contract with the Théâtre-Lyrique and left two operas, including Bizet's, without a heroine. The next candidate, Jane Devriès, who subsequently created the part, satisfied Bizet but not the rest of the syndicate, who wanted Mme Carvalho. But Bizet, though told he might lose 10,000 francs thereby, stuck to his guns; and rehearsals began in July with the first night planned for September. The next postponement was due to Bizet himself. There was a Grand Exhibition in Paris that summer, and he preferred to wait until the cosmopolitan public, whom he suspected of following only the great names, had dispersed. Rehearsals were therefore broken off and resumed only in early

[1] To this period (March 1867) belongs his condemnation of Verdi's *Don Carlos*. 'It is *very* bad. You know I am eclectic; I adore *Traviata* and *Rigoletto*. *Don Carlos* is a kind of compromise. No melody, no expression; it aims at style, but it only aims. It made a disastrous impression. It was a complete and utter *flop*.' And in another letter: 'Verdi is no longer Italian; he wants to write Wagner. . . . It has neither head nor tail. He has discarded his faults, but his virtues have gone with them. He aims at style and achieves only pretentiousness.' He did however admit that the attempt did credit to Verdi's integrity as an artist, and in later years he greatly admired *Aida*. 'You will find in it things that will astonish and delight you,' he wrote to Guiraud.

December. However, Bizet had the satisfaction of selling the score to Choudens on excellent terms, which he said rivalled those given to Gounod. He was to receive 3,000 francs at the first performance, 1,500 at the thirtieth; if he had 120 performances within three years he would get 16,000 francs in all. It is doubtful if *La Jolie Fille de Perth* has yet reached 120 performances.

Meanwhile in the spring the organizers of the Exhibition had offered prizes for the best cantata and the best hymn, each composed on a given text. Bizet entered for both competitions under the pseudonym of Gaston de Betsi [*sic*]. He gives an amusing account of what happened when he and Guiraud delivered their entries.

The porter received us very unceremoniously. 'Oh! So every one is a musician! Good Lord, it's time that was stopped!' I replied drily: 'I am no more a musician than you are, I would have you know; but a poor fellow whom I'm looking after entrusted me with this parcel, and I ask you to deliver it faithfully.' All the staff then bowed on learning that we were not musicians. What a coward I am!

According to Galabert Bizet and Guiraud both took the cantata seriously but tried to be as vulgar as possible in the hymn. The cantata competition (the piece was called *Les Noces de Prométhée*) was won by Saint-Saëns. There were 103 entries, of whom Bizet was among the first fifteen. He was pleased that Saint-Saëns had won the prize, but furious that his own handwriting had been recognized and his participation known—another sign of his lack of confidence and horror of humiliation. The hymn competition was annulled, the jury being unable to decide between so many entries of equal merit.

Bizet was on good terms with most of his fellow-composers, and particularly with Saint-Saëns, with whom he used to discuss his difficulties. Saint-Saëns once suggested that as they were not welcomed in the theatre they should go back to the concert hall. 'That's all very well for you,' replied Bizet, 'I am not made for the symphony; I need the theatre, I can do nothing without it.' This was not always his opinion; he was apt to change his mind on such matters, and when taxed with inconsistency would reply: 'Yes, but since then I've been thinking.' Saint-Saëns well expressed the difference between his approach to music and Bizet's: 'We pursued a different ideal, he

BIZET AGED ABOUT TWENTY-FIVE

seeking passion and life above all things, I running after the chimera of purity of style and perfection of form.' On one occasion Bizet was working in his study at Le Vésinet when he heard a tenor voice declaiming the romance from *Les Pêcheurs de perles* in the street. It was Saint-Saëns, who, not knowing the number of Bizet's house, chose this method of attracting attention. Bizet liked Massenet, admiring in particular his oratorio *Marie-Magdeleine*, and wrote of him: 'We must pay attention to this little chap, he's going to leave us standing.' He respected Thomas, but could not abide Auber. Once when both composers had had an opera produced within a short interval Auber met him in the street and said, in the tone of one repeating a banal formula: 'I've heard your work. It's very good.' Bizet replied: 'I accept your praise, but I do not reciprocate it.' Then, as Auber made a face, he added quickly: 'A simple soldier may receive the praises of a marshal of France; he does not return them.'

Early in 1867 he acquired another correspondence pupil. This was a young composer named Paul Lacombe, who lived at Carcassonne and wrote to Bizet without introduction. He was much more of a musician than Galabert, and Bizet's letters to him, if they tell less of his personal life, are of greater musical interest. In the first letter,[1] writing to a man he has never seen, he makes an engagingly frank statement of his position.

I am 28 years of age. My musical baggage is pretty slender. An opera very much discussed, attacked and defended—in fact a failure, honourable, brilliant if you allow me the expression, but none the less a failure. Some songs—seven or eight piano pieces—some symphonic fragments performed in Paris—and that's all. In some months' time a big work, but that is to count my chickens—don't let's speak of it.

The final sentences give a picture both of the man and his preoccupations:

As for terms. I don't know what answer to give. I don't much like dealing with that side. If I had money of my own, I would be happy to give you some of my leisure. I should think myself amply paid by the progress I should be helping you to make. Unhappily I have no leisure. Lessons, vast quantities of work for several publishers, extensive correspondence—

---

[1] Dated 1866 by Imbert, but almost certainly belonging to the early months of 1867.

all that swallows up my life. I am thus forced to accept, not the price of my advice, but the price of the time I spend on you. I charge 20 francs for my lessons. On an average, my time is worth 15 francs an hour to me. Will you base our arrangement on this consideration? We shall be able to work out a general average on the amount of work you send me. . . . The important thing is that we should talk no more about it, for these details are particularly disagreeable to me.

In the summer he found a more public opportunity of stating his views of music. The editor of the periodical *La Revue Nationale et Étrangère*, which had recently been converted from a monthly to a weekly in order that more space could be devoted to current affairs, asked him to take the vacant post of music critic. He agreed, and his first article appeared on 3rd August under the pseudonym of Gaston de Betzi (this time with a *z*), an anagram of his own name. This witty and sensible piece of criticism [1] contains a great deal that is still apposite. It also shows that Bizet had a real literary gift, a fact since confirmed by the publication of his letters. It is a forcible plea for honesty and impartiality in musical criticism. 'I shall tell the truth, nothing but the truth, and as far as possible the whole truth.' He protests against the increasing tendency to judge music according as it conforms or fails to conform to a pre-ordained system, whether national, philosophical, political or purely musical. 'For me there are only two kinds of music—the good and the bad.' [2] Two further sins, as green as ever to-day, receive no less trenchant treatment: the habit of praising one composer only by damning several others, and the fashionable admiration of good taste rather than genius.

Let us be unaffected [*naïfs*] and genuine, not demanding from a great artist the qualities he lacks but learning to appreciate those he possesses. When a passionate, violent, even brutal personality like Verdi endows our art with a work that is vigorously alive and compounded of gold, mud, blood and gall, don't let us go up to him and say coldly: 'But my dear sir, this lacks taste, it is not gentlemanly [*distingué*].' Gentlemanly! Are Michelangelo, Homer, Dante, Shakespeare, Beethoven, Cervantes and Rabelais *gentlemanly*?'

[1] Printed as Appendix E, p. 248. It has never before been reproduced in full.
[2] Chabrier, who had much in common with Bizet, later in a similar context added a third kind—the music of Ambroise Thomas.

This is a truth that needs to be uttered from time to time in the history of art. We do not know how Bizet's article was received; but it was his last as well as his first venture into journalism. Immediately after it appeared the editor of the paper retired, and his successor endeavoured to censor Bizet's second contribution. He took exception to some criticism of Azevedo, Rossini's biographer, and asked him to cut out a passage about Saint-Saëns. Bizet, true to his principles, refused and resigned his post; this may have cost him some sacrifice, for it was particularly well paid.

In October 1867 he wrote a jubilant letter to Galabert:

I am completely happy! Never did an opera have a better start! The general rehearsal produced a great effect! The piece is really very interesting; the interpretation is most excellent! The costumes are rich! The settings are new! The director is delighted! The orchestra and singers are full of keenness! And what matters more than all that, dear friend, the score of the *Jolie Fille* is a GOOD PIECE OF WORK! I mention it to you *because you know me!* The orchestra gives it all a colour, a relief, that I admit I didn't dare hope for! I am sticking to my path. Now, forward! I must climb, climb, always climb. No more evening parties! No more fits and starts! No more mistresses! All that is finished! Absolutely finished! I am talking seriously. I have met an adorable girl whom I love! In two years she will be my wife! From now on nothing but work and reading; thinking is life! I am talking seriously; I am convinced! I am sure of myself! The good has killed the evil! The victory is won!

The girl was Geneviève Halévy, second daughter of Bizet's old teacher, and within two years she was indeed his wife; but all biographers seem to have overlooked the fact that no sooner was the engagement made than it was broken off—by the girl. That is the only explanation of the tone and language of Bizet's letters in the next two months, which contain such phrases as: 'The hopes I had formed have been broken. The *family* has resumed its rights! I am very unhappy' (October). 'I am still very much depressed. The blow I have received takes away all the hopes that were dear to me' (November). We can only guess at the cause; but it is possible that some breath of scandal about Céleste Mogador had reached the ears of the Halévy family. Nor do we know when they eventually agreed to the marriage; probably not till shortly before it took place, in June 1869. It was in this gloomy mood that Bizet wrote an act for an anonymous joint operetta called *Malbrough s'en va-t-en guerre* (words by Siraudin and Busnach). He described the circumstances in a letter to Lacombe:

I sent the Athénée packing. But they came weeping to me, and I polished them off the first act. Legouix is charged with the second, Jonas with the third and Delibes with the fourth. The secret was well enough guarded; but a woman has just revealed it, all is lost. I shall disown it shamelessly. I have a mind to hiss the first act—apart from the fact that the public will do it quite well without me! I have been totally dished and done for. I was reproached with not keeping my word, they set up a wail, and I *gave* them my first act. It won't bring me in a brass farthing. I certainly don't make much progress in business matters.

The piece was produced at the Athénée on 13th December; the air which gave it its title was sung, with variations by one Bernadin, before the rise of the curtain. Pigot says that at some period during the next two years Bizet wrote music for another piece of the same kind, with the illuminating title of *Sol-si-ré-pif-pan*, which was produced, also anonymously, at the Menus Plaisirs. But the only discoverable work with this title, a so-called 'bouffonnerie musicale' in one act by William Busnach, was produced at the Château d'Eau on 16th November 1872 with music by one H. Vincent. There was a contemporary Viennese composer called H. J. Vincent who did write operettas (and incidentally devised a new system explaining the principles of harmony by reference to geometry), but it is not impossible that the name was a pseudonym of Bizet's. The music of both operettas has disappeared [1]—a matter for little regret.

The first performance of *La Jolie Fille de Perth* at last took place on 26th December 1867. It seems to have been well performed and well received. Lutz as Ralph and Massy as Smith were excellent; Devriès (Catherine) began nervously, but was at her best from the middle of Act III; the Bohemian Dance was encored. Bizet wrote cheerfully to Galabert:

My work has obtained a genuine and serious success! I was not hoping for a reception so enthusiastic and at the same time so severe. . . . I have

---

[1] According to Pigot an attempt was made to reconstruct *Sol-si-ré-pif-pan* from the orchestral parts after Bizet's death.

been taken seriously, and had the great joy of moving and gripping an audience that was not predisposed in my favour. . . . The press is excellent! Now, are we going to make money?

This was in fact the one opera of Bizet's that was reasonably well received by the press. *Le Ménestrel* called the second act 'a master-piece from beginning to end.' Edmond Tarbé in *Le Figaro* praised the orchestration and the dramatic perspective, but found the work, judged by the highest standards—and he maintained that Bizet deserved to be so judged—lacking in originality. Reyer in *Le Journal des Débats* considered the style eclectic, but excused the con-cessions to public taste and to the whims of the prima donna on the ground of Bizet's youth and still unestablished position. He gave particularly high praise to the Bohemian Dance and Ralph's song in Act II. The severest critic was Johannès Weber in *Le Temps,* who pointed out that, so far from the charge of Wagnerism being justified, Bizet was in danger of lapsing too far the other way; and he instanced the entry of Catherine and Glover in Act I, with its en-semble in the style of Auber accompanied by copious *roucoulades* from the soprano. Bizet, who was never afraid of criticism provided it was fair, at once wrote to Weber, whom he did not then know:

No, sir, no more than you do I believe in false gods, and I will prove it to you. This time, I admit, I have made some concessions [1] which I regret. I should have plenty of things to say in my defence—you can guess them. The school of *flonflons*, trills and falsehoods is dead—dead as mutton! Let us bury them without tears, without regrets, without emo-tion and—forward! [2] Needless to say, sir, this letter is not an advance which would be as unworthy of my character as I am convinced it would be of yours, but I repeat, your criticism pleased me, and I felt the need to tell you so sincerely.

This was the line he had taken in his article in August, and he stuck to it: there is nothing in his later work that can be qualified as a concession either to public taste or to singers.

[1] He told Galabert that they had been forced upon him.

[2] It is typical of Gauthier-Villars's treatment of facts that he should sneer at Bizet for saying this 'just at the time that he was writing without remorse' the passages Weber had complained of. He had written them over a year before, and was now abjuring them!

But a good press did not save *La Jolie Fille de Perth*. It had eighteen performances, the same number as *Les Pêcheurs de perles*, and then disappeared from the Paris stage till 1890. The reasons were probably twofold: a series of indispositions in the cast and the imminent financial collapse of the Théâtre-Lyrique. That bad luck rather than failure was the cause is made clear by its production at Brussels as early as 14th April 1868. Bizet went to see it there, and reported that, though the performance was monstrous, the work was a success with both public and press.[1] The St. Valentine chorus rapidly became a favourite in the Paris salons.

Bizet's musical activities during the next three years are bewildering. He began or projected at least six operas without finishing any of them, and it is often difficult to determine exactly when he was composing what and why he abandoned it. In June 1867, in connection with the exhibition, the three opera-houses each announced a competition. The Théâtre-Lyrique invited a work on any libretto the composer chose; the Opéra-Comique put forward a libretto by Saint-Georges, *Le Florentin*; while the Opéra began with a preliminary libretto competition. Bizet's first typical reaction was: 'If I compete, no one except you [Galabert] and Guiraud will know of it, and *my copying will not be recognized.*' In April 1868 the Opéra announced that its winning libretto (out of 168 submitted) was *La Coupe du Roi de Thule* by two young authors, Louis Gallet and Édouard Blau. Bizet advised both Galabert and Lacombe to set the piece as an exercise, adding (June): 'It is more and more probable that I shall not compete.' The reason for this was that Perrin, the director of the Opéra, was pressing him to set a piece, still only in scenario, by Arthur Leroy and Sauvage. The title of this piece is not known. At the same time he refused a request from Bagier of the Théâtre-Italien to write an opera in the old Italian style. He spent the summer in a state of vacillation.

I am very much embarrassed at the moment; I don't know what to do. If I compete without getting the prize, I'm afraid the good opinions that are held of me may be modified to my disadvantage. If I win the prize, that will put off my big affair for two years, perhaps. If I do not compete and my big affair miscarries I shall find myself between two stools!

---

[1] Tenth letter to Lacombe, misdated 1869.

The big affair was presumably the Leroy and Sauvage opera, over which he was at first very enthusiastic. While waiting for the libretto he concentrated on other compositions. During the summer he at last finished *Roma*, completely rewriting the first movement, which had originally been a set of variations, and finding that the second theme of the finale fitted 'marvellously' in the middle of the andante. The first movement 'bears no resemblance to any known first movement. It is new, and I count on a good effect.' He considered, however, that the finale was not up to the standard of the rest, and later upbraided Guiraud for not telling him how bad it was. He also composed some songs,[1] which did not greatly please him, and some piano music, which did. This (which according to Galabert was inspired by his hearing Delaborde play on one of Erard's pianos) comprised the *Variations chromatiques*, based on a theme sketched the previous winter, the *Nocturne* in D major and probably *Marine*.

In July, and again in August, he had very severe attacks of angina, accompanied by some kind of spiritual crisis.

An extraordinary change is taking place in me. I am changing my skin, as artist and as man; I am purifying myself, I am becoming better: I feel it! Come, I shall find something in myself if I look hard enough. . . . A change so radical from the musical point of view is taking place in me that I cannot risk my new manner without preparing myself several months in advance. I am making use of September and October for this trial.

He was making 'a summary study of the history of philosophy from Thales of Miletus to the present day.' This was not his first attempt to chart his philosophical position. In 1866, disgusted by the battle of Sadowa and the aggressions of Bismarck ('aided by cholera, his worthy colleague in mincemeat'), he had tried to formulate his views on progress, political, religious and artistic. He saw no hope in nationalism—he was convinced that 'notre belle Frrrrrance' would soon be soiling her hands in the fray—and organized religion, though it had served a purpose, seemed to him outmoded and misused.

---

[1] These were the six originally published by Hartmann in 1868: *Pastorale, Rêve de la bien-aimée, Ma vie a son secret, Berceuse, La Chanson du fou* and *La Coccinelle*.

Religion is for the strong a means of exploitation against the weak; religion is the cloak of ambition, injustice and vice. This progress of which you speak moves slowly but surely; it destroys little by little all superstitions. Truth breaks free, science is popularized, and religion totters; soon it will fall, in the course of centuries—that is, to-morrow. That will be all right, but don't let us forget that this religion, with which you can dispense—you and I and some others—has been the admirable instrument of progress; it is religion, and above all the Catholic religion, that has taught us the precepts which enable us to dispense with it to-day. . . . The Jews had to have altars, Sinais with Bengal fire, etc. One had to speak to their eyes; later it was enough to speak to their imagination. In good time we shall only have to deal with reason.

But this prospect had its drawbacks too.

I believe that the whole future belongs to the perfecting of our social system (with which politics are always so confoundedly mixed up). Society once perfected, no more injustice, and so no more malcontents, hence no more assaults on the social system, no more priests, no more policemen, no more crime, no more adultery, no more prostitution, no more inflamed emotions, no more passions—but wait! no more music, no more poetry, no more legion of honour, no more press (bravo for that!), above all no more theatre, no more error, and so no more art! . . . The societies most deeply tainted with superstition have been the greatest promoters of art. . . . Art decays in proportion as reason advances. . . . The imagination lives on chimeras, on visions. You suppress the chimeras, and good-bye imagination!

Faced with this dilemma, or with the greater implied dilemma that lay beneath, Bizet for a time took refuge in something approaching sheer pessimism ('Don't count on anything! The longer I live, the more I mistrust our poor human kind'). His survey of 1868, superficial as he admitted it was, brought him a conclusion of sorts. He found talent, genius, outstanding personalities . . . but not a philosophical system that stands up to examination. With morality it is different. Socrates (that is to say, Plato), Montaigne (excellent, because he has no system)—but spiritualism, idealism, eclecticism, materialism, scepticism, all are downright useless. Stoicism, despite its errors, did make men. In fact, the true philosophy is: examine known facts, extend scientific knowledge and ignore *absolutely* everything that is not proved up to the hilt! That positivism is the only rational philosophy, and it is grotesque that the human spirit should have taken nearly three thousand years to discover it!

However inadequate an answer this may seem on the part of Bizet the man (and it is hard to think he really believed it), it is very possible that it was a help to Bizet the artist. Gounod, faced with a more acute conflict between the fleshly and the spiritual, developed something like religious mania, with disastrous effects on his music.[1] Bizet remained critical, detached, half idealist, half sceptic; and in the remaining years of his life he wrote music that showed a remark, able power to enter into and interpret, as it were from within and without at once, the emotional and psychological states of all manner of persons, from an Arabian slave-girl to Parisian children at play, from young men turned into criminals by a passion stronger than themselves to a couple of old peasants meeting at last to declare the love they have concealed for fifty years.

The results of what he described as this changing of his skin appear in the unfinished and unpublished *La Coupe du Roi de Thule*. The Leroy-Sauvage libretto still hanging fire, Perrin prevailed upon Bizet 'with the *compelling authority* which a director of the Opéra exercises over a composer whom he holds between finger and thumb' to enter for his competition. Two acts were written by October, and Bizet was at first greatly pleased, considering them far superior to anything he had done before.[2] Yet though Perrin assured him, somewhat irregularly, that whatever the jury (which included Berlioz) decided, he would see that he got the prize, Bizet was still suspicious. He thought that Perrin's object was to make sure of getting a tolerable

---

[1] It has been assumed that Bizet was all his life a devout admirer of Gounod. This is far from the case. In December 1868 he wrote to Lacombe: 'Gounod is leaving for Rome to take orders. He is absolutely mad! His last compositions are dreadful. To hell with Catholic music!' He admired Gounod's early operas, *Ulysse, Sapho*, etc., which he found 'full of verdure and sap,' and Gounod's musical influence of course persisted; but his admiration for both the man and his music seems to have waned during the sixties. There are surprisingly few references to Gounod in the letters of this period.

[2] Though as usual he soon wavered. 'I have reviewed my first act of *La Coupe* on two different occasions,' he wrote to Guiraud. 'The first time I found it altogether admirable; the second time it seemed to me nauseating!'

score, but that if he received one better he would be quite pleased to drop Bizet's; and he found himself up against the old problem: 'Not to get the prize would be annoying and a black mark as far as the Opéra is concerned. To let it be carried off by a gentleman who would do less well than I would be galling.[1] What am I to do?' He did nothing; in December he told Lacombe he was thoroughly sick of the subject. *La Coupe du Roi de Thule* remains the most tantalizing of all his fragments. Nor did he write a note of the Leroy-Sauvage opera. On the other hand we find him in September in negotiation with Léon Halévy, brother of the composer and father of Ludovic, over a five-act opera called *Les Templiers*. He spent a week on Halévy's scenario and declared himself ready to undertake it. 'How happy I should be if you would be willing in collaboration with M. de Saint-Georges to write this magnificent opera-poem for me.' Some sketches believed to belong to this work were found after Bizet's death, but he does not seem to have progressed very far. The statement [2] that he sent in a setting of *Le Florentin* for the Opéra-Comique competition is almost certainly untrue; there is no mention of it in the letters. There is, on the other hand, a letter of uncertain date projecting an opera called *Vercingétorix*; Bizet writes that he has long been in love with the idea, 'but the insurmountable obstacle is

---

[1] It was in fact carried off by an amateur, Eugène Émile Diaz de la Peña, whose opera was a complete failure. So were the winning entries in the Opéra-Comique and Théâtre-Lyrique competitions. Pigot says that in all three competitions there was so much back-stage work and so little regard for impartiality that most serious musicians refused to compete. But Diaz defeated both Massenet and Guiraud. A pleasant story is told of his getting into difficulties with the scoring of his opera. He went to Bizet and Guiraud and said: 'Shall I have the flute accompanying here, or the horn?' Bizet suggested the horn, Guiraud the flute. Diaz, perplexed, went to his father, an elderly and distinguished painter, who pondered hard and replied: 'Don't run any risks, my boy. Have them both.' Massenet was told by Massé, one of the judges, that his setting contained such an abuse of Wagnerian formulae that it engendered nothing but weariness and fatigue.

[2] Soubies and Malherbe, *Histoire de l'Opéra-Comique*, vol. ii, p. 202. The authors also seem to think Bizet actually submitted his entry for *La Coupe du Roi de Thule*.

Caesar! These wretched emperors are generally not too musical!'
Bizet's muse certainly was not equipped to deal with emperors.

On 28th February 1869 Pasdeloup performed three movements of
the Italian symphony under the title *Fantaisie symphonique, Souvenirs
de Rome*. This title, as well as those of the individual movements,
was concocted at the last minute, possibly by Pasdeloup, who was
also responsible for the omission of the scherzo, apparently because
of its hostile reception six years earlier. This was against Bizet's
will, but Pasdeloup said that as soon as the work obtained the
success it deserved he would 'slip in the scherzo like a letter into
the letter-box.' The performance went quite well. Bizet reported
the public reaction concisely: 'First movement: a round of applause,
some hisses, second round, a whistle, third round. Andante: a
round of applause. Finale: great effect, applause three times repeated,
hisses, three or four whistles. In fact a success.' This was a modest
ration of hisses for a new work at this date; in the same year the
overture to *Die Meistersinger* was twice nearly howled down by
Pasdeloup's audience.[1] But despite the fair reception, the Symphony
seems to have been totally ignored by the press, and it was not
repeated till 1880, five years after Bizet's death, when the scherzo
was restored. The publication of the score, prepared in 1869, was
also delayed till 1880, when the work appeared under the title *Roma*.

Early in 1869 Camille du Locle, a man of progressive ideas but
no great musical understanding, joined de Leuven in the management of the Opéra-Comique. He at once wrote to Bizet about a
possible work in three or four acts. Bizet was eager to co-operate:
'I shall be delighted to drop the competition and try to change the
genre of *opéra-comique*. Down with *La Dame blanche*!' Much time
was spent in finding a libretto; Sardou and du Locle were busy with
one piece, probably *Grisélidis*, while Bizet was keener on another.
In fact he composed no music at all in the first nine months of the
year. There were distractions, the chief of them being his marriage.
This took place on 3rd June and ushered in six years of complete

[1] The first Paris performance of *Rienzi*, at the Théâtre-Lyrique in April
1869, also baffled the public. Bizet gave Galabert an amusing description
of the dress rehearsal; he described the opera, not inaptly, as 'a noise of
which nothing can give you an idea.'

domestic happiness. This summer, and the following, he was a member of the jury chosen to award the Prix de Rome; with him were the ancient Auber and a number of nonentities. In the autumn he settled down at 22 Rue de Douai, sharing the house with some of his wife's relations, including her cousin Ludovic Halévy, already known for his collaboration with Henri Meilhac in libretti for Offenbach. Here his first task was the completion of his father-in-law's biblical opera *Noé* (libretto by Saint-Georges). This must have been an ungrateful task; he had in fact already made one unsuccessful attempt to polish it off in 1868. He had a contract with the Théâtre-Lyrique (now under Pasdeloup), binding him to complete it by the end of November, but a clause allowed him to postpone the production until he was satisfied with the cast. He at once availed himself of this; the Théâtre-Lyrique went bankrupt; the Franco-Prussian War broke out; and *Noé* was not produced till Mottl staged it at Karlsruhe in 1885. It has never been played in France.

The fruit of his deliberations with the Opéra-Comique was not one projected opera, but three; and again, though all seem to have been begun, not one was finished. During the winter he was much taken with *Calendal*,[1] a libretto by Paul Ferrier based on an epic poem by the Provençal Frédéri Mistral; but he soon abandoned it, apparently because it did not appeal to du Locle. The attraction of the Provençal subject is noteworthy, especially as Bizet had been considering it for some time. The other two pieces were *Grisélidis* by Sardou and *Clarissa Harlowe* by Philippe Gille, based on Richardson. In June 1870 Bizet and his wife went to Barbizon for the summer, and he set to work on both libretti at once. But he was soon overwhelmed by greater events that menaced the very existence of France.

[1] So much so that he copied out the libretto in different-coloured inks, one for each part. It was this copy that he sent back to Ferrier, who gave it to his widow after his death. The libretto was set later by Henri Maréchal.

CHAPTER IV

MATURITY (1870-5)

ON 15th July 1870 Napoleon III, provoked by Bismarck, declared war on Prussia and began the disastrous campaign that terminated his own dynasty and lost Alsace and Lorraine. Within a few weeks the Second Empire had fallen, the emperor himself was a prisoner, and Paris was besieged. Bizet's reaction to these events was not that of most Frenchmen; the jingoism of his Rome days had given way to a broad detachment that does him credit. Eschewing the cheerful bellicosity of his countrymen, he wrote sadly to Galabert:

And our poor philosophy, our dreams of universal peace, world fraternity and human fellowship! Instead of all that we have tears, blood, piles of corpses, crimes without number or end! I can't tell you, my dear friend, in what sadness I am plunged by all these horrors. I remember that I am a Frenchman, but I cannot altogether forget that I am a man. This war will cost humanity five hundred thousand lives. As for France, she will lose all!

Still more revealing of his unhappiness and unsatisfied longings is a dream which he recounted to Guiraud:

I dreamed last night that we were all at Naples, installed in a charming villa; we were living under a purely artistic government. The Senate consisted of Beethoven, Michelangelo, Shakespeare, Giorgione and people like that. The National Guard was replaced by an immense orchestra under the command of Litolff. The suffrage was withheld from idiots, spongers, intriguers and ignoramuses. I need not tell you it was thus the most limited suffrage imaginable. Geneviève was a little too friendly with Goethe, but despite this inconvenience waking up was a cruelly bitter business.

A few days after the outbreak he went to Paris and enlisted in the sixth battalion of the National Guard, complaining loudly of Napoleon's failure to rouse and arm the nation ('the *uncle* at least knew where to find the enemy'). He remained in Paris with his wife throughout the siege; he refused to leave on the ground that it was more dangerous to be a coward than to do one's duty. Work did not come easily. He shrank from writing a popular song on the Marseillaise pattern, but considered setting Victor Hugo's 'Ceux qui pieusement sont morts pour la patrie' under the title *Morts pour la France!* Choudens, whose efforts to preserve a satisfactorily escapist frame of mind are amusingly described in a letter to Guiraud, dissuaded him from this, but demanded songs about spring, love and roses. Not surprisingly Bizet could not oblige. By December he was living on horse, and Geneviève dreamed every night of chickens and lobsters (as for Choudens, he had given up eating and was growing fat). Nevertheless he could still applaud the fall of the Empire and the removal of 'the thick coat of shame and ordure' with which it had bespattered the country.

Paris surrendered in February, only to plunge into an experience still worse than the Prussian siege. Bizet paid a short visit to Bordeaux on business connected with his wife's family, but he was back in time to see the insurrection of the Commune (18th March) and the ensuing civil war. His impressions of these events, in which as a member of the National Guard he was at first involved, are given in an interesting series of letters to his mother-in-law and her brother. At first he was appalled by the sheer inefficiency, stupidity and cowardice of both sides. All discipline had collapsed; Bizet was among those who put their services at the disposal of the government, but after being in position for eighteen hours during which they neither saw a superior officer nor received an order, they were advised to go home. He found the citizens out on holiday, cigar in mouth. The position, he said, would have made him burst with laughing were it not the sure sign of the death of a society. He was no reactionary; he admitted that the Communards were better disciplined than the garrison, and confessed that his greatest fear was a Catholic monarchy. At first he declared that Paris had fallen too low for bloodshed, but he was soon proved wrong. On the outbreak of fighting at the barricades, looting and political murder he took his wife, whose nerves were seriously upset, to Compiègne and then to Le Vésinet, where for weeks they listened to the cannonade of the guns in Paris, which was loud enough to keep them awake at night. At Le Vésinet they were safe, thanks to the German garrison, a circumstance on which Bizet comments bitterly. He was disgusted by the excesses of the Commune ('it is assassination and incendiarism raised to the level of a political system'), though still afraid of the reaction: he lost his temper with a man at Versailles who spoke of the return of the emperor. He began to feel that there was no future for the arts in France.

Between the fury of the whites and the reds there will be no place for honest men. There is no future for music here. We must go abroad. Shall I go to Italy, England, America? . . . Germany, the country of music, is impossible for any one who bears a French name and heart. It's all very sad. Life had begun so well for us!

This was on 19th April; a month later he was taking a more philosophical attitude and noting the great powers of recovery that France always displayed on the morrow of disaster. On 24th May MacMahon's army entered Paris, and within four days the fighting was over.

These events had caused Bizet much heart-searching, and not only in regard to his material future. In April, responding to Mme Halévy's expressed interest in his career, he reviewed progress.

To tell the truth, I have never been spoiled. That is doubtless due to the lack of flexibility in my character. I have little affection for what is known as the world, and even less esteem. So-called *honours, dignities* (in the plural), *titles,* etc., would profoundly disgust me if I were not indifferent to them. Of all my comrades I am one of the two or three who have obtained good artistic results, slender enough in truth, but seriously and honourably acquired.

He has seen colleagues obtain lucrative appointments by backstairs methods which he would disdain to use; he is prepared to face a future that holds out no prospect of official encouragement. He goes on to criticize, with ample reason, the administration of the state theatres and the Conservatoire. 'Saint-Saëns, Guiraud, Massenet, myself and some others could rejuvenate this school, which Monsieur Auber has turned into a house I shall not qualify honourably because it is not honourable.' A few weeks later he heard of Auber's death and recognized it as the end of a period in French musical history: 'The poor man could not survive the destruction of all that life meant to him.' Auber's successor, as Bizet had hoped,

was Ambroise Thomas, whose *Hamlet* he regarded (with little justification) as compensating for many other musical weaknesses.[1] Bizet
looked forward to his future career with a certain sober confidence.

The doors are opened to me, and opened by me. But as for begging
something from whosoever it may be, that I shall never be able to do at
any price. Ten years ago I believed in the world, consorted with it and,
I confess, was amused by it. To-day I am not misanthropic, I am indifferent: I do not hate, I despise. . . . The road I have taken is long,
but I know where it is leading me.

And a little later he reviewed the old question of success, both
immediate and ultimate: 'The beautiful, that is to say the union of
idea and form, is always beautiful,' but few contemporaries can
assess it.

What makes success is *talent*, not *ideas*. The public (and I speak of
intelligent people, the rest don't count: that's democracy for me)—the
public only *later* understands the *ideas*. To reach this *later*, it is necessary
for the artist's talent, by means of an attractive form, to make the road easy
for him and avert an immediate repulse. Thus Auber, who had any
amount of talent but few ideas, was nearly always understood, while
Berlioz, who had genius without any talent, was scarcely ever understood.
. . . The artist does not find his true level till *a hundred years* after his
death. Is it sad? No. Merely stupid.

It is significant of his detachment from prejudice, whether musical
or national, that he should be able at this time to give a balanced
opinion of Wagner. He had for some time admired the musician
but been repelled by the man. In 1868 he had been furious with
Wagner ('this cardboard republican,' who was equally ready to
accept money from the King of Saxony one year and take a shot at
him from the barricades the next) for calling Gounod's *Faust* 'musique
de cocottes.' 'Genius certainly, but what a poseur! what a bore!
what a blackguard [*goujat*]!' In 1871 he bade his mother-in-law
set aside Wagner's political writings, particularly *Une Capitulation*,
the typical and revolting piece of tactlessness he had just perpetrated
on the fall of Paris.

[1] Bizet's letter of congratulation to Thomas is printed by Marc Pincherle,
Musiciens peints par eux-mêmes (1939).

It is the fate of great geniuses to be misunderstood by their contemporaries. Wagner is no friend of mine, and I hold him in indifferent esteem; but I cannot forget the immense pleasure I owe to his innovating genius. The charm of his music is unutterable, inexpressible. It is voluptuousness, tenderness, love! If I played it to you for a week you would be infatuated! Besides, the Germans, who alas! are quite our equals musically, have understood that Wagner is one of their strongest mainstays. The German nineteenth-century spirit is made incarnate in that man. You personally know well enough what cruelty disdain brings to a great artist. Happily for Wagner, he is endowed with a temper so insolent that criticism cannot touch his heart—even admitting that he has a heart, which I doubt.

He dismisses the claim that Wagner's work is the music of the future, a meaningless term: it is 'the music of all time, because it is admirable.' And in a postscript he answers one of the favourite charges of his critics.

Of course if I thought I was imitating Wagner, despite my admiration, I would not write another note in my life. *Imitation* is a fool's job. It is much better to write bad music of one's own than other people's. And besides, the finer the model, the more ridiculous the imitation.

Meanwhile, uncertain of the future of the theatres, but seeking distraction, he resumed work on *Grisélidis* and *Clarissa Harlowe*. The former had been well advanced by February, though Sardou wanted to change the last act; *Clarissa Harlowe* was then hardly begun. His plan was to complete both works by the autumn, and he tackled them conjointly throughout May and June. But neither was ever finished, and it is uncertain how much was written down. Of *Clarissa Harlowe* at least one act was composed, for he wrote to Guiraud:

My wife says it is good; as for me, I know nothing about it whatever. I await your opinion before having one of my own. I am always the same! Yesterday my act seemed to me bad, this morning mediocre, and just now excellent. I am dropping it and remaining under this last impression, which a new examination will clearly modify.

Grisélidis was abandoned because the Opéra-Comique refused to mount it on the score of expense. This theatre was now under the joint direction of two men of very different temperament. The one,

Adolphe de Leuven, had been the librettist of certain operas by Adam, which he accordingly regarded as the most up-to-date works in the repertory; he was a true-blue conservative with a fanatic horror of innovation.[1] Camille du Locle, on the other hand, was possessed of a reforming spirit. He held strong views on the future of the operatic stage and proposed to put them into practice at the Opéra-Comique. He wished to break with the Auber-Scribe tradition and create a form in which exoticism, poetry and the symphonic element had a large part; unfortunately, although he wrote libretti for Reyer and was part-author of Verdi's *Don Carlos*, he does not appear to have had great musical perception or much understanding of the drama. Needless to say the collaboration was not very happy. After a flop at the Opéra-Comique du Locle would be seen grinning and whispering to his friends 'That's one in the eye for Leuven!' After the next flop de Leuven would return the compliment. Du Locle had acquired rights in several of Gounod's operas from the Théâtre-Lyrique, and since the failure of that concern he was trying to attract the young composers who had begun to make their name there. He now hit upon Bizet as his chosen instrument, and on the withdrawal of *Grisélidis* offered him in compensation a one-act piece by Louis Gallet based on Alfred de Musset's *Namouna*. This had been in the hands of one Jules Duprato, who had expressed himself charmed but omitted to set it to music. Du Locle recalled the libretto and shortly afterwards induced Gallet to change the title to *Djamileh*,[2] a name he had met on one of his periodical visits to Cairo. Bizet was told to get busy at once—he spoke to Galabert of pistols pointed at his head—and he seems to have composed the score in a few weeks. Now at last he had the chance, to which he had looked forward more than two years before, to change the genre of *opéra-comique* and deliver his counterblast to *La Dame blanche*, an opera in his opinion fit only for sappers, nursemaids and porters.

[1] His real name was Adolphe de Ribbing. He had been writing for the theatre since 1825, often in collaboration with Saint-Georges: his stage works number over a hundred and fifty, and occupy seven pages of the British Museum catalogue.

[2] Du Locle, according to Pigot, inspired the whole thing, subject words and music: certainly both are dedicated to him.

Unfortunately Gallet, though a cultivated man and a great improvement on Saint-Georges, was more fitted to supply du Locle's requirements than Bizet's. In his preface to the libretto of *Thaïs*, where he abandoned strict metre, he wrote: 'A lyrical poem is a work in verse that is handed over to a musician to convert into prose.' In fact he thought more of poetry and atmosphere than of the stage. He has left a delightful picture of Bizet at Le Vésinet during the composition of *Djamileh*:

He walked about in a straw hat and loose jacket with the easy assurance of a country gentleman, smoking his pipe, chatting happily with his friends, receiving them at table, with a conviviality that always had a touch of bantei in it, between his charming young wife and his father, who was his host and spent all day gardening as a change from the fatigue of giving lessons.

It was Bizet's habit always to converse or talk business on the move, either in the open air or walking about the room; it was a bad sign if any one found him sitting down.

Djamileh was not his only care this year. He was still working at *Clarissa Harlowe*. There was some question of Pasdeloup's reviving *Roma*, which seems to have undergone further touching up at this time, and Bizet was apparently offered the post of chorus-master at the Opéra. This would have eased his financial position, and the duties were not heavy; but for some reason the negotiations came to nothing. A small but important work that dates from this time is the set of twelve pieces for piano duet entitled *Jeux d'enfants*. These were sold to the publisher Durand on 28th September 1871; the date 1872 usually assigned to their composition is due to a mistake of Imbert's in dating the eighteenth letter to Lacombe. The assumption that the *Petite Suite d'orchestre*, Bizet's orchestral version of five of the pieces, was later than the duet version is also unproven. Certainly the orchestral suite was finished by September, when the duet pieces numbered only ten. *Les Bulles de savon* and *Les Quatre Coins* were written later; *La Toupie* was originally *La Toupie d'Allemagne*, and *Trompette et tambour* appears (if indeed it is the same piece) as *Les Soldats de plomb*. Bizet also names *Les Chevaux de bois* as one of the pieces already scored, though it was subsequently replaced by *Trompette et tambour*—which we know had existed in orchestral form since 1865, when it appeared in the opera *Ivan le Terrible*. It is thus possible that Bizet's scoring of *Les Chevaux de bois* remains to be unearthed.

The production of *Djamileh* was delayed, and Bizet spent a harassed winter struggling with lessons and rehearsals and, as he put it, strengthening himself against the little emotional upsets of life, to which his temperament was peculiarly susceptible. At last on 22nd May 1872 the opera was produced. It was not a success. Du Locle had taken immense trouble with the settings and costumes, going to the length of pedantry in his effort to achieve an authentic background. He even installed a special multicoloured lamp for the sunset. He was much less successful with the singers. Bizet had wanted either Priola or Galli-Marié to play Djamileh, but the choice lighted on one Aline Prelly, pseudonym of the Baroness de Presles, whose physical potentialities were overwhelming, and indeed notorious, but seem to have been her only qualification to appear on the stage of the Opéra-Comique. This voiceless Venus, as Gauthier-Villars aptly terms her, was splendid at her first entrance, when she does not have to sing a note; but she suddenly jumped thirty-two bars in the Ghazel, and the orchestra, under Deloffre, had a desperate race to catch her up. The tenor Duchesne (Haroun), an inexperienced singer at the outset of his career, was also weak, and Potel (Splendiano), though a good artist, had very little voice. Bizet watched in the prompt box and said to Gallet at the end: 'There, a complete flop!' The scene in front of the curtain is amusingly described by Adolphe Jullien:

I s infamous! cried one. It's odious! cried another. It's very funny! said a third, more philosophically. What cacophony! What audacity! He's making fun of us all! That's where the Wagner cult leads—to madness. Neither tonality nor shape nor rhythm! It's no longer music —it's macaroni. What! Is it Italian music then? Not a bit, I mean it has neither beginning nor end.

Djamileh struggled on for eleven performances (not four or ten, as various writers have stated) and then disappeared from the French stage till Bizet's centenary in 1938.

This was a tragic fate for a charming work, full of music as original as it is delightful; but though much may be set down to the inadequacy of the singers, there was a basic weakness as well. De Leuven in his own way had already put his finger on it when he suggested that the action might be gingered up if one of the characters suddenly dropped a plate. Bizet himself wrote a month later that the poem was anti-theatrical. Du Locle and Gallet in their love for atmosphere had forgotten that the stage also requires action. The press was not slow to point out this and other supposed deficiencies. Bizet, surprisingly enough, expressed entire satisfaction with his press notices; perhaps he did not read many: for the majority were overwhelmingly antagonistic. All but three or four renewed the charge of Wagnerism at full blast; even Reyer detected a whiff of *Die Meistersinger*. Others condemned the opera as pretentious, monotonous and incomprehensible. Albert Wolff in *L'Avenir National* expressed the majority opinion when he wrote that it breathed 'an odour of boredom that only the composer's friends can resist. . . . From first to last *Djamileh* is a succession of laments. . . . The composer seems to have but one aim, to render his art incomprehensible.' Frédérick in *Paris-Journal* found no trace of an original idea in this 'laborious' score, but 'an aspect dim, vague, confused, without relief, contour or colour.' Certain individual numbers came in for particular attention. The slaves' march that opens the overture, declared Jouvin in *Le Figaro*,

lacks character, melody and rhythm. The tonality in an affected manner eludes the comprehension of the ear that would grasp it. To make this clear by a bodily parallel, imagine the listener walking on a mass of superimposed dissonances and losing his balance in following the musician as he steps off into air.

The critic of *Le Soir*, after accusing Bizet of 'the pitiless and deliberate suppression of every sign of rhythm and tonality,' pounced on Djamileh's lament. He analysed the bold progression at the beginning ('one of those audacities of which M. Wagner would be jealous'), apologizing for the technicalities, and added: 'This is so horrible, so savage in its effect, that I could not resist pointing it out for the edification of persons possessed of sufficient musical instruction to understand me.' But the height of absurdity was touched by Félix Clément in his imposing *Dictionnaire des Opéras*. To him the music was

> so extraordinary, so bizarre—in a word, so disagreeable that one might suppose it the result of a wager. Wandering in the tracks of M. Richard Wagner, he has exceeded his model in bizarrerie and strangeness. That melody is absent goes without saying. . . . But that the successions of sounds and chords, the processes of harmony and accompaniment, belong for the most part to no known or classified system of composition is an error of judgment very regrettable in a composer so skilful as M. Georges Bizet.

As for the overture, the music of the age of Rameses and Sesostris could not have appeared more extraordinary to modern ears, and the whole opera was 'packed with dissonance and harmonic cacophony in comparison with which the audacities of Berlioz were mere child's play.'

This was not the whole story, but it is curious to find even the most favourable critics concerned about the extent to which Bizet had removed the centre of interest from the voice to the orchestra. Joncières (*La Liberté*), in an appreciative notice in which he applauded Bizet for turning his back on conventional *opéra-comique*, remarked that even the common herd, lost in the new lands to which Bizet was leading them, seemed not unmoved by the subtle atmosphere they encountered there. The most discerning criticism came from Guillemot in *Le Journal de Paris*; he picked out at once the two great qualities of *Djamileh*, the extraordinary charm and freshness of the oriental colouring with its novel harmonic and orchestral effects, and the dramatic presentation of the heroine herself. Jullien too was favourable, finding fault only with the final duet. Whereas the others found traces of Wagner, he complained (with more justification) of the preponderance of Gounod. He found the opening of the overture 'extremely original and picturesque,' praised the scoring and the dramatic aptness of the music, and summed up the work as showing 'a curious spirit, in search of novelty but afraid of the banal. He is still searching; perhaps one day he will find.' But perhaps it was Reyer who gave Bizet most pleasure. He noted traces of Wagner, Schumann and Gounod in the music, but defended Bizet on the sensible ground that 'the composer who stumbles in taking a step forward is worth more attention than the composer who shows us how easily he can step backwards.' He praised the treatment of the exotic element, which never transgressed the boundary separating art from realism, and acclaimed him as the leader of the young French school.

There is in this work more than the manifestation of a talent, there is the expression of a will. And I think that if M. Bizet knows that his work has been appreciated by a small number of musicians judging without prejudice, he will be more proud of that than of a popular success.

One of this small number was Saint-Saëns, who paid his tribute in the unexpected form of a sonnet, in which 'Le bourgeois ruminant dans sa stalle serrée' opens one glassy eye, eats a sweet and goes to sleep again, bored by this 'perle aux porceaux jetée.'

Bizet felt that *Djamileh* despite its failure was a great advance, and he was right. 'What gives me more satisfaction than the opinion of all these gentry,' he wrote to Galabert on 17th June,

is the absolute certainty of having found my path. I know what I am doing. I have just been ordered to compose three acts for the Opéra-Comique. Meilhac and Halévy are doing my piece. It will be *gay*, but with a gaiety that permits style.

This was the genesis of *Carmen*, though the subject may not have been chosen yet; it was Bizet himself who suggested Mérimée's novel to his new collaborators. There were other projects too. 'It seems decided that I shall be asked for something for the Opéra. The doors are open; it has taken ten years to get there. I have ideas for oratorios, symphonies, etc.' In July he was nominated to the jury of a fugue competition and wrote to Marmontel: 'A wrong answer is only a very slight fault if the mistake makes the answer more *musical*. . . . Long live Bach! Saint-Saëns will probably think as I do, but the others!' And as if to multiply his high spirits and hopes, on 10th July Geneviève Bizet gave birth to a son, Jacques,[1] who instantly became a vocal force to be reckoned with in the household.

[1] He was Bizet's only child. In later years a journalist and author of light dramatic pieces, and secretary of a commission appointed by the Minister of Fine Arts in connection with the Paris Exhibition of 1900, he died on 3rd November 1922.

The next commission was not long in arriving. After his failure at the Théâtre-Lyrique Carvalho had migrated to the Vaudeville, a theatre where straight plays were the staple diet. Not wishing to sever his connection with music, he decided to revive the almost extinct form of *mélodrame*, that is, a play with incidental music. Although Gounod had written such music to Legouvé's *Les Deux Reines* in 1866, the form had fallen into the hands of mediocrities whose stock device, according to one writer, was to accompany every mention of the Virgin Mary with a banal tune on violins, two clarinets and three cornets in unison over a tremolo on one cello and one double bass. Carvalho invited Bizet to write music for Alphonse Daudet's play *L'Arlésienne*. For reasons of economy he was allowed an orchestra of only twenty-six players, though he was given latitude in his choice of instruments. This restriction seems to have stimu-lated rather than hindered him, for not only did he produce a master-piece both of dramatic insight and orchestral balance, but he wrote the whole score in a matter of weeks. Once more, however, he was unlucky in the production. Carvalho intended to open his season with a play called *Madame Frainex* by Robert Halt, and all the advance press notices dealt with this. On 21st September it was suddenly banned, and *L'Arlésienne* was put forward at the last minute. The first performance took place on 1st October before a bored and unappreciative audience. The overture and entr'actes were drowned by perpetual chatter, people coming and going, doors opening and shutting, and chairs being pushed back; a group of literary folk demanded loudly why this confounded Wagnerian Bizet had to interfere with his orchestral cacophony. 'They're not even listening,' Bizet whispered to Daudet in great agitation. Only the Intermezzo (the Minuet of the first Suite) made a hit. Daudet told Bellaigue that as the evening advanced he and Bizet had the sensa-tion of drowning with a collar of stones hung about their necks. It was not the fault of the production; the acting seems to have been good and the scenery admirable. The orchestra, according to Reyer, played with rare perfection and irreproachable ensemble, like a handful of virtuosos—which indeed they must have been to realize the delicacy and subtlety of the score. The chorus was not thought good enough to be seen on the stage (the only number in which it should so appear, 'Le flutet se marie' in the last act, was cut), but it seems to have given satisfaction in the wings, where it was accompanied on the harmonium by Bizet or Guiraud or occasionally Antony Choudens, the publisher's son. The conductor was Constantin, of the Athénée theatre. The *mélodrame* form had such a low reputation that most of the musical critics did not even attend, and Bizet's work, which ran for less than three weeks, passed almost unnoticed by the press. Reyer however acclaimed it as a masterpiece, and both he and Johannès Weber noted the unobtrusive skill with which rare artistry was subordinated to the psychological demands of the drama. Reyer ended by sounding a challenge:

Go and hear *L'Arlésienne*, you young musicians who as yet hold out no hopes to your professors, and perhaps you will be encouraged and more assiduous in your studies when you see the degree of talent reached by one who, only a few years ago, was sitting like you on the school benches.

It is interesting to observe that Francisque Sarcey, the leading dramatic critic of the day, in a long article devoted to demolishing Daudet's claims as a dramatist, dismissed the music as 'in no respect integral with the work; it is an addition applied afterwards' (the ineffable Clément made the same charge). In criticizing the 1885 revival at the Odéon Sarcey attributed the great success wholly to the music. Bizet was a frequent sufferer from this time-serving kind of criticism; the grotesque contortions performed by Arthur Pougin with regard to the libretto and score of *Carmen* make fascinating if disillusioning reading.

Four extracts from *L'Arlésienne*, forming the familiar first Suite, were rapidly rescored by Bizet for full orchestra and performed by Pasdeloup on 10th November. This time the success was immediate, the Minuet being encored. The Suite was repeated by Colonne at the Châtelet on 9th November 1873, at two different concerts on 18th January 1874 and at the Concerts du Conservatoire on 21st February 1875. There were now many more openings than at the outset of Bizet's career. The war of 1870 had been followed by a great national revival in the arts: operetta and salon virtuosity, symbols of the giddy Empire, were replaced by more substantial forms. The great date in this movement, and indeed in French nineteenth-century musical history, was 25th February 1871, when Saint-Saëns and a professor of singing named Bussine founded the Société Nationale de Musique, which (under the slogan 'Ars Gallica') had as its main object the encouragement of young French musicians and the performance of their works. The original committee included Franck, Guiraud, Fauré and Lalo, and one of the earliest members was Bizet. The society prospered from the first, for it was rooted in fertile soil. It became the nursery for the brilliant flowering of French music in the ensuing half-century. Soon it was giving an average of nine or ten concerts a year, devoted entirely to contemporary French music (in 1886 Saint-Saëns and Bussine resigned in protest against a proposal to let in the classics); the earlier concerts were confined to chamber music, but orchestral works quickly followed. Nor was the society's influence confined to direct encouragement. Before the new demand the old institutions began slowly to open their doors (all except the Opéra, whose doors had rusted into a solid barrier). Pasdeloup was soon playing a French work at every concert: du Locle at the Opéra-Comique put on pieces by Saint-Saëns, Massenet and Paladilhe as well as Bizet (he proved to be too far in advance of his public, the most notoriously backward in Paris, which took acute exception to all of them); and early in 1873 a new society, the Concert National, began to function at the Odéon under the conductor Édouard Colonne.[1] It was at the first of Colonne's concerts, on 2nd March 1873, that the *Petite Suite d'orchestre* from *Jeux d'enfants* was first played in public. Bizet derived great benefit from these new outlets; unfortunately he had little time in which to enjoy them. Had he lived a few years longer he would doubtless have made further attempts to realize those symphonic projects which he never ceased to cherish; he might even have left posterity deep in debt to that unexplored talent for chamber music which lurks in the pages of *Jeux d'enfants* and *L'Arlésienne*.

Immediately after the production of *L'Arlésienne* Gounod, who was abroad, asked Bizet to take charge of the negotiations for the revival of *Roméo et Juliette* at the Opéra-Comique. During the correspondence that ensued Bizet, apparently by way of explaining the 'quasi-

[1] Colonne's great achievement was to persuade the French to recognize their greatest composer, Berlioz.

silence' (Gounod's term) that had come between them, wrote that he had been uneasy about his musical personality being absorbed by Gounod's. The latter professed himself much astonished; but the incident emphasizes Bizet's greater self-awareness. *Roméo* was given on 20th January 1873, and Bizet, who had taken a great deal of trouble, received a charming letter of thanks from the composer. It seems to have been about this time that he began work on *Carmen*. The first act (and probably a good deal more) was finished before the summer, but some hitch with the Opéra-Comique intervened, and he turned to another project. His collaboration with Gallet over *Djamileh* had borne fruit in an unexpected quarter. Jean Baptiste Faure, principal baritone at the Opéra, had proposed that Gallet and Édouard Blau should write a libretto for Bizet to compose and himself to sing in. The first suggestion was Musset's *Lorenzaccio*, but Faure did not like the moral character of the hero (on hearing this, Bizet said 'He wants everything. Not only must he be great, handsome, generous and strong, but the other characters must be praising him when he's not on the stage'). The next idea came from Bizet himself. He found a translation of Guilhem de Castro's *La Jeunesse du Cid* and instantly told Gallet:

That's what I want to do. It's not Corneille's *Cid*, it's the original Cid with real Spanish colouring. There is one scene, that with the beggar, which is marvellous. Have a look at it. Faure, I'm sure, will be satisfied. The Cid amorous, filial, Christian, heroic, triumphant—what more could he want?

Bizet insisted that there should be no quotations or echoes of Corneille and that the piece should have a new title. It was accordingly named *Don Rodrigue*. He composed the whole five acts during the summer and autumn, which he spent at 17 Rue de Paris, Port-Marly. His correspondence with Gallet during this period throws light on his methods. He took immense pains over details and was always asking for minor alterations in the libretto, emphasizing (as he had done to Galabert years before) the vital importance of dramatic timing. On one occasion he asked pardon for rewriting the verse, excusing himself on the ground that the music sometimes came 'with an authority that I would call inspiration if the word were not ridiculously pretentious.' The scene in which Rodrigue, at the lowest ebb of his fortunes, protects a beggar and is rewarded by a vision in which Lazarus foretells the turn of the tide, he regarded as the climax of the opera; Massenet, when he came to set a revised version of the libretto, omitted it altogether. Towards the end of October Bizet invited Faure, Guiraud and the librettists to hear him run through the work at the piano. He played from a score containing only the vocal parts, supplying the accompaniment from memory. Gallet speaks of the vivid expression he infused into every part, though his voice was a poor reedy tenor, and says that he played all five acts at a sitting with scarcely a pause. The listeners were very much impressed by the vital passion and colour of the music, as more than one of them has left on record, and the outlook for the future seemed bright. On the following day Bizet wrote Gallet an anxious note: 'What is your impression of yesterday's session? What did you say when you went home? What are your hopes and fears?' Another note reports the cordial attitude of Faure, whose influence it was hoped would thaw the frozen portals of the Opéra. But it was left to a stronger agency to perform this rare feat: on 28th October the Opéra was burned down. The company migrated to the Salle Ventadour and at once began to play for safety; after a period of suspense the management announced that the reputation of neither Bizet nor his librettists was sufficiently established, and in place of *Don Rodrigue* put on *L'Esclave,* a work of profound obscurity by one Membrée, whose immediate failure drove them farther than ever behind the entrenchments of Meyer-beerian tradition.

Don Rodrigue was probably not such a loss as Guiraud and others imagined. Only the vocal parts and a few half-legible indications of the scoring survive in the manuscript—presumably the one from which Bizet played to his friends—and these fragments, so far as it is fair to judge them, show less character than might be expected from a work on a Spanish subject written at the same time as *Carmen.* But Bizet was thoroughly discouraged, swore he would have nothing more to do with the stage (*Carmen* was still held up), and asked Gallet to prepare him the text of an oratorio to be entitled *Geneviève de Paris.* The recent success of Massenet's *Marie-Magdeleine* probably influenced him here. This mood may not have lasted long; at some point he said to Guiraud, with acute self-criticism: 'Your place is at the Opéra; I'm afraid of making a poor showing there, of not having the necessary fullness. I shall shine at the Opéra-Comique; I shall enlarge and transform the genre.'

Meanwhile Pasdeloup, true to the spirit of the time, had commissioned three symphonic overtures, from Massenet, Guiraud and Bizet. The results of this were *Phèdre, Artewelde* and *Patrie*. Bizet composed the last during the winter of 1873–4, taking its main theme from a march in Act V of *Don Rodrigue*. There is some mystery about the title. It has nothing to do with Sardou's play *Patrie*, then being converted into an opera by Paladilhe. Pigot says that this rumour was put about by malignant persons who wished to suggest that Bizet wanted to set Sardou's work, but had been rejected in favour of Paladilhe. It may be so; but Pigot goes on to say that Bizet, though he had the war in 1870 in mind, did not wish to reopen a sore subject in an age of appeasement, and so by a poetic fiction substituted for France 'the mighty shade of Poland in her death agony, always conquered but always resurgent, whose ineffaceable memory and sacred name live for ever in the hearts of her scattered children.' But did Bizet bring Poland into it? There is no such hint in the score, which is merely entitled *Patrie!* [*sic*] Possibly a note was inserted in the programme at the first performance. At any rate, the real inspiration was certainly the war of 1870. *Patrie* was first played under Pasdeloup on 15th February 1874, and met with immediate success. It was repeated more than once in the same year, and so this most dramatic composer met his only success in life with two concert works for orchestra—one a suite torn from its stage context, the other the feeblest and most uncharacteristic progeny of his later years.

Some time during the winter things began to move at the Opéra-Comique. Even during the composition of *Don Rodrigue* Bizet had continued to work at *Carmen*, and there was talk of rehearsals beginning in December. They were now put forward to August 1874, and Bizet, after a renewed and very acute attack of angina, accompanied by abscesses of the throat, left for the country to finish the score. This year he found a new summer residence at Bougival

(1 Rue de Mesmes), a quiet spot right on the Seine. Here *Carmen* was finished, and the 1,200 pages of full score were orchestrated within two months. He was pleased with the result. He said to a friend:

They make out that I am obscure, complicated, tedious, more fettered by technical skill than lit by inspiration. Well, this time I have written a work that is all clarity and vivacity, full of colour and melody. It will be amusing. Come along; I think you will like it.

He told Lacombe that for three or four years he had been dreaming of a piano concerto, but could not bring himself to write piano and symphonic music at the same time. During the winter he attended César Franck's organ class at the Conservatoire, where his silent attentiveness made an impression on the young d'Indy. Till the eve of the production of *Carmen* none of the pupils knew the identity of the stranger in their midst. It is interesting to speculate on what fruit Franck's teaching might have borne had Bizet lived longer.

Meanwhile *Carmen* had been once more postponed till the spring. The long delay may have been due to de Leuven's implacable hostility to the libretto. When Halévy first tackled him he flew into a panic at the mention of the subject: 'We have five or six boxes let every night for marriage interviews! Impossible!' Halévy pointed out that the story would be considerably sweetened, especially by the introduction of Micaela, and the final murder softened by ballet [1] and brilliant spectacle; but de Leuven could not reconcile himself to the murder—there had never been such a death on the Opéra-Comique stage—and finally cut the Gordian knot by resigning in 1874. Early on there may also have been difficulty in finding a leading lady. Galli-Marié's acceptance is dated 18th December 1873,[2] and she was

---

[1] There was no ballet in *Carmen* as first produced; probably this was one of the many points at which Bizet resisted the sweetening process. The ballet in Act IV was first inserted at Vienna in October 1875 (with music taken from *La Jolie Fille de Perth* and *L'Arlésienne*). It is a shocking dramatic solecism that should never be repeated.

[2] Her letter was first printed by Delmas, *Georges Bizet* (1930). By a strange coincidence there is extant a letter from Victor Massé to Sardou projecting an opera on *Carmen* with Galli-Marié in the title-part. It is dated 11th August 1864.

to create the part in October 1874 at a fee of 2,500 francs a month for four months, twelve performances a month. If her engagement were prolonged owing to the success of the piece she demanded a minimum of 3,600 francs. At first Zulma Bouffar seems to have been considered for the part, but the statement of H. Sutherland Edwards [1] that Bizet wrote it for Marie Roze must be dismissed as complete fiction. Edwards states among other things that Bizet and the librettists visited Marie Roze for suggestions in 1874, that she accepted the part and that only her engagement in England prevented her carrying it out; whereupon Bizet rewrote the whole thing for Galli-Marié. Had there been the slightest truth in this story (which was denied by Bizet's widow), it would surely have been mentioned in *The Mapleson Memoirs*, for not only does Mapleson say a good deal about early productions of *Carmen*, but he was Marie Roze's father-in-law.

On 15th January 1875 Bizet sold the score of *Carmen* to Choudens for 25,000 francs. On 3rd March the first performance took place at the Opéra-Comique. That same morning Bizet's appointment as chevalier of the Legion of Honour was announced in the *Journal Officiel*, and the omen seemed favourable, although some wit put it about that the authorities made haste to decorate him in the morning as they would never dare to do so in the evening, owing to the scandalous nature of the new work. The rehearsals had been trying for Bizet. He met with a good deal of hostility inside the theatre; d'Indy, who often attended, says that 'every one from the director to the concierge turned his back on Bizet'—till the opera showed signs of success. The orchestra, accustomed to the routine scoring of the Auber-Adam school, at first resented the greater elaboration and difficulty of Bizet's music, even finding some passages unplayable, and Deloffre, the veteran conductor, though a conscientious musician, had little authority. It was the same with the chorus, who after two months' work declared their music in the cigarette girls' and quarrel scenes impossible to sing, especially as they had to act instead of following their usual practice of standing in a line with their eyes on the conductor. On 13th February Bizet asked for additional female voices in Act I, a request which du Locle granted only after asking

[1] *The Prima Donna* (1888).

Halévy if it was absolutely necessary. Nor were the librettists very helpful. Apprehensive of the outraged moral sense of the public, they prevailed on the singers to tone down their parts; they stopped Escamillo (at his first entrance) patting the cheeks of a couple of the gipsy girls in the chorus and even put some restraint on Galli-Marié. In this policy they were acting directly contrary to Bizet's wishes; the latter resisted every attempt to soften down both word and gesture. He refused to shorten the duet in Act II (which was thought too 'naturalistic') and break it up into sections for applause. In Act I he wished the chorus to enter by ones and twos instead of in a dense mass, but du Locle protested that this was against all tradition. Du Locle's whole attitude is puzzling. He seems to have liked Bizet personally, and he mounted the opera with great care, but he was unhappy about the libretto and he loathed the music. He kept repeating in his 'sour and derisive voice' (Saint-Saëns's phrase) that it was Cochin-China music, no one could understand it. Saint-Saëns even accused him of deliberately sabotaging *Carmen's* chances in order to leave the field clear for his favourites, Verdi and Gounod. This is probably unfair, but he certainly did not put his weight behind the work. When a minister applied for a box on the first night he invited him to the dress rehearsal, saying that the piece was so improper that before taking a box for his family he ought to see if it was suitable. The probable explanation of his conduct, which can hardly have encouraged the cast, lies in the precarious financial position of the Opéra-Comique. Early in 1876 he was compelled to surrender the management, and perhaps he was already beginning to count up the results of the fiasco which he was convinced *Carmen* would be.

Nevertheless by the first night most of those taking part had been won round to enthusiasm, and the last rehearsals had been excellent. Ludovic Halévy in his diary records both the initial mystification of those behind the scenes (including himself) at the novelty of the music and their subsequent confidence of its success. Perhaps it was too much to hope that the most notoriously conservative audience in Paris would reach the latter state of mind without passing through the former. At any rate the reception was disappointing—not openly hostile as has sometimes been stated, but frigid, shocked and un-

PORTRAIT OF GENEVIÈVE BIZET BY ÉLIE DELAUNAY

comprehending. Halévy described it thus in a hurried letter to a friend written the following day:

Act I well received. Galli-Marié's first song applauded, also the duet for Micaela and José. End of the act good—applause, recalls. A lot of people on the stage after this act. Bizet surrounded and congratulated. The second act less fortunate. The opening very brilliant [the entr'acte was encored]. Great effect from the Toreador's entry, followed by coldness. From that point on, as Bizet deviated more and more from the traditional form of *opéra-comique*, the public was surprised, discountenanced, perplexed. Fewer people round Bizet between the acts. Congratulations less sincere, embarrassed, constrained. The coldness more marked in the third act. The only thing applauded was Micaela's air, of old classical cut. Still fewer people on the stage. And after the fourth act, which was glacial from first to last, no one at all except three or four faithful and sincere friends of Bizet's. They all had reassuring phrases on their lips but sadness in their eyes. *Carmen* had failed.

The performance seems to have been fair, though the chorus, especially the women, were inclined to sing out of tune and put little conviction into their acting. Bouhy (Escamillo) and Mlle Chapuy (Micaela)—afterwards the wife of a general who became Minister for War—were good, and Galli-Marié excellent. Lhérie (José) was a poor actor and erratic in pitch. The orchestra was no more than moderate. There were the usual mishaps. Once when Galli-Marié was singing *pianissimo* the big-drum player, miscounting his bars, stupefied the house by coming in with two loud bangs. Some of the ladies of the chorus, accustomed to the unhurried entries and exits of *La Dame blanche* and now obliged not only to dance and fight but even to smoke on the stage, were taken ill as a result. D'Indy, who with Camille Benoît was the lucky winner of a free ticket which Bizet had offered to Franck's organ class, went to congratulate the composer in the first interval. According to his account, which does not quite square with Halévy's, they found him and his friend the publisher Hartmann walking up and down on the pavement outside the stage door. Both seemed dejected. Bizet thanked them for their congratulations, adding that they were the first he had received that evening and would doubtless be the last. When someone else mentioned his success he replied: 'Success! Don't you see that all these bourgeois have not understood a wretched word of the work I have written for them?' During one of the intervals, on catching sight of the critic Victor Wilder, he broke through a circle of friends and begged him to say what he really thought of *Carmen*, as he was not the kind of man who had to be told that everything he did was admirable. After the performance he took refuge in du Locle's office, where some of his friends tried to comfort him, and he was one of the last to leave the theatre. Of what followed, two flatly contradictory accounts have been given. According to Pigot, who had it from Guiraud soon after the event, Bizet took Guiraud's arm and wandered about Paris for half the night pouring out the bitterness of his soul. Halévy on the other hand, thirty years later and when he was an old man of over seventy, stated that Bizet went quietly home with himself and Meilhac. Pigot's account is the more probable. Halévy, who was living with Bizet at the time, may have been thinking of another occasion, perhaps the dress rehearsal (his account is inaccurate in several other respects). For some reason that has never been explained, he seems to have been at pains to minimize the depressing effect that the reception of *Carmen* had on Bizet, whose nature he clearly did not understand; the evidence of others who knew him well—Guiraud, Gallet, Maréchal, and most notably Mme Bizet—points all the other way.[1]

The first press reviews of a work that has since been accepted as a masterpiece are always interesting; those of *Carmen* throw a light half lurid, half humorous, on the state of French musical criticism in 1875. It would hardly be too much to say that both libretto and music caused something approaching pandemonium in the press. The general opinion was that Mérimée's novel was far too obscene to be staged, the characters were, in Arthur Pougin's words,[2] 'of an

[1] Galabert agrees with Halévy; but his correspondence (and it seems his acquaintance) with Bizet ended abruptly in 1872. All that he writes of the last years is from hearsay.

[2] Pougin is quoted rather than others whose vocabulary was even stronger, because in 1903 he published in *Le Ménestrel* an article (since much quoted) entitled *La Légende de la chute de Carmen et la mort de Bizet*, in which he posed as a great admirer of the libretto ('a masterpiece'), supported statements of Galli-Marié's (*a*) that Bizet was much less severely handled than the

antipathetic nature and devoid of interest,' and Galli-Marié over-emphasized the seamy side of her part to such an extent that 'it would be difficult to go much farther without provoking the inter-vention of the police' (François Oswald in *Le Gaulois*). The actress's gestures, wrote Léon Escudier in *L'Art Musical*, 'are a very incarnation of vice, and there is something licentious even in the tones of her voice.' Or, as succinctly put by Noël and Stoullig in their *Annales du Théâtre et de la Musique*: 'Quelle vérité, mais quel scandale!' This in a sense is a tribute to the actress, but the critics found more scandal than truth in the music. The more conserva-tive trumpeted unanimously about Wagnerism, the decrepitude of melody, the surrender of the voice before the confused and clamorous roar of the orchestra. It seems astonishing that *Carmen* of all operas should within the memory of some people alive to-day have been condemned for lack of melody, but that was the opinion of more than half the Paris press. Oswald remarked that the tunes were given to the orchestra, the accompaniments to the voice, and con-trasted Bizet's erudite melody with the natural flow of Auber, Adam, Hérold and Boieldieu. Baudouin in *La République Française* spoke of 'complete absence of light—music dwelling from start to finish

---

librettists, (*b*) that the success of *Carmen* was assured before Bizet's death, and concluded: 'It is absolutely untrue to say that the public understood nothing of the music and felt only indifference or disdain towards it.' The whole article is a complete distortion of the facts, apparently inspired by a guilty conscience. The second of Galli-Marié's statements was explicitly denied by Bizet's widow; the first is disproved by reference to the printed word. Pougin wrote two reviews of *Carmen* in 1875; in the first (7th March) he described Bizet as 'one of the most ferociously intransigent of our young Wagnerian school,' but gave the music considerable praise; in the second (11th March) he was a good deal cooler. In 1878 he contri-buted the article on Bizet to Fétis's *Biographie universelle*. Having now, it appears, seen the writing on the wall, he became patronizing and con-temptuous. Bizet is held up as 'the most deadly enemy of *opéra-comique*,' and rebuked for having shown antipathy to 'the genius of one of its most glorious representatives in the past—Boieldieu.' The 1903 article completed the volte-face. In 1878 Pougin also made the extraordinary assertion that the critics welcomed *Carmen* with the greatest pleasure.

in a limbo of greyness.' Henry de Lapommeraye in *La France* found José's air behind the scenes (Act II) 'indecisive in shape and pretentious in harmony,' though this is the one item in the score that is sung unaccompanied (it is possible however that the critic heard one of the later performances when d'Indy supported Lhérie with a harmonium in order to keep him in tune). Another charge, nearly as surprising, was that the music was not dramatic. A typical summing-up is that of Oscar Comettant in *Le Siècle*, who thought that only Rossini could have done justice to so sensual a libretto.

Certainly no one will accuse M. Bizet of melodic prodigality. . . . It is impossible to give musical expression to Carmen's erotic fury by ingenious orchestration; melody is the only thing that can realize MM. Meilhac and Halévy's brutally realistic characters. I do not mean to say that there are not what are called themes in M. Bizet's music. Unfortunately, as a rule, they are anything but original and they lack distinction. . . . There is no unity of style in *Carmen*, but its greatest fault is that it is not dramatic. . . . M. Bizet has learnt everything that can be taught, but unhappily he has much still to learn of what no one can teach him. He thinks too much and does not feel enough, and his inspirations, even when most happy, lack sincerity and truth, two qualities that are worth all the erudition in the world.'

To the supporters of the old Auber school everything that savoured of erudition was suspicious, and Bizet's scoring fell under this ban. Escudier, who could stomach neither scoring nor harmony, even ranked *Carmen* below Bizet's first two operas.

In *Carmen* the composer has made up his mind to show us how learned he is, with the result that he is often dull and obscure. He makes a point of never finishing his phrases till the ear grows weary of waiting for the cadence that never comes.

Most of these gentry allowed him a certain talent and occasional glimpses of inspiration, and nearly all had a kind word for Micaela. Many of them showed a remarkable ignorance both of the history of music and of the most elementary details of craftsmanship. It would thus be otiose to multiply quotations, and indeed they are worth quoting at all only because a historian must take note of the contemporary atmosphere in which an artist worked, and the voice of criticism is a very potent element in that atmosphere. Pierre Berton thought that part of the press was bribed. This is unlikely, but some explanation is required of the simultaneous appearance in several papers, on the *morning* of the first performance, of short notices announcing that the Opéra-Comique could no longer be the theatre of marriage interviews and family parties, owing to the risky and improper nature of the coming opera. Was this du Locle reinsuring himself against a possible scandal?

Carmen was not condemned in these terms by the whole Paris press. There was a section from which sounder judgment could be expected. Joncières in *La Liberté* praised most of the music, especially the card scene and the final duet, though he wanted more rage *à la* Verdi at the end. The subtlest appreciation came from the poet Théodore de Banville in *Le National*, who alone showed some grasp of Bizet's aims and achievements in *Carmen*: 'M. Bizet has sought to show (in place of the puppets of *opéra-comique*) real men and real women, with the orchestra, turned creator and poet, interpreting for us their agonies, jealousies and mad impulses.' Reyer in *Le Journal des Débats* wrote a rather dull article, notably less enthusiastic than his criticisms of Bizet's earlier work, but ended with the much-quoted sentence: 'But *Carmen* is not dead, and at the Opéra-Comique we have seen plenty of others come back to life after such an experience.' Weber in *Le Temps* was both cautious and captious. He thought the cigarette girls' chorus mediocre and the final duet too long, and came a bad tumble over the opening chorus of Act IV, which he damned as a mere quadrille despite the fact that it is in 3-4 time throughout. When the score was published a week or two later he ate many of his words; Reyer also, and even Jouvin, took the opportunity of modifying their original coolness. There remains Jullien, who in *Le Français* uttered a piece of invective that left all the efforts of the Comettant-Escudier school in the shade. He considered the work 'a vulgar *opéra-comique* with a dash of the pathetic and a final murder that is almost inexplicable' (his reason for this last epithet is that Carmen had done nothing wrong, and if José was seduced by her it was his own fault!). Meilhac and Halévy had travestied Mérimée, and Bizet's music was always contemptible where he was in contact with the former, sometimes interesting when he was dealing with Mérimée. The quintet was banal, Act III 'bad almost from beginning to end.' In particular Jullien renewed the old charge about concessions.

The composer has naïvely imagined that it would be enough for him to attenuate his preferences, repudiate his juvenile audacities, timid and modest as they were, rally openly to the traditional *opéra-comique* genre, whose sacred forms he had believed he could stretch or modify according to the exigences of his libretti—in fact to write plenty of lively *couplets* and easily memorized refrains, in order to win those precious praises that most of the critics obstinately refused to bestow on him. . . . This *opéra-comique* is nothing but a long string of compromises, in the poem as much as in the music.

Bizet, in fact, knew what he ought to do, but for discreditable reasons refused to do it. The flaws in Jullien's self-important bombinations are obvious enough. It was a classic and literal case of prejudice: Jullien, a passionate Wagnerian, had decided beforehand in which direction French music should go, and if Bizet tried to lead it elsewhere he was automatically guilty of a sin not only against France and music, but against his own nature. Jullien was only the first of many French writers to approach Bizet in this state of mind. There was, indeed, a certain duality in Bizet's nature, though it was not the mere pull of genius versus self-interested ambition that Jullien maintained. And *Carmen* in 1875 did fall between two stools, though not the two so unctuously placed on either side by Jullien. Most of the critics expected a sort of apotheosis of Auber (or even Offenbach, for Meilhac and Halévy were then known exclusively as Offenbach's librettists) and, not finding it, damned the result as Wagnerian; while Jullien and his followers, desiring the exact opposite, waxed mightily indignant when they saw a revitalized form of *opéra-comique*. There is no need to look farther than this to account for *Carmen's* failure in 1875. As with *Pelléas et Mélisande* twenty-seven years later, neither the conservatives nor the radicals were satisfied, because neither party had envisaged the possibility of Bizet's creating something that was equally remote from both of them.

And *Carmen* really was a failure in 1875, though attempts have been made to maintain the opposite. It is true that it had forty-five performances during the year (more than any other work at the Opéra-Comique), together with three more early in 1876. But it was very nearly taken off owing to poor support after four or five performances, and there seems to be little doubt that, though its admirers certainly increased, two things only kept it running: the widely spread and attractive rumour that it was very shocking and Bizet's sudden death on the night of the thirty-first performance. It had at best a brief *succès de scandale*—an impression confirmed by the subsequent refusal to revive it till 1883, even though its success at Vienna in October 1875 had led rapidly to a world-wide reputation. Towards the end of the run, too, the management was giving away tickets wholesale. The effect on the man in the street is illustrated by an experience of Charles Malherbe, later librarian of the Opéra. He was present on the second night, in a half-empty theatre; a gentleman entered and sat down by him, watched the first act with an expression of growing stupefaction on his face and finally beat a precipitate retreat (banging the door) when Galli-Marié broke a plate for her dance in Act II. Halévy tells a pleasant story of the ancient librettist Dupin, whose first work had been staged in 1808. He found *Carmen* a criminal breach of the Scribe tradition, for which he soundly rated his friends Meilhac and Halévy, and declared that it would not be played twenty times. Yet he lived to see the three-hundredth performance in the ninety-sixth year of his age. Tchaikovsky on the other hand prophesied that within ten years it would be the most popular opera in the world. Servières quotes figures for the receipts, which show that though *Carmen* did not empty the theatre, it seldom if ever filled it. At no time did the takings equal those of the 1883 revival; they averaged about half and were sometimes down to a fifth. On the day of the second performance Bizet appeared at Franck's class and asked for a volunteer to attend regularly and play the harmonium to support José's song behind the scenes in Act II. When the request was received with amusement, Bizet explained that Lhérie was incapable of sustaining the pitch: 'he begins in G and finishes in E major—unless it should be E minor, and even (horrors!) E flat minor.' D'Indy undertook the task with enthusiasm and fulfilled it to the last. 'I saw the house gradually empty. I was present at the last performance in February 1876.'

Du Locle must have had some confidence in Bizet, for immediately after the first performance of *Carmen* he commissioned another opera from the same three collaborators. Probably the subject was never settled. Late in March Bizet had a severe attack of angina. Normally in these circumstances he would stay a few days in bed, and no one was worried. But this time his recovery was slow and only partial, and was accompanied by extreme mental depression. Two or three weeks after *Carmen* Henri Maréchal, a young winner of the Prix de Rome who used to dine with him every week, found him so upset that he dared not mention the subject. Suddenly Bizet burst out: 'Ah! I've had enough of writing music to surprise three or four comrades who then go and scoff behind my back!' He complained to the critic Weber about the perpetual outcry of Wagnerism. To Gallet 'he seemed to fall into profound melancholy, which showed itself in words that escaped his lips as if in his own despite,' though on the surface he was his usual ironical self, 'speaking of everything in that same bantering tone which disguised so well from people who did not know him his sensitiveness and kindness of heart.' Berton described him as ultra-sensitive and impressionable, and all the more at the mercy of his emotions from his attempts to conceal them. Gallet adds that even when in good health he always carried deep within him the obscure idea of some grim catastrophe. Perrin too says he was haunted by the fear of early death. One evening about this time he had some friends in and was running through *Carmen* with a young singer whose voice and musical aptitude had charmed him. Towards the end he suddenly interrupted and asked her to sing some Schumann. He listened in a corner with his head in his hands, greatly moved, till she finished something from *Manfred*. Then he exclaimed: 'What a masterpiece, but what despair! It's enough to make you long for death [*C'est à vous donner la nostalgie de la mort*].' He went to the piano and played Schumann's funeral march (presumably the slow movement of the Quintet), followed by Chopin's—which not many days later played him to the grave.

When, about the beginning of May, the usual time came for going into the country, he was still convalescent, and his wife tried to persuade him to wait till his recovery was complete. 'No, no,' he cried, 'let's go; I want to go at once; this Paris air is poisoning me.' It was not until 31st May that he left Paris. Meanwhile he had

another attack. An undated note to Guiraud tells its own tale:
'Colossal angina. Don't come on Sunday. Imagine a double
pedal A flat–E flat going through your head from the left ear to
the right. I'm quite done in. I shall write to you.' He recovered
sufficiently to see Lamoureux about *Geneviève de Paris*; Gallet had
read the poem to Lamoureux, who expressed lively interest. Bizet
proposed to write the music in the first three months of the summer.
There were to be five scenes, representing (I) Geneviève as a child
receiving the blessing of Bishop Germain of Auxerre; (II) Geneviève
triumphing over the spirit of evil and consoling fugitives fleeing from
the approach of Attila; (III) Attila's camp; (IV) Geneviève exorcising
the storm and miraculously leading a vessel full of wheat to the
hungry and besieged city of Paris; (V) Geneviève strengthening the
courage of the Parisians and finally triumphing over Attila solely by
the efficacy of prayer. Probably not a note of the music was written,
and it is difficult to agree with Tiersot that French music here lost
one of its supreme masterpieces. About 29th May Gallet visited
Bizet for the last time; it was the only occasion on which he remembered him conversing seated. Guiraud came round on the evening
of the 30th and in response to Bizet's invitation sat down at the
piano to play passages from *Piccolino*, the opera he was then composing. Bizet stopped him; in a shrill and shaky voice that horrified
Guiraud he said he could hear nothing with his left ear, and came
round to the other side. They discussed Guiraud's music and other
things, till at midnight the visitor rose to go. At the bottom of the
staircase he remembered something he had promised to discuss, and
for twenty minutes they chatted, Guiraud at the bottom, Bizet at the
top in his dressing-gown, with a candle in his hand. That was the
last Guiraud saw of his friend.

On the morrow the Bizets went to Bougival. The first day
(1st June) passed well; husband and wife went for an enjoyable walk
with their friend the pianist Delaborde. That night Bizet awoke in
terror, complaining of suffocation. Delaborde and the doctor were
hastily summoned. The latter after an examination reassured the
family that there was no danger; only calm and rest were needed.
He declared finally that it would be useless to disturb him if another
such crisis occurred during the night. On the next night, 2nd June,

the same thing occurred. They hesitated to call the doctor, till the crisis took an even sharper turn and the patient could hardly breathe. The doctor and Delaborde took their time in coming: when they arrived they found Bizet dead. His wife still thought he was asleep; then that he had fainted. It was 1 a.m. on the morning of 3rd June, Bizet's wedding-day. An hour or so before, the curtain at the Opéra-Comique had fallen on the thirty-first performance of *Carmen*. When playing the scene in Act III in which Carmen reads her death in the cards—'moi d'abord, ensuite lui, pour tous les deux la mort!'—Galli-Marié had been overcome with terrible foreboding and fainted on leaving the stage. She managed to continue, but burst into tears at the end and refused to be comforted.[1] Du Locle, suspecting some personal crisis, was more amused than upset—till a few hours later he received a telegram from Bougival: 'The most horrible catastrophe; our poor Bizet died last night.—LUDOVIC HALÉVY.'

The exact cause of death has never been determined. During the last illness there was talk of an open abscess of the throat and cardiac rheumatism. It is certain that Bizet had always been subject to some weakness in the throat, perhaps of streptococcal origin, and a burst abscess may have spread the infection to the heart. It is of course fanciful to attribute his death directly to the bad reception of *Carmen* —just as it is fanciful to suppose that Keats was killed by reviewers— but it is by no means impossible that worry and disappointment after the prolonged strain of the rehearsals had weakened his resistance to an infection which he had been able to throw off when in better health. Modern research has proved that psychology is more intimately concerned with physical illness than was once supposed, and even in the eighties one doctor [2] suggested that 'physical and moral depression brought on by the failure of *Carmen*' may have been the last straw. It is perhaps significant that for several years after his marriage Bizet had been quite free from his old trouble.

The funeral took place on 5th June at the church of La Trinité in Montmartre. Four thousand people attended. The musical arrangements were in the hands of Pasdeloup, who had hurried back from Caen, where he was conducting a regional festival, and got together

[1] This telepathic experience is vouched for by Reyer.

[2] G. Lefèbvre, quoted by Pigot.

the programme in a few hours. It was remarkable for loyalty to the dead rather than artistic taste. The organist Bazille played fantasies on themes from *Les Pêcheurs de perles* and *Carmen*; Pasdeloup's orchestra contributed the *Patrie* overture and the Adagietto and second half of the Prelude from *L'Arlésienne* (besides Chopin's funeral march); the vocal numbers consisted of the now notorious *Agnus Dei* and a *Pie Jesu* arranged by Guiraud from the famous duet in *Les Pêcheurs de perles*. The pall-bearers were Gounod, Ambroise Thomas, Camille Doucet (President of the Société des Auteurs Dramatiques) and Camille du Locle; behind them came Bizet's old father,[1] leaning on Ludovic Halévy's arm, and a distinguished company that included Léon Halévy, Massenet, Guiraud and Paladilhe. Among the wreaths was one from the young competitors for the Prix de Rome, who could not attend because their examination was then in progress. At the interment in the famous cemetery of Père Lachaise speeches were made by Jules Barbier, du Locle and Gounod, who after quoting a statement of Geneviève Bizet's that there was not an hour or a minute of her married life that she would not gladly have again, broke down and was unable to continue. The special performance of *Carmen* that night was, according to all accounts, almost unbearably moving; and the press which had so damned the opera three months before for a whole week proclaimed its composer a master. A year later, on 10th June 1876, a monument of red Jura stone was unveiled at Père Lachaise; it was designed by Charles Garnier, with a bust by Paul Dubois after the well-known Carjat photograph. A replica of the bust, which is described as an excellent likeness, was set up in the foyer of the Opéra-Comique, but perished in the disastrous fire of 1887. Among the eighty-three subscribers were many names famous in the theatrical and musical world, and the

---

[1] He survived his son by over eleven years, dying on 19th December 1886. In that year (8th October) Geneviève Bizet married Émile Straus, a well-known advocate. The Strauses became intimate friends of Marcel Proust, a volume of whose correspondence with them has been published. Proust's portrait of the Duchesse de Guermantes is said to have been modelled on Madame Straus, who lived to a ripe old age. She died in December 1926, four years after Proust and her son Jacques, and over half a century after her first husband.

proceedings were graced by eulogistic speeches from Barbier and Perrin. The city of Paris named a street in the district of Passy after Bizet.

A few words may be added on the posthumous history of *Carmen*. The day before his death Bizet signed a contract for its production at Vienna. This duly took place in October in a version for which Guiraud had replaced the spoken dialogue by recitatives.[1] It is from this Vienna production, seen and highly praised by Brahms and Wagner among others,[2] that the success of *Carmen* dates. It had fair success at Brussels in February 1876; in 1878 it triumphed in St. Petersburg, London, Dublin and New York. In London it narrowly missed performance by two companies simultaneously. (The impresario Mapleson gives an amusing account of its first performance here—by an Italian company. The tenor returned the part of José, saying that he would do anything to oblige, but could not think of undertaking a part in which he had no romance and no love duet except with the *seconda donna*. The Escamillo and the Micaela each declared that their parts must have been intended for one of the chorus. For the methods, worthy of a company promoter, by which Mapleson ensured the success of the opera with the public, see *The Mapleson Memoirs*.)

For the next few years *Carmen* continued to sweep Europe and America, often with Galli-Marié in her original part (at Genoa in 1881 she was wounded in the cheek by the knife of an over-realistic José); but Paris, though it heard many of Bizet's works in the concert-hall,[3] steadfastly refused to revive *Carmen*. It was only after

[1] Not all of them were used, however, the director (Jauner) preferring a mixture of spoken dialogue and recitative. Guiraud's version or Jauner's compound seem to have been the only ones used outside France till about 1928, when various German theatres began to restore the spoken dialogue. This—the only authentic version—has never been performed in England.

[2] Tchaikovsky first saw one of the last Paris performances, early in 1876, but he had already received the vocal score from his pupil Vladimir Shilovsky, who was an enthusiastic spectator on the first night. For his interesting reactions to the opera, see his *Life and Letters* by Modeste Tchaikovsky, translated by Rosa Newmarch.

[3] On 12th December 1880 Colonne gave the first performance of the *Marche funèbre* from *La Coupe du Roi de Thule*, which the critics found worthy but rather crude. Has this fine work been performed since?

a lively press campaign that Carvalho reluctantly brought it out at the Opéra-Comique on 21st April 1883. He seems to have been terrified of his own public, for he watered down the production in a manner to make Bizet turn in his grave. The title-part was entrusted to Adèle Isaac, who played it in a style of demure respectability.[1] Lillas Pastia's tavern-cum-brothel was turned into a glorified Corner House café, with sixty to a hundred guests and at least twenty dancers. The fight with knives became a token duel, and the music was prettified and dragged. In fact it was a caricature. No trouble was taken with the dramatic side, for Carvalho was sure it would be a failure. He must have had the shock of his life. The public flocked to see it, and the critics—many of them survivors from 1875 —raised an uproar, not this time against the opera, but against the director who had dared thus to travesty one of the masterpieces of the French stage. Various explanations have been given for this odd behaviour by a man who had always supported Bizet: that he was unwilling to revive a work closely associated with his predecessor, that there was no part for his wife, that he wanted to set his stamp on the production by merely being different, that the Opéra-Comique received twenty per cent of its takings from bridal couples, who used it as a rendezvous with their families—and how could a decent man take his betrothed to see the illicit amours of such as Carmen? Whatever is the truth, Carvalho was quick to see his mistake. On 27th October of the same year he brought back Galli-Marié in a rejuvenated production, and since that time *Carmen's* success has been as assured in France as it was already elsewhere. The hundredth performance at the Opéra-Comique took place on 22nd December 1883, the thousandth (with Calvé) on 23rd December 1904. There has been no sign of its losing its position among the established masterpieces of the operatic stage.

[1] According to Maurice Lefèvre (*Musica*, June 1912), a journalist who had taken the lead in the press campaign for the revival, Meilhac and Halévy were as much opposed as Carvalho to the re-engagement of Galli-Marié. 'Mme Galli-Marié may have played Mérimée's Carmen, she did not play ours!' There is no doubt that she played Bizet's.

CHAPTER V

ORCHESTRAL WORKS

AT the head of Bizet's output stands a work which, for sheer precocity of genius, rivals the best early work of Mozart and Mendelssohn. The Symphony in C major, begun on 29th October 1855 and finished by the end of the following month, has had a curious history. For eighty years after its composition the manuscript lay unknown to the world, until Mr. D. C. Parker, the author of the first English life of Bizet, found it in the library of the Paris Conservatoire and brought it to the attention of Weingartner. Since its first performance under that conductor, at Basle on 26th February 1935, it has made up in well-merited popularity for its long years of neglect. Tardy performances of unknown works by eminent composers often bring a sense of anticlimax; a recent instance is Schumann's violin Concerto. But Bizet's symphony made all the greater impression since there was no evidence that at the age of barely seventeen he either had produced, or was capable of producing, work of such quality. In fact Gauthier-Villars, for whom any stick was good enough to beat Bizet with, had maintained without challenge that the last thing that could be claimed for him was precocity. The discovery therefore helps to correct a wrong perspective.

The Symphony is in the usual classical four-movement form and is scored for an orchestra of moderate size, without trombones or harp. Any seventeen-year-old composer is bound to lean obviously on his models, and Bizet's are clear at once. The simple construction of the opening theme on a rising arpeggio of the tonic chord tells of a grounding in the Haydn-Beethoven tradition. The *crescendo* in the bridge-passage with its *tremolo* strings and repeated rhythm on the trumpets is a memory of Rossini (there are others later). Touches here and there recall the Mozart whom Bizet loved so much, and the deftness of the scoring perhaps owes something to Mendelssohn. There are surprisingly few signs of Gounod, and the one passage that obviously owes its existence to him, the soaring string melody in the slow movement, shows that influence at its unpretentious best and not, as so often in the next twelve years, at its sanctimonious worst. But the closest affinity is not with any of these composers, but with Schubert; and the fact is very remarkable. In the fifties Paris had (outside the limited programmes of the Société des Concerts du Conservatoire) no regular orchestral or chamber concerts, and if it had, it is very doubtful if Schubert's works would have been a feature of them. Not many years had passed since the great C major Symphony had been laughed off the platforms of Europe, though championed by such a conductor as Mendelssohn. Many of the works by which we know Schubert best to-day had not then been published. Paris could at most have been acquainted with his songs; and even they did not suit the frivolous tastes of the Second Empire. It is noteworthy that Bizet, who in his letters from Rome gives a clear picture of his musical tastes at a slightly later period, never at any time mentions Schubert. Yet the parallel is obvious. The second subject of the first movement has two characteristics that at once recall Schubert: the momentary glance at the relative minor and the unexpected extension of the melody (this also appears in the main theme of the slow movement). The corresponding theme in the finale not only takes a similar glance at the relative minor, but proceeds to modulate with an absence of clamour thoroughly Schubertian into the remote key of B flat major and back again. More pervasive, though less tangible, is the general similarity of mood and approach—the effortless flow of singing melody, the gay impulsiveness of rhythm, the tendency in the development section to serve up the same material repeatedly in sharply contrasted keys instead of treating it organically (a habit shared by Schumann). On the other hand the Schubertian long-windedness which might have been expected in a youthful work on this scale (compare Schubert's own early symphonies) is notably absent; there are already signs of a terse epigrammatic quality, typically French, that was to come to full flowering in *Jeux d'enfants* and *L'Arlésienne*. What these points suggest is an affinity of genius rather than any direct influence, still less conscious imitation. It has been suggested that Bizet, had he lived, might have developed into a French Verdi; if he had continued on the lines of this Symphony and if self-consciousness had not intervened, he might equally have become a French Schubert. He wsa to be something Schubert never was—a great dramatic composer; but though none of his later works shows such a kinship with Schubert, he never lost two of the gifts he shared with his great predecessor, an ever-springing melodic invention and a gift for sudden breath-taking modulation and equally unexpected but triumphant return.

Of Bizet's four movements, the *Adagio* is the most prophetic and the scherzo the most perfect. The former opens with a brief introduction, built on a figure

which, besides raising a nice sense of expectation, is used with considerable subtlety later in the movement. The main theme, played by the oboe over pizzicato violas:

marks the first appearance of a type of melody which runs all through Bizet's work. In *Les Pêcheurs de perles* and perhaps *L'Arlésienne* it might be taken to have an exotic significance, and it may be influenced by current French experiments with oriental colouring, such as David's *Le Désert*; but it is clear from its appearance here that it represented something in Bizet's musical make-up and was not simply turned out when he was confronted with a demand for local colour. It is one of many signs that Bizet's later preoccupation with themes remote from the Parisian scene was not an exterior thing, a searching for novelty in the Meyerbeerian sense, but corresponded to a need in his own nature. The tune is admirably treated and extended, and is followed by the soaring string melody, mentioned above, which both recalls Gounod and looks forward to such things as the Flower Song in *Carmen*. The fugal central section has been condemned as drily academic, and indeed it hardly fits the context. But the fault lies not in the fugue itself, which is academic only in the sense that it is extremely skilful, but rather in the fact that the young composer, having hit on the happy idea of developing his subject from the introductory figure, evidently could not resist the temptation to drag it in regardless of the unity of the movement. Even so he almost disarms criticism by the neatness of his return, the oboe melody being at once combined with the opening, thus tying it very happily not only to the introduction but to the fugue as well. Towards the end there occurs another prophetic passage, a slow descending chromatic scale over a tonic pedal, which adds a wonderful touch of rich colouring:

This device was to become very characteristic of the mature Bizet; like the 'exotic' oboe melody it formed a part of his musical personality from the earliest years.

The scherzo (it is marked only *allegro vivace*) not only typifies the joyous vitality that Bizet brought into French music; it has some striking technical features. The opening theme with its gay rhythm that breaks refreshingly away from the current 4-bar and 8-bar phrase, not only supplies a counterpoint to the delightful tune for strings in octaves that follows, but forms the chief material for the trio as well. This is no barren ingenuity; the music sounds entirely fresh and natural. The use of the device at all is hard to parallel at this date (though Schumann in his D minor Symphony had built the trio of his scherzo on a theme from the slow movement); for a boy of seventeen to bring it off triumphantly—however well it reflects on his teachers at the Conservatoire—betokens a native talent of no common order. The whole movement, especially the trio with its drone-bass, is admirably finished and rounded.

The opening subject of the finale:

as surely looks forward to the bull-fighting music in *Carmen* as the little march-like bridge theme does to the chorus of street urchins in the same opera:

In some ways, indeed, the whole Symphony seems closer in spirit to *Carmen* than to many of the works that intervene. The lilting Schubertian second subject leads by a brilliant extension to a cadence that, perhaps more clearly than anything else in the work, carries Bizet's personal stamp:

The weakness of the movement is the development, which belies its name, the themes, especially the second subject, being merely repeated in a many-coloured variety of keys.

However, the surprising thing is not that the work has too little of the genuine symphonic quality, but that it has so much. In later years Bizet told Saint-Saëns that he could do nothing without the theatre; he was not made for the symphony. Yet even without the evidence of this newly discovered work we know that in his early years he was much preoccupied with the form. His Rome letters are full of symphonic as well as operatic projects. He began and abandoned at least two symphonies in Rome, apart from the scherzo that later grew into *Roma*. And this early work shows, as *Roma* does not, that he really had some talent in that direction. Apart from its obvious failings, already mentioned, it shows a notable sense of balance. The *adagio* is not perfect in this respect, but considering the variety of its constituent elements it keeps its figure better than might have been expected. In the two sonata move-ments the exposition of the themes is neither cramped nor over-weighted, and the recapitulations are shortened just sufficiently to give conciseness to the summing-up of the argument. Bizet makes no innovations in the symphonic form, but he manages it easily and pours into it a wealth of music that varies in originality but never loses its freshness, never degenerates into padding or bad taste. Also, it is clothed in an orchestral dress that matches it for lucidity and charm. Bizet was a born orchestrator: like Mendelssohn, he seemed to have an instinctive grasp of the potentialities of each instrument. There is no superfluous doubling, no smudging of the lines; the colour is clear and vivid. The varied use of the woodwind in the trio of the scherzo is masterly, and the march theme in the finale is not only as appropriate to the wind as the opening subject is to the strings, but supplies a telling contrast.

The unpublished Overture in A minor-major probably belongs to about the same date as the Symphony. Though less finely wrought, it has many of the same qualities and deserves to be pub-lished. It is scored for larger orchestra, including piccolo, trombones and ophicleide. The form is somewhat lop-sided; Bizet may have been thinking of the overture to *William Tell*. There are four sections: *andante ma non troppo* in A minor, *allegro vivace* in the manner of romantic storm music, a very Italian *andante espressivo* in E major and an energetic *allegro vivace* (A major) in condensed sonata form. The themes are not original, but their treatment shows considerable vitality, and the bridge-passage in the final section is characteristic:

The *Marche funèbre* of 1861, also unpublished,[1] is more ambitious but much weaker. Rome had made Bizet self-conscious, and nothing could illustrate better than this march how unfitted he was for the expression of grandiosity. Even his customary felicity in scoring deserted him. He adds English horn, trombones, ophicleide, tenor drum and two harps to the orchestra of the Symphony, but this inflation of the currency only draws attention to a depreciation in the value of the goods. Neither the fanfares of the opening nor the would-be pathos of the broken second theme ring true. The main theme was later used for Leila's entrance in Act III Scene ii of *Les Pêcheurs de perles*.

Bizet's first Symphony was written in a month. His second occupied him on and off for at least eight and possibly eleven years. For the work we know as *Roma* was to Bizet always 'my symphony.' The history of its composition is chequered and in places obscure. His third *envoi* from Rome consisted of a Scherzo and *Marche funèbre* for orchestra (bearing the title 'Symphonie') and an overture, *La Chasse d'Ossian*. Of these three pieces, the second was discarded and has already been described, while the third has disappeared altogether (attempts to identify it with the first movement of *Roma*,

[1] For the published (and mistitled) *Marche funèbre* see *La Coupe du Roi de Thule*, p. 156.

at one time entitled *Une Chasse dans la forêt d'Ostie*, fall to the ground, for this movement got its title only in 1869 and *La Chasse d'Ossian* is mentioned in Halévy's report of 1861; also the former was originally a set of variations and would hardly have been accepted by Halévy as an overture without comment). The Scherzo, little altered, formed the nucleus of *Roma*, the first version of which was finished (though apparently not scored) by July 1866. In the early summer of 1868 the first movement was completely rewritten, only the theme of the variations being preserved (with modifications), and the *Andante* also underwent alteration; it was at this time that the C major theme from the finale was inserted, Bizet remarking how wonderfully it fitted. This second version was finished in June. In October Bizet expressed dissatisfaction with the finale. On 28th February 1869 three of the movements were performed by Pasdeloup (the scherzo, hissed when done by itself in 1863, was omitted) under the title *Fantaisie symphonique, Souvenirs de Rome*. Bizet continued to call it a symphony, and seems to have revised it a third time in the summer of 1871.[1] It was not performed complete till October 1880, when Pasdeloup preint roduced it as *Roma, Symphonie en quatre parties*; in the same year it was published by Choudens as *Roma, troisième suite de concert* (the first two suites presumably being those from *L'Arlésienne*). Mr. Martin Cooper has kept the game alive by referring to it as a symphonic poem.

But this is not the whole story. At the performance of 1869 the movements appeared on the programme as *Une Chasse dans la forêt d'Ostie, Une Procession* and *Carnaval à Rome*. These descriptive titles were added at the last minute, possibly at Pasdeloup's suggestion (he was certainly responsible for the suppression of the scherzo). A new symphony by a native composer was quite a bold step at this date, and they may have been intended to sugar the pill. They were dropped in the published score,[2] except in the case of the finale, which is headed simply *Carnaval*. The question at once arises:

[1] An unpublished letter in the Conservatoire library speaks of the difficulty of finishing it.

[2] Choudens began to engrave this in 1869, but for some reason—probably because Bizet was dissatisfied with the work—it did not appear till after his death.

What was Bizet really aiming at when he wrote the music—a genuine symphony in the classical tradition, as his letters imply and Galabert positively asserts, or a programme suite? Perhaps we should ask, Which was the predominant aim? There is no doubt that the work suffers from a confused purpose, and probably this had persisted from its inception. As early as August 1860 Bizet announced in a letter to his mother that he had in mind a species of Italian symphony with four movements entitled *Rome, Venice, Florence* and *Naples.* 'That works out wonderfully: Venice will be my *andante,* Rome my first movement, Florence my scherzo and Naples my finale.' At this date, incidentally, he had not visited Venice. How far he got with this scheme is not known. It is not even certain if the Scherzo of 1861 had originally any part in it, and a funeral march hardly seems in place, least of all for Venice. Nor do we know the connection, if any, between this work and the two abortive symphonies of 1859 (Bizet claimed to have destroyed these in December of that year, but his destroyed works, like those of Berlioz and others, had a habit of reappearing later). Yet the hope of recording his impressions of Rome in orchestral dress may have persisted and been incompletely fused with those symphonic ambitions which he never abandoned. This would account both for the prolonged birth-struggles and the marked unevenness of the final product. It is clear from internal evidence that the *Andante* is a patched-up affair. The C major tune was a late and unhappy insertion, and the long opening melody and its codetta, the four-bar phrase with triplets that immediately precedes the change to 12–8 time, were lifted bodily from a song (possibly an operatic fragment) called *Le Doute.* This was published posthumously in *Seize Mélodies,* and though the date of composition is unknown the song version is undoubtedly the original. Thus the *Andante* can have no Roman or Italian associations: nor is the 1869 title *Une Procession* at all appropriate. Indeed the only movement which does show any signs of Italian origin is the final *Carnaval.*

Whatever its original inspiration, Bizet wished *Roma* to stand on its own feet as absolute music. Unfortunately as a symphonic work it is a complete failure, and compares very badly with the Symphony of 1855. It is too haphazard in form, too loosely articulated, especially the first and last movements, and contains too much that is at the same time pretentious and feeble. There are things beyond the boy of seventeen, but there is also much that the boy of seventeen instinctively and rightly avoided. Much of the freshness has gone; the vitality has suffered a Mendelssohnian dilution, and the faint exotic charm, neatly executed, has yielded to a surge of sanctimoniousness laid on with a trowel—or whatever is the equivalent ecclesiastical implement. The hand of Gounod lies heavy on this score, not the modest Gounod of *Mireille*, but the pretentious religiosity of the last scene of *Faust*. Bizet's so-called concessions were, indeed, chiefly made, not to any outside influence, but to this artistic fifthcolumn for long entrenched within the composer himself. Only in its orchestration, a point of technique in which he seldom failed, is *Roma* consistently successful. Whether he could have written a mature symphony we cannot judge; *Roma* is too obviously a misfire. But it may be doubted: he was too much the musical dramatist, and of all composers with a genius for the stage only Mozart has achieved equal distinction in the symphony.

The opening theme on four horns no doubt owes something to Weber's *Freischütz* as well as to Gounod. Bizet wrote worse tunes, but there is no mistaking the flavour of insipid solemnity. The motive (*a*) introduced by solo trumpet supplies the germ from which the main theme of the *allegro agitato ma non troppo* soon springs, following a conventional boil-over on diminished sevenths. This is quoted (*b*) in its original form, from a letter of June 1868, and (*c*) as it appears (with improvements) in the published score:

It is somewhat Mendelssohnian in character (compare the scoring—strings in octaves with staccato wind chords—with the opening of

the 'Italian' Symphony) and has that composer's tendency to amble
when setting out to gallop. One passage of stormy suspense is very
reminiscent of *Der Freischütz*. The wind instruments are charmingly
used, and the quiet (*ppp*) division of the strings into many parts in
the coda is a happy touch. The figure (*a*) especially when given
to the horn looks forward to the accompaniment of Micaela's 'Je dis
que rien ne m'épouvante.' The scherzo is by far the best movement,
and significantly is much closer to the 1855 Symphony both in spirit
and date. It is less self-conscious, more spirited, less inflated than
the rest. It opens with a fugato on the following admirable subject:

The little figure (*a*) pervades the whole movement and is woven into
the accompaniment not only of the broader second theme, but of
the trio as well. This again recalls the Symphony, though here the
main theme of the trio is new—or as new as the spirit of Gounod
will allow. It is however easily saved from banality by the jostling
of figure (*a*) and the fascination of the two-against-three rhythm.
The whole movement, as Mr. Cooper points out, owes something
to the *Menuetto capriccioso* of Weber's A flat piano Sonata. Two
harps are employed in the orchestra.

The main theme of the *andante* is an obvious though inferior fore-
taste of the *Adagietto* in *L'Arlésienne*. There is less concentration, less
refinement here, but the shape and style of the melody and the lay-
out (strings in four parts) are the same. The effect is not unpleasing,
especially when the tune returns on the wind with violin arabesques.
The great blot is the C major tune in 12-8 time, one of Bizet's very
worst, rather blatantly scored for a mounting aggregate of wind
octaves against arpeggios on the harp. It is a sad comment on his
taste at this period that, having used it to spoil his finale, he should

have chosen to deal a similar blow at the *Andante*. This movement curiously uses bigger orchestral forces than the rest of the work.

The finale comes nearest to programme music. In form it is little more than a string of tunes, based in great part on an *ostinato* of alternate dominant and diminished sevenths. There are four main themes: the first, a brilliant and elastic affair on the flute:

brings a glimpse of the *Carmen* quintet; the second is a lilting Italian tune in thirds; the third with its distinctive rhythm echoes the finale of Mendelssohn's violin Concerto; while the fourth is the C major tune of the *Andante* now taken at a brisk trot. The movement is brilliantly scored, and there are excellent pages, especially where the third theme disappears in fragments on individual instruments (a device put to admirable use in *Carmen*), to be revived at once in stimulating counterpoint with the flute melody; but, as is the way of the world, the most blatant element comes more and more to the front, and the coda, in which it is twice directed to be played *plus vite* and ends *fff*, only serves to emphasize its essential complacency. There is no balance of keys or regular recapitulation, the fourth tune being left to assert the tonic, which it does in no uncertain fashion.

The overture *Patrie* is the one thoroughly poor production of Bizet's maturity. Inspired by the recent memory of the Franco-Prussian war, it is an awful warning of the danger of confusing art with patriotism. Formally it is unorthodox and not uninteresting, but the extreme poverty of the ideas damps all enthusiasm. The opening theme, a sufficiently noisy affair in C minor,[1] repeated in

[1] Some critics have discovered an echo of the Rakóczy March, but the similarity is so remote and so obviously fortuitous that much subtlety is required in order to perceive it.

C major and briefly developed, is succeeded by one of those weak sequential tunes, narrow in compass and limp in rhythm, of which Gounod so well knew the secret. This tune (*un peu animé*, F major), first cousin to that which disfigures the last two movements of *Roma*, is introduced by clarinets, bassoons and violas in unison and presently pounded out *fortissimo* in full orchestral dress. Two more prominent themes follow, a species of funeral march on violas and cellos (*andante molto*, A minor, marked *piano mais sonore* like the opening theme of *Roma*), and a bucolically good-humoured tune in 3–4 time on first clarinet, English horn and violas against muted violin arpeggios (*andantino*, A major), that sounds as if it had strayed into the wrong work. The opening C minor theme then returns *ppp* on a single flute over chromatic *tremolando* cellos and basses, with deft touches from the percussion — one of the few characteristic passages in the overture. It is soon contrapuntally combined in a long *crescendo* with the F major theme, which at length, as the *Roma* precedent leads us to fear, rises in full state-robes—C major, *moderato maestoso, tutta forza*, 6–8 time—to declare the proceedings closed. Perhaps the most effective touch is the unexpected appearance of the A major tune in the very last bars.

Bizet uses a large orchestra including, besides harps and a heavy battery of percussion, both cornets and trumpets and an ophicleide. The appearance of the ophicleide at this late date is not a conscious archaism, but indicates a preference, shared by other French composers, over the more German and specifically Wagnerian tuba.[1] In the same way his preference throughout his life—even in *Carmen* —for natural rather than valve horns need not be attributed to backwardness: he was quite capable of using modern developments when he wanted them, as he showed with the E flat saxophone in *L'Arlésienne*. The use of trumpets as well as cornets—the former

---

[1] He seems, however, to have had difficulty in making up his mind about the bass of the brass family. He uses an ophicleide in the early Overture, *Te Deum, Vasco de Gama, Marche funèbre* (1861) and *Don Rodrigue* as well as *Patrie*; bass trombone in various early works; contrabass trombone in *La Coupe du Roi de Thule* and *Noé*; tuba in *Les Pêcheurs de perles*; and bass and contrabass saxhorns in *Ivan le Terrible* and *Don Rodrigue*.

particularly for fanfares and solemn moments, the latter for melodic passages—was also a French habit. In *Patrie* these lavish forces, though well handled, hardly suit Bizet's orchestral style, which loses much of its delicate variety of colouring; there is more doubling than usual, and the contrasts are cruder and less subtle.

Patrie marks Bizet's last attempt to chase the wrong hare. Like most French composers of all ages he was constitutionally quite unfit to thump a tub. But a lapse of this kind need not be dwelt upon: *Patrie* should be consigned to that limbo which houses Beethoven's *Battle Symphony,* Tchaikovsky's *1812 Overture* and other such aberrations of the loftiest public spirit.

CHAPTER VI

KEYBOARD AND NON-DRAMATIC VOCAL MUSIC

IT is curious that a composer with Bizet's gifts as a pianist should have written so little for the instrument, and that much of his small output should be painfully unsuited to it. It seems probable that, though he loved to play genuine keyboard music like Bach's preludes and fugues, his greatest interest in the piano lay in its power beneath his fingers to evoke the different colours of the orchestra. It was as a score-reader that he was most renowned, and no doubt his countless operatic and orchestral transcriptions affected his style (though the unpublished early works are almost as unpianistic as the later). His original music for the piano suffers from a double disadvantage: it is too clumsy to reward the concert pianist and too difficult for the moderate amateur. But not all of it is musically negligible.

Little need be said of the unpublished pieces, all written before the age of sixteen. Some have a flashy brilliance borrowed from the pyrotechnical school of Liszt and Thalberg; a curiosity is the *Thème brillant*, written on three staves with an orgy of tremolos and rapid repeated notes. The *Nocturne* in F major has Chopin's mannerisms without anything else of Chopin. The most interesting is the *Romance sans paroles*, whose middle section foreshadows a rhythm and lay-out characteristic of the later Bizet (*cf.* prelude to *La Coupe du Roi de Thule* and Frédéri theme in *L'Arlésienne*):

The first of the published pieces, the inaptly named *Chasse fan-tastique* (? 1865), shows little advance. There is nothing fantastic about it except its badness. It is a long, flashy and insipid produc-tion that looks like a Liszt transcription of Mendelssohn at his worst, with a dash of Weber thrown in. The six *Chants du Rhin* (1865), described as 'Lieder sans paroles' and based on trashy poems of the Christmas-card type by Méry (at this date the French could still be wistfully romantic about the Rhine), are very uneven in quality. Here Bizet pays tribute to Mendelssohn and Schumann; the main theme of *Le Retour* is an obvious half-sister of the opening of the former's B flat major cello Sonata. This was the period when Bizet was declaring himself a German heart and soul. Of the six pieces, the first has little character and the last two are poor; but the other three are worth performing, perhaps in an orchestral transcription.[1] *Le Départ* is lively and charming, with characteristic and nicely extended rhythms; an odd feature is the outburst of Puccini octaves. The opening of *Les Rêves* with its long double pedal in seconds is striking for its date and brings to mind Borodin's song *The Sleeping Princess*. The main theme is cleverly reintroduced at intervals in the inner parts, and the mood faintly foreshadows that of *Colin-Maillard* in *Jeux d'enfants*. But the best is No. 4, *La Bohémienne*: even as early as this there was something about a gypsy that touched hidden depths in Bizet. The piece is full of character and shows great freedom of modulation. It is also the most operatic of the set: some nameless José courts the gypsy throughout the last two pages.

Another set that would repay orchestral performance is the *Trois Esquisses musicales* for piano or harmonium (? 1866). This is admirable light music in the best French style, polished, virile and neatly con-structed. *Ronde turque* is an excellent specimen of Bizet's exoticism on a small scale, full of sap and well sustained by rhythmic and harmonic tension. The bareness of the opening theme, ineffective on the piano, would be vindicated on the orchestra. The two other themes recall the chorus of the Watch in *La Jolie Fille de Perth*, composed about the same time; indeed *Ronde turque* has much of the

[1] This dubious procedure is justified in Bizet's case by the orchestral nature of the keyboard-writing. Much of it sounds like a transcription from an imaginary full score.

epigrammatic skill of that little masterpiece. It also points the way to *Trompette et tambour* in *Jeux d'enfants*. *Sérénade* is remarkable as much for neat construction as for charm. It is in simple A B A form, A being in D flat major and 3–4 time, B in A major and 3–8. The two sections are well contrasted and cleverly bound together: in B the sudden incursions of the chord of C sharp major remind us enharmonically of the opening, and the little rhythm ♫ ♪ ♩, characteristic of B,[1] persists throughout the reprise of A and finally takes complete control. The tune of B:

is a Bizet fingerprint (see p. 216). *Caprice*, which is almost in sonata form, is the least original movement. The polka-like tune in the middle proclaims Bizet's debt to Weber.

The last three piano works date from 1868. *Marine* is insignificant. The *Nocturne* in D major (called No. 1, though it had no successors) is a failure, though not without harmonic interest, particularly in its avoidance of the tonic chord for the first page and a half. It is the most Lisztian of all Bizet's works, from the melodic feebleness of its main theme to the inorganic flourishes at the end. Of much greater interest are the *Variations chromatiques*. The theme itself is sufficiently memorable, consisting merely of a rising and descending chromatic scale in 3–4 time over a pedal C. The combination of chromatic scales with pedal-note had interested Bizet since the early Symphony of 1855. He had already put the device to dramatic use to characterize Zurga's jealousy in *Les Pêcheurs de perles*, and was to repeat it for the entrance of Mitifio and Frédéri's fatal leap in *L'Arlésienne*. In the variations he explores its possibilities in the realm of pure music. The result, though not a masterpiece, is so striking that its complete neglect is difficult to explain. An orchestral version has been made by Weingartner and was once broadcast by the B.B.C.

[1] Compare the accompaniment to the second stanza of the song *Douce Mer*.

There are fourteen variations, seven in C minor, seven in C major and a coda ending in the minor. Bizet draws a great variety of mood and suggestion from the theme, while never abandoning the framework. There are glimpses of a number of old friends, past and to come: Catherine Glover in the tenth variation (a great improvement on her vocal polonaise 'Vive l'hiver,' which it so much resembles), Micaela in the eleventh, Frédéri in the fourteenth. The fifth and sixth are full of fire and passion, while the seventh, in which the theme appears in contrary motion against a four-octave pedal in a mighty crescendo from *ppp* to *fff*, produces some remarkable harmonies for its date:

Unfortunately the double tremolo is not the way to the pianist's heart. The real weakness of the work is the coda, where Bizet, having said all he has to say, seems unable to make an end. Instead of a cogent summing-up we are given a mixture of fireworks and recitative, and the return of the theme in the last bars hardly makes up for lost ground. This is a pity, for throughout the variations interest has been sustained in mounting tension. The conception of the work was probably influenced by Beethoven's thirty-two Variations in C minor, which Bizet much admired. The other published piano pieces are all transcriptions, mostly of songs and excerpts from the dramatic works.

One keyboard work remains, the suite of twelve pieces for piano duet called *Jeux d'enfants*. Composed in 1871, this was by far his most perfect work to date and reveals a fresh brand of talent. Certain episodes in the operas, such as the chorus of the Watch in *La Jolie Fille de Perth*, had shown a formal and emotional power of concentrating atmosphere within a small compass; but the miniaturist's skill of *Jeux d'enfants* comes with all the surprise of a new departure. Music in this form is usually called into being by special circumstances, and is bound to appeal to the domestic rather than the public consumer. But it need lose nothing in musical value on this account, and Bizet's suite, having (even in the shortened orchestral form which the composer gave it) no headline appeal, has not always been rated as the little masterpiece it is. In France it was the forerunner of a number of similar works: Debussy's *Petite Suite* (1888), Fauré's *Dolly* (1893) and Ravel's *Ma Mère l'Oye* (1908) all owe it a debt, though none has quite the freshness and perfection of Bizet's original.

The names of the movements speak for themselves: *L'Escarpolette* (Rêverie), *La Toupie* (Impromptu), *La Poupée* (Berceuse), *Les Chevaux de bois* (Scherzo), *Le Volant* (Fantaisie), *Trompette et tambour* (Marche), *Les Bulles de savon* (Rondino), *Les Quatre Coins* (Esquisse), *ColinMaillard* (Nocturne), *SauteMouton* (Caprice), *Petit Mari, petite femme* (Duo) and *Le Bal* (Galop).[1] Each is vividly illustrative of a facet of childhood, but there is not a trace of triviality, selfconsciousness or false sentiment. Their quality is essentially musical; and their forms, though slight, are turned with a neatness that leaves no loophole for criticism. Here is a typically French wit and detachment combined (as not too commonly in French music) with a warmth and a sympathy that recall Schumann, but without a trace of the grownup nostalgia that marks the *Kinderscenen*. The essential originality of the music is apparent in almost every bar; in melodic distinction and harmonic piquancy *Jeux d'enfants* represents Bizet at his most personal and least derivative. *L'Escarpolette* influenced Debussy's *En Bateau*. The final fifteen bars of *La Poupée* illustrate Bizet's power both of extending a melody (here a particularly beautiful one) and rounding off the whole in an exquisite coda. The brilliant colour and elastic rhythm of *Trompette et tambour* is contrasted with the simple evocative charm of *ColinMaillard*, and the delicate partwriting of *Petit Mari, petite femme* with the busy gallantry and Haydnish capriciousness of *Le Bal*. The modulations in this finale are enchanting in their unexpectedness. For the bogus return of the main theme in the

[1] *The Swing, The Top, The Doll, Wooden Horses, Battledore and Shuttlecock, Trumpet and Drum, Soap Bubbles, Puss in the Corner, BlindMan'sBuff, LeapFrog, Little Husband, Little Wife, The Ball.*

submediant, followed after four bars by an exhilarating plunge back into the tonic, there is historical precedent in Beethoven and Schubert, but the effect remains fresh and brilliant. The piece ends with true childlike exuberance, marked *fff, furioso*. Bizet's harmonic resource is particularly evident in these pieces, many of which show signs of an impressionism that was to achieve ripeness in Debussy's Preludes a generation later. And the experiments with pedals and chromatic scales now reach forward to a composer not yet born—Maurice Ravel:

SAUTE-MOUTON

It is notable how often such passages are marked *p* or *pp*. Doubtless Bizet would have stood better with posterity had he made a clamour of his harmonic audacities.

Five of these pieces—*La Toupie, La Poupée, Trompette et tambour, Petit Mari, petite femme* and *Le Bal*—were orchestrated by Bizet himself under the title *Petite Suite d'orchestre*. It is strange that this version is not more popular to-day, especially as the scoring is executed with Bizet's usual aptness and includes certain details, such as the gay trumpet flourish in the last bars of *Trompette et tambour* [1] that do not appear in the duet version. In later years five more pieces were scored by Karg-Elert—far more heavily and clumsily, if the version recorded by the London Philharmonic Orchestra under Antal Dorati is indeed Karg-Elert's—and the ten have been used for a ballet. Unfortunately the two pieces that were never scored—*Les Bulles de savon* and *Saute-Mouton*—are harmonically among the most interesting of the series.

Bizet was not a great song-writer, but he left some attractive music in this form, including one or two neglected gems. The French song before Fauré and Debussy did not, as has been too readily assumed, consist solely of faded romances for fashionable drawing-rooms. There was of course much rubbish of that kind, but Gounod was a charming song-writer in his own right: his lyrical gifts, so often drowned in pretentiousness on the stage, were at home in this small form, and he often found the perfect musical dress for poems of a

---

[1] Most of the differences occur in this piece, which originally appeared in *Ivan le Terrible*. The orchestral version is the more brilliant, and one of the themes is slightly altered. There is also a curious variant at bar 10 of *Petit Mari, petite femme,* in the cello counter-melody.

pastoral or amorous lyricism, quite free from the meretricious taint of the salon. Bizet was for the most part content to follow Gounod without attempting any innovations, though his emotional range was wider. The prevalent weaknesses of his songs are uncritical repetition of the same music to every stanza, accompaniments all too obviously conceived in terms of the orchestra and a facile resort to padding when inspiration fails. Their good qualities are charm of melody, happy modulation and on occasion a dramatic capture of the essentials of a situation and their translation into an inevitably right musical setting. His Arabian girl or his Gascon, once known, remain characters to be reckoned with in the memory. Unfortunately these moments are rare. It is disappointing to find so little of the subtle miniaturist of *Jeux d'enfants*, but the great majority of the songs belong to the early formative years; indeed he seems almost to have given up song-writing after 1868. He himself held a very low opinion of them, and on the whole their chief interest lies in the light they throw on his dramatic powers; they show him instinctively responsive to character and atmosphere, but not always able to epitomize a mood or transcend a mediocre text. He was always less sensitive to words themselves than to the human emotions behind them. It may as well be said at once that Bizet, like many French composers, paid very little attention to prosody in either his songs or his dramatic works. The verbal distortions are, however, a light fault to be set against the dramatic truth of his best vocal writing, and they are far less offensive in French, which is not a strongly accented language, than in English.

Bizet's first published works were two songs, *Petite Marguerite* and *La Rose et l'abeille,* issued (together with a very inferior song by Bizet *père*) in 1854, when he was barely sixteen. The words are the sorriest drivel (when Choudens reissued the songs in 1888 new poems were supplied by Armand Silvestre), but the music has charm and promise, marred only by a lapse into Gounodesque uplift in the major-key refrain of *Petite Marguerite*. *La Rose et l'abeille* anticipates *Chanson d'avril* in its effective modulation into the flattened submediant.

Bizet published two volumes of songs in his lifetime. The six *Feuilles d'album* of 1866 were pot-boilers undertaken during the composition of *La Jolie Fille de Perth* and are of little interest. The most enterprising is *Guitare*, which shows him responsive as ever to bolero rhythm; the return of the piano ritornello for the second stanza before the voice has finished with the first adds a characteristic thrust. But the song is still inferior to its forerunner in *Vasco de Gama*. The *Vingt Mélodies* of 1873 (the date is misleading, for nearly all had been published separately some years earlier) are very uneven in quality. It would have been better for Bizet had the last two never seen the light, and some of the others are negligible; but about half a dozen are well worth preservation. *Chanson d'avril* and *Vieille Chanson*, though in the Gounod tradition, have a delicate charm and refinement peculiarly Bizet's own. The modulation from E flat to C flat in the refrain of the former is most happily characteristic, and the touch of archaism in the latter never degenerates into pastiche. *Pastorale* exploits the age-old device of a strophe in the minor key followed by a refrain in the major with a wayward charm that keeps it wholly fresh. *Berceuse*, of which the accompaniment is based on a folk-tune used also by Fauré in *Dolly* and Debussy in *Jardins sous la pluie* (and earlier by Couperin), beats Gounod at his own game. Melodic charm is combined with a clever use of the traditional tune (note the bass of the last bars) and subtle harmonic touches, such as the immediate repetition of the opening in F on an E flat (tonic) pedal, to produce a veritable little masterpiece. In complete contrast is *Vous ne priez pas*, a passionate C minor song remarkable for fire and sweep of melody, whose one weakness is the repetition of the same music for three stanzas, with only the pace indication altered. But the best of Bizet's songs is the intensely dramatic *Adieux de l'hôtesse arabe*, which owes nothing to Gounod or any one else. Composed as early as 1866, this is a worthy ancestor of the Ghazel in *Djamileh*. Here again [1] we find the exotic and dramatic elements leading Bizet into harmonic experiment (see p. 124). The rhythmic accompaniment figure is kept up throughout in an ever-varying harmonic colour, often enriched by pedals, that reflects the rise and fall of the singer's passion. This is not a rigidly strophic song: the scheme—first stanza E minor ending in A major, second stanza E major ending in A minor—admirably solves both the

[1] See p. 140.

Bel é·tran·ger, hé·las! a·dieu!

musical and the literary-dramatic problem. For the rest *Chant d'amour* has the triumphant succulence of parts of *Samson et Dalila*, *Rêve de la bien-aimée* (which has sometimes been inserted without justification in *La Jolie Fille de Perth*) spoils the effect of a charming start by the old diminished seventh lapse at the end of each stanza, and *Ma vie a son secret* redeems a dullish vocal line by a striking ritornello prophetic of José's flower song:

Ex. 16.

The posthumous *Seize Mélodies* (1886) consist largely or wholly of fragments of unfinished operas, assembled and edited by Guiraud, with new words commissioned by the publisher, who thus made it difficult to identify the source of each number. With one or two exceptions the musical quality is not high; several are the merest sketches torn from a context which we cannot even assess. Two of the best, *Ouvre ton cœur* and *La Sirène*, are taken from *Vasco de Gama* and *La Coupe du Roi de Thule* respectively, though the fact is not stated. *N'oublions pas!*[1] shows real dramatic power at the outset and anticipates the melody of José's 'Dût-il m'en coûter la vie.' *Aubade* has a deft charm that would be underlined by the scoring Bizet no doubt had in mind, and *La Chanson de la rose* is remarkable for its modulations and neat two-part writing. There is one master-piece—*Le Gascon,* a little humorous character-study turned with exquisite grace:

Ca-dé-dis! lorsque je me fâche, Tordant ma moustache D'un air ca-va-lier

This does not read like a fragment: if the lilting tune was not originally set to these words, then Catulle Mendès was visited by genius when he put them to it. Seldom has a musical moustache been worn at a more gallant angle. Of four unpublished songs preserved at the Conservatoire the serenade *Oh, quand je dors,* with a charming piano interlude between each stanza, is much the best. The accompaniments supplied by Bizet for the six traditional *Chants des Pyrénées* have the sterling merit of unobtrusiveness.

The four vocal duets with piano accompaniment are of little consequence. Three of them, published posthumously, include material that appears in three of the songs in *Seize Mélodies* (*Voyage, La Nuit* and *Aimons, rêvons*), and are clearly chips from the dramatic workshop. In two cases the words also are much the same, though they are attributed to different authors. One point of interest concerns the duet *Rêvons*, whose middle section has an accompaniment figure [2]

---

[1] See additional note at end of Chapter VII, p. 163.

[2] This does not appear in the version for solo voice.

identical with that for the cellos in Micaela's 'Je dis que rien ne m'épouvante.' This air is said to have been taken over from *Grisélidis*, but it seems likely from internal evidence that the duet *Rêvons* (+*Aimons, rêvons*), like *Les Nymphes de bois* (+*La Nuit*), comes from Act II of *La Coupe du Roi de Thule* (see note, p. 163). Did Bizet use the cello figure three times? The fourth duet, *La Fuite*, was published in 1872, in the same year as the song *Absence*. Both have words by Gautier, both amble along with repeated chords in triplets and rising scales in the bass, and both show Bizet's lyricism not at its best.

Still less important are the four so-called *Motets et hymnes*. Fortunately Bizet is probably not responsible for the sins here inflicted on the long-suffering church. He certainly had no hand in *Regina Coeli*, a dreadful arrangement by one Flégier of the original duet [1] in the last scene of *Les Pêcheurs de perles*. Nor is it likely that he perpetrated the *Ave Maria* and *Agnus Dei*, carved from the Prelude and E flat Intermezzo of *L'Arlésienne*. The *Agnus Dei* was sung at his funeral, together with a *Pie Jesu* fashioned by Guiraud from the duet for Nadir and Zurga—surely a classic example of double sacrilege. *L'Esprit Saint* is a fattened version, with organ obbligato, of the worst song in *Vingt Mélodies*. The male-voice part-song *Saint Jean de Pathmos*, composed for a Belgian choral festival, equally deserves its oblivion. It is notable for appalling prosody, a second bass part reminiscent of a military band which it must be difficult to sing with a straight face, and the only complete fugue that Bizet published—an ingenious but barren monument to his Conservatoire training.

There are a number of miscellaneous vocal works on a larger scale, mostly unpublished. The early cantatas and choruses are of very poor quality. *Clovis et Clotilde*, which won Bizet the Prix de Rome, is able but colourless. The influence of Weber is very marked, especially in the themes which are used (without any idea of development) to distinguish each of the three characters. The music of Leila's 'O courageuse enfant' in Act II of *Les Pêcheurs de perles* (p. 94 of vocal score) first appears here. The *Te Deum*, with the exception of the *Judex crederis* section, is a wretched work; most of

---

[1] This does not appear in modern vocal scores or in the full score. It can be found (if necessary) in the vocal score of 1863.

the music is of the kind that seems to presuppose Blackpool pier and somebody's silver tuba band. 'Rex gloriae' begins with a trombone solo accompanied by the strings in a rhythm rendered notorious by misuse in Italian opera and frequently parodied by Sullivan. It is pleasant to record that part of 'Pleni sunt coeli' was afterwards fitted to the words 'O Brahma divin' (*Les Pêcheurs de perles*, p. 60). The expected four-square fugue appears at 'Fiat misericordia.' Another work that illustrates Bizet's unfitness to compose religious music is *La Mort s'avance*, for four-part chorus and large orchestra with two English horns taking the place of the oboes. This is based on two Studies by Chopin, in C minor (Op. 25, No. 12) and C major (Op. 10, No. 1); but the ingenuity with which Chopin's themes are worked into the texture—the former, without its distinctive arpeggios, is turned into the Frédéri rhythm—does not make up for the flatulence of the conception as a whole.

Two works for solo voice, mixed chorus and piano, *La Chanson du rouet* and *Le Golfe de Bahia*, were among the posthumous pieces published in 1880. It is unlikely that we have them in the form that Bizet intended as final. *La Chanson du rouet* in particular looks like an operatic fragment. It is a spinning-chorus in G major with three stanzas, the first and third on the same music being choral, and the second in E minor confided to a solo voice (presumably soprano). The music is attractive, with a hint of Weber, and the E minor section contains a striking and typical chromatic pedal passage:

Le Golfe de Bahia also exists in a shortened version for piano solo. It is not of great significance, though the refrain with its attractive syncopations has a languorous charm. In the piano version this refrain (which incidentally bears a characteristic fingerprint: see p. 216) supplies the main theme, the music of the second verse—that of the first is quite distinct—forming a kind of trio. A third version with different words occurs in Act IV of the unpublished opera *Ivan le Terrible*.

CHAPTER VII

THE EARLY OPERAS

BIZET'S first dramatic work, the one-act *opéra-comique La Maison du docteur* with words by Henry Boitteaux, was probably designed for private performance among a circle of friends. The manuscript contains a list of his teachers and colleagues at the Conservatoire. It is obviously very early, and was never scored. In the absence of the spoken dialogue it is difficult to grasp the plot, though the appearance of a *buffo* bass called Lord Harley suggests an appropriate situation for the doctor's house. The music displays an easy flow of melody influenced by Weber and the Italians, and a native knack of extending a tune a bar or two longer than one expects.

The libretto of *Le Docteur Miracle* conforms to a familiar type. It concerns a young officer in love with the daughter of a magistrate who loathes soldiers. The officer consequently disguises himself as a cook and serves the magistrate an omelette so bad that he believes himself poisoned. A doctor (the officer again disguised) is hastily summoned and promises to cure the magistrate in return for the hand of his daughter. The music is a trifle, but a very engaging one. It shows the eighteen-year-old Bizet in complete command of the light Italian style before he went to Rome (Paris was full of Italian opera, and was still graced by the presence of Rossini, who a month after *Le Docteur Miracle* presented Bizet with his autographed portrait). Nothing is original, but nearly everything sparkles with wit and vivacity, and the scoring too is that of Rossini. After a tripping overture an off-stage band comprising clarinet, tenor trombone, big drum and cymbals strikes up a gay tune, leading to a trio in which Bizet takes a naïve delight in playing with words like 'un charlatan.' Both the romance for soprano and the tenor *couplets* are pretty, but the high light is the 'Quatuor de l'omelette.' The dish is acclaimed by all the characters in turn—by the magistrate 'avec émotion,' by his daughter 'avec indifférence'—to the words 'Voici l'omelette,' which are then worked into an elaborate mock-heroic ensemble. After a flute cadenza the magistrate sits down to eat in commodious 6–8 time, interrupted by the statutory diminished seventh at the words

'Quel goût bizarre et singulier!' An admirably important *mélodrame* introduces the doctor, and the happy 6–8 finale echoes that of *Don Pasquale*.

Don Procopio comes still closer to *Don Pasquale*, for the two plots are almost identical. An old man, Don Andronico, wants to marry his niece Bettina to a fellow miser, Don Procopio, because he thinks a young man will only run through her money. Bettina, however, is attracted to a gallant colonel, Odoardo, and with the help of her aunt Eusebia and her brother Ernesto a plot is hatched to teach the old men a lesson. Procopio, threatened with the gay dissipated minx which Bettina makes herself out to be, takes fright and tries to get out of the marriage; faced with her insistence, he insults her, abandons his contract and flees, thus converting Andronico to the side of the lovers, as they had planned.

Bizet set the libretto in Italian, and in consciously writing Italian music he was only supplying an artistic requirement. Again his score is largely an imitation, but by no means a shoddy one; it is surprising how much of the freshness and vitality of his model he contrives to reproduce, an achievement to which natural high spirits and sure technical accomplishment equally contribute. In places the music bubbles and sparkles as if it were a genuine scion of the *Don Pasquale* stock. The ensembles in particular, which employ all the stock devices, voices in thirds, staccato chord accompaniment, endless repetition of words, show a very light touch, and some of the arias and duets, such as the love scene in Act II, 'Per me beato,' and Ernesto's cavatina 'Non v'è, signor,' an obvious descendant of Malatesta's 'Bella siccome un angelo' (an exact parallel: in each case the baritone describes his sister's charms to the miser-bridegroom in the key of D flat), are also purely Italian. There is little room for other influences, though Mozart and Weber (e.g. in Bettina's 'Voler che sposi') both left their mark. Flashes of genuine originality are few and far between—fewer than in the C major Symphony. One cadential figure in 'Voler che sposi':

bears witness to that lyrical exuberance that overflows from Bizet's best scores, and the expressive phrase that heralds Bettina's entry in the middle of the first finale at once stamps the composer:

Moderato allegretto

There is little attempt at characterization beyond a generalized defini-tion of the old *opera buffa* types, and no use of leading themes. The entr'acte and recitatives, which do employ certain phrases in this way, were added by Malherbe when the opera was published, though this is not made clear in the score. Malherbe made the mistake of imitating the self-conscious Bizet of a few years later and thereby falsified this spontaneous little opera.

Several episodes in *Don Procopio* are familiar elsewhere. Odoardo's entry at the head of his regiment is signalized by the march-theme that forms the bridge-passage in the finale of the Symphony, but without the attractive modulations that follow. The three themes of the initial 2-4 section of the first finale reappear in the Carnival chorus in Act II of *La Jolie Fille de Perth*, and that of the chorus

'Cheti piano!' [1] is found again in Act I of *Les Pêcheurs de perles* (to the words 'Ah! chante, chante encore'); in each case the unpretentious original is killed by translation to a grander sphere. More interesting is the fate of Odoardo's serenade, 'Sulle piume,' the main theme of which is well known as that of Smith's serenade in *La Jolie Fille de Perth*. In *Don Procopio* Odoardo sings two stanzas, the second of which has an added counterpoint on the mandoline with an attractive cross-rhythm, omitted in the later work but worth preservation:

Bettina replies in the tonic major (an effect reserved for the last act of *La Jolie Fille*); both then sing a passage for which Bizet later substituted the tune in F major known in the Beecham arrangement as 'Aubade'; and the piece ends with a remarkable cadence that sounds like a faint striving after some such effect as he achieved in the Flower Song in *Carmen*:

If the later version of the serenade is more effective from the dramatic point of view, this earlier version can claim an equal if not greater musical interest, and the scoring, with two English horns, mandoline and guitar, is more unusual.

In *Don Procopio* Bizet does not seem to have allowed his creative (as opposed to his imitative) faculty free rein, and to that extent it is

[1] There is a curious discrepancy here between the manuscript and the published score of *Don Procopio*. In the former the tune is exactly the same as in *Les Pêcheurs de perles*; in the latter it has been modified, presumably by Malherbe.

disappointing. Yet he has certainly matched the libretto with appropriate music, and its high spirits are so genuine that if well sung the opera (and *Le Docteur Miracle* as well) might still be worth occasional revival.

The symphonic ode *Vasco de Gama,* though not a stage work, may be conveniently discussed here. Written a year later than *Don Procopio*, it is more ambitious, more uneven and in some ways more interesting. It was modelled on David's *Le Désert,* the prototype of a bastard form that was neither dramatic nor symphonic nor oratorio, but somewhere between the three. It would take a mature genius to fashion such a piece into a coherent work of art, and in addition to his immaturity Bizet was hampered by a text frigid in conception and comically inept in execution. It is not surprising that much of the music is perfunctory in the extreme; the interest lies in observing how the appeal of local colour or the slightest opportunity for dramatic treatment at once fired Bizet's imagination. There is little enough to justify Halévy's strictures on the harmony, though a few modulations and pedal-points do hint at future development.

The text deals with Vasco da Gama's voyage of exploration to Asia; it takes the ship's company from the Tagus, through a calm and a storm stirred up by the giant Adamastor (sung by six basses), to their rescue through prayer and first glimpse of the promised land. There is little attempt at characterization, either of the principals (of whom Vasco has a most ungrateful part) or of the expedition as a whole. But Bizet does try to give the piece some sort of unity by means of a rocking figure in 6–8 time to denote the sea. The introduction follows David in its use of declamation against a slowly shifting harmonic background over a long pedal.[1] The sailors' chorus is simple Gounod, the soldiers' chorus almost as square and banal as Gounod's notorious prototype (which Bizet may have known, though *Faust* was produced after his arrival in Rome); the combination of the two is a very academic piece of counterpoint. There follows something much better, though it has nothing to do with the story. Léonard, a young officer with the rare gift of a soprano voice, offers to amuse the becalmed company with the 'joyful love-song

[1] It is significant that ten years later Bizet used the same music to indicate the desert in *Noé.*

which Ines with her gentle voice used to sing me every day.' The hint of local colour was enough for Bizet: this bolero might have been written at any period in his life. With its lively melody and persistent accompanying rhythm it is the ancestor, not only of the song *Adieux de l'hôtesse arabe* but of the Almée and Ghazel in *Djamileh* and the *chanson bohème* in *Carmen*.[1] It is in fact un-mistakable Bizet. The first phrase:

is a fingerprint that constantly reappears, notably in the F sharp minor chorus in *L'Arlésienne* (where it is combined with a very similar rhythmic figure). A storm follows, conventionally rendered by diminished sevenths, and the chorus describes it in music that looks forward to the first movement of *Roma* and backward to almost any movement of Mendelssohn marked *agitato* in 6–8 time (for instance, the opening of the 'Scottish' Symphony). Adamastor, however, though he has to utter such remarks as 'Respectez cette barrière, Retournez vite en arrière,' at once evokes Bizet's talent for the dramatic, and the music rises to a higher plane. One recurring phrase with a distinctive harmonic twist which seems to depict the giant:

---

[1] The first seven notes of the oboe counterpoint in the second verse of the bolero are actually identical with Carmen's opening phrase, 'Les tringles des sistres tintaient.'

may have worried Halévy. The prayer is tamely conventional, except for a chromatic passage at the end over a long tonic pedal, and the final chorus dreadfully square and empty. But between the two comes a flash of real beauty when the look-out sights land:

The libretto of *Les Pêcheurs de perles*, by Carré and Cormon, is typical of its era. The scene is laid in Ceylon and concerns the love of two men, Zurga king of the pearl fishers and his friend Nadir, for the same woman, the priestess Leila. They saw her first in Candy and vowed to part both from her and each other. In Act I they meet again, apparently recovered from their passion; but in the veiled priestess, who under a strict oath of chastity is appointed by the pearl fishers to ward off the wrath of Brahma during the fishing season, Nadir recognizes Leila, and mutual love springs up between them. Nadir is caught with her in the sanctuary; the high priest Nourabad tears off her veil, and Zurga, recognizing her in his turn, in jealous fury condemns them both to death. Meanwhile it has transpired that Zurga was once beset by robbers and rescued by a girl, to whom he gave a necklace in gratitude. When Leila takes off her necklace before execution and asks for it to be sent to her mother, Zurga recognizes his own gift. At the last minute he starts a fire in the pearl-fishers' tents and releases the prisoners, only to be denounced by the fanatic Nourabad and killed [1] while they escape.

The structural weaknesses of this plot are obvious enough: it depends too much on coincidence, and the introduction of the neck-lace episode puts Zurga's noble action on a *quid pro quo* basis worthy only of Hollywood. But the worst fault is that the whole back-ground is false. It is impossible to believe in these 'Indians' and their worship of Brahma and 'blanche Siva.' [2] They are only the regulation sopranos, tenors, etc., with their faces blacked. Conse-quently no atmosphere of illusion is established, and none of the characters comes to life. There are some effective stage situations of the conventional sort, and the 'exotic' setting, bogus as it is, does draw sparks from a composer uniquely gifted for the imaginative depiction of atmosphere; but that is little credit to the librettists. They were perfectly aware of the shortcomings of their work; after the first night Cormon is reported to have said, 'If we had realized M. Bizet's talent we should never have given him *cet ours infâme.*'

If in *Don Procopio* Bizet looks musically backwards, with *Les Pêcheurs de perles* he is at the crossroads. It is the most uneven of his operas, both in style and quality. Contemporary critics discovered the influence of Gounod, Félicien David, Verdi and Wagner; and, if for Wagner we substitute Meyerbeer, they were right. That master of the meretricious was still alive, and the attempted grandiosity of parts of Bizet's score, resulting in stiffness and occasional bathos, bear witness to his example. The libretto in fact was very much in the Meyerbeer-Scribe tradition, with its emphasis on situation rather

[1] This was an afterthought. In the printed libretto and the 1863 vocal score he survives.

[2] The librettists themselves seem to have taken a somewhat cynical view, for all their sympathy is on the side of Leila's perjury. The sacred virgin who yields to love was a favourite theme of nineteenth-century opera: e.g. *La Vestale* and *Norma.*

than character; hence it tended to lead Bizet away from the true bent of his genius, which lay in the interpretation of human emotion, dramatic conflict and atmosphere, towards the statuesque and heroic conceptions current at the Opéra, for which he was little gifted. His attitude to opera was much more akin to Mozart's than to Gluck's. He did his best to bring the four characters of the libretto to life, but the result is not very convincing. Leila remains the typical suffering soprano, Nadir the aspiring tenor who is all emotion, no brain and little brawn (it is hard to imagine him stalking, 'le poignard aux dents,' the various wild beasts to which he lays claim), while Zurga, like other stage baritones, is required to veer between ferocity and magnanimity as the situation demands. The various conflicts between love and religious vows (Leila), love and friend-ship (Nadir) and love, jealousy and kingly obligation (Zurga) are not well dramatized; Bizet, besides being hindered by his libretto, was not yet equipped to deal with them. But he clearly recognized the existence of the problem and tried to solve it by the use of leading themes. Thus the beautiful tune of the Prelude with its characteristic *ostinato* figure:

symbolizes Leila the virgin priestess, and of several other recurring motives the most prominent is that of the duet for Nadir and Zurga, 'Au fond du temple saint.' This is brought back repeatedly when-ever the friendship of the two men is in question. The stroke is often dramatically effective, but the tune itself, a fair specimen of the Gounodesque type, is not strong enough to bear the weight put upon it, especially as it is not in any way developed. Bizet had not yet learned that leading themes must have a musical as well as a dramatic aptness: if they are to be used repeatedly without development, they must be of a type, preferably brief and epigrammatic, that will fit naturally into varied contexts. The principal motive in *Carmen* answers these requirements, but not the duet in *Les Pêcheurs de perles*.

That theme illustrates another of the opera's weaknesses: most of the solo music is derivative (usually from Gounod) and some of it insipid. But here a distinction must be made. Where the Gounod influence is primarily melodic (and Gounod was most successful as a melodist), as in the Prelude or Nadir's 'Je crois entendre encore' or Leila's cavatina 'Comme autrefois,' Bizet's music retains a considerable charm. Leila's cavatina, with its 9–8 time, more agitated middle section [1] and accompanying horns and cellos, strikingly anticipates Micaela's 'Je dis que rien ne m'épouvante.' It is where Bizet follows Gounod's worst feature, his rhythmic ineptitude, as in the choruses 'Voilà notre domaine,' 'Sois la bienvenue,' 'Brahma, divin Brahma' and 'Ah! chante, chante encore' (taken over from *Don Procopio*), that he writes really bad music. It is notable that whereas the solo music is fairly even in quality, if not very individual, nearly all the best and the worst passages occur in the choruses and concerted numbers. Gounod is not the only influence. The shadow of Meyerbeer over the conception as a whole has already been noted; it is most explicit in the dreadful trio 'O lumière sainte' [2] in the final scene, which is not only musically lamentable but holds up the action to an extent that must make the dénouement ludicrous on the stage. There is also an Italian strain, not so much Donizetti this time as Verdi; the accompaniment figure in the final pages of the duet 'Je frémis, je chancelle' is the clearest of many hints of *Il Trovatore*. This eclecticism of style, though of course a defect, is not to be

[1] The resemblance here to a tune in the duet 'La brise est douce' in Gounod's *Mireille* is deceptive, for Bizet's work was written first.

[2] This was a later addition. The 1863 vocal score, which shows many differences in the last scene, has a duet for Leila and Nadir on the same words, but with different music. This occurs before Nourabad's denunciation and is therefore dramatically rather more defensible. The music, which should have been allowed to die, was perpetuated in a *Regina Coeli* in which Bizet had no hand. There are other variants in the 1863 score, including an abysmal end to the duet 'Au fond du temple saint.' When Bizet made the alterations—if indeed it was he who made them—is not known: the opera was never revived in his lifetime.

confused with the notorious eclecticism of Meyerbeer. Bizet did not, as it were, put into his shop-window all the devices he could pick up here and there from his intercourse with the world. On the contrary, a multiplicity of influences in a young composer is a healthy sign: it shows him prepared to found his own style on the widest basis. It is as a rule easier to eliminate alien influences than to generate a creative originality out of a vacuum—a lesson too often forgotten in the present century.

It is significant that most of the genuinely original music in *Les Pêcheurs de perles* is concerned with the exotic element. Though very superficially treated in the libretto, this clearly released something in Bizet's imagination. It is here that the influence of David's *Le Désert* has been detected; but though no doubt Bizet did owe something to that rather frigid work, an immediate difference is apparent. Whereas with David exoticism was an end in itself, an attempt to paint coloured pictures because the colour was strange and exciting, Bizet is already using it as a vehicle to convey character and dramatic atmosphere. The opening chorus and dance conjure up a much more vivid picture than a reader of the text could believe possible; with its incisive rhythms, sharp modulations and touches of chromaticism it launches us well into the story, and a discerning listener in 1863 might have seen (as Berlioz did) that a new and genuinely dramatic composer had arisen. The neat orchestral coda, with the tune dying into the distance in fragments over a long tonic pedal, is prophetic of *Carmen*. Equally fine is the bloodthirsty C minor chorus 'Dès que le soleil' in the last scene, which adds to its dramatic fire something of the nimbleness of a Mendelssohn scherzo. The exotic touch is apparent too in the finest of the solo numbers, Nadir's 'De mon amie,' which with its subtle rhythms (12–8 with occasional bars of 9–8), alternating major and minor key and harp accompaniment has a haunting beauty all its own. Its introductory phrase:

strikingly recalls the oboe theme in the slow movement of the Symphony.

Harmonically also Bizet's exoticism is much more enterprising than David's. Most of the latter's special effects are based on either long pedals or repeated accompaniment rhythms such as ♪♪♫♪ ♩ ♩ or both together. But he runs both devices to death and is very careful to avoid serious harmonic clashes. His contribution lay in opening a new door; he had not the original genius to enter and take possession of the territory that lay beyond it. Bizet was the first to do this, and if the ground has since been trampled by many feet, his contributions often retain their beauty and freshness where much exotic music of a later date has tarnished. The reason lies of course in their musical quality. Bizet shared David's fondness for long pedal notes, but by using them as a basis for vivid patches of chromatic harmony he greatly extended their functional possibilities and evolved one of the most characteristic and fertile elements of his style. So far from avoiding clashes, he used the novel harmonic effects thus derived to add a whole new range to his powers of expression. His audacities (which greatly startled his contemporaries) are of course commonplaces to-day, but taken in their context they still strike the listener with all the force of a fresh sensation. And this is what matters: no technical innovation is of the slightest importance apart from the use to which it is put. It is the fact that Bizet reserved his special effects for the appropriate moment instead of making a parade of them that accounts for the treatment of his harmonic originality with almost universal neglect or contempt. He used his chromatic pedal-passages for three main purposes: (*a*) simply to add variety to a piece of non-dramatic music; (*b*) to express 'exotic' colour or atmosphere, nearly always for a genuinely dramatic purpose; (*c*) to heighten dramatic tension at moments of crisis. Examples of (*a*) have already been quoted from the early Symphony and the *Variations chromatiques* for piano. The second purpose is much in evidence in *Les Pêcheurs de perles* (e.g. in the opening chorus) and of course still more so in *Djamileh* and *Carmen*. But it is the third method that he uses in the widest, subtlest and most original manner, thereby contributing something quite new to opera, especially French opera. Already *Les Pêcheurs de perles* abounds in such touches. It was probably this, quite as much as the use of leading themes, that brought down on his head the fatuous charge of Wagnerism. In Act II Nourabad, after reminding Leila of her oath, the spirit of which she has already half broken, goes out, leaving her troubled and afraid, while the orchestra plays this:

The effect is extraordinarily impressive. The jealous Zurga's entrance at the beginning of Act III is depicted by quiet chromatic scales in contrary motion over a tonic pedal—a device later brilliantly transferred to Mitifio's entrance in *L'Arlésienne*. We are again reminded of *L'Arlésienne* in the opening chorus of Act II, 'L'ombre descend,' sung behind the scenes. The bass voices in fifths together with a tambourine keep up their persistent rhythm throughout, and the only other instruments used (very sparingly) are two piccolos, whose trills and arpeggios give the scene a remote magic very characteristic of Bizet:

There is already no doubt of Bizet's exceptional musical and dramatic gifts; but they are inconstant (especially the former) and often insufficiently fused. He is too apt at climaxes to take refuge in the diminished seventh or the tremolo, and a certain rhythmic deficiency is apparent in some of the choruses, notably in the excessive use of an ambling 6–8 time. In the last act his inspiration flags badly: except for one chorus and one or two passages, such as Zurga's entry mentioned above, the music is very weak. In the duet for Zurga and Leila, where she comes to beg for Nadir's life, unaware that Zurga also loves her, Bizet misses a great dramatic opportunity. This is exceptional, however. In general his dramatic sense is surer than his musical style. The finale of Act II, with its piled-up climaxes as the chorus demand the culprits' death—especially the passage in dotted rhythm 'Ni pitié, ni merci'—is very good theatrical music, though not yet mature Bizet. Here and there he hits on the musical *mot juste* that sums up and intensifies the dramatic situation in the most economical way—which is after all the highest aim of the dramatic composer. Such a stroke is Leila's oath of chastity in Act I:

These are her first words in the opera, and the phrase is twice repeated, each time a minor third higher. A moment later she and Nadir recognize each other. Zurga is aware of her hesitation, though not of its cause, and offers to release her before it is too late. She at once pulls herself together and replies in accents not heard again till the great duet in the last act of *Carmen* [1]:

Je reste i - ci quand j'y de-vrais mou - rir!

Here is the first hint of that flexible melodic recitative that Bizet used so subtly in *Carmen* (e.g. Seguidilla, card scene, final duet) and which he would surely have further extended had he lived.

One of the features that most troubled contemporary critics was the scoring. They found it painfully noisy and overloaded (one referred to the opera as a 'fortissimo in three acts'), and it may well have offended an ear attuned to Auber. But the more grandiose passages, which are the least typical of Bizet, owe not a little to Meyerbeer and Gounod, whose scores then seemed the height of romantic extrava-gance (Berlioz's were still regarded as merely eccentric). Certainly *Les Pêcheurs de perles* is (with the exception of the unheard *Ivan le Terrible*) the most massive of Bizet's operatic scores, and the least rich in subtlety. The trio 'O lumière sainte,' where everything is thrown in, including one of the earliest operatic appearances of the tuba,[2] is Meyerbeerian in execution as well as in conception; and Nadir's 'Des savanes et des forêts,' where the voice is doubled by cellos and bassoons beneath a long string tremolo, reflects the prac-tice of Meyerbeer as well as early Wagner. Bizet is more sparing than later in the use of solo instruments and groups, but he already shows an eye for colour and the combination of timbres. The exotic parts, as we should expect, are scored with most skill. The dance

[1] Compare Carmen's 'Mais que je vive ou que je meure, Non, je ne te céderai pas!' (p. 349 of the Choudens vocal score), where the same sentiments are expressed in almost the same striking phrase.

[2] Its sole appearance in Bizet's scores; but it is possible that another hand has been at work here. See footnote, p. 138.

in the opening chorus (p. 12 of vocal score), in which melody and harmony are entrusted to three solo wind instruments while violas, cellos, tambourine and triangle keep up a rhythmic drone in open fifths, admirably suits colour to action. The first chorus of Act II is supported only by two piccolos and a tambourine, all behind the scenes, and Nadir's 'De mon amie' by a single oboe and harp (again behind the scenes): in both cases a very individual and poetic atmosphere is evoked by the simplest means. This is the method that Bizet brought to perfection in *L'Arlésienne*. Already the flute and harp, instruments which he used with special understanding, take a prominent part. Together they introduce the theme of the duet 'Au fond du temple saint,' over whose later appearances one or both of the flutes, supported by tremolo strings, almost exercise a prescriptive right. The English horn, whose first appearance in Nadir's charmingly scored romance is most effective, and the percussion are used sparingly. If parts of the score pay service to current convention, there are clear signs of the piquancy, suppleness and economy that distinguish Bizet's later practice.

In later years Bizet thought very little of *Les Pêcheurs de perles*, judging it quite as severely as the critics. It remains, however, an opera of interest and promise, justifying perhaps more than *Djamileh* Reyer's wise words: 'The composer who stumbles in taking a step forward is worth more attention than the composer who shows us how easily he can step backwards.' Here we see in embryo, intermingled with much dross, many of the qualities that were to make Bizet the foremost dramatic composer in France.

His next opera remains unpublished. The score of *Ivan le Terrible*, long believed to have perished, reached the Conservatoire library from the executors of Bizet's widow and her second husband in the 1920s. It is complete except for portions of the last act, of which the voice-parts only are sketched. The libretto, a sterling specimen of the ponderous and improbable type by Leroy and Trianon, seems to have been designed for the Opéra rather than the Théâtre-Lyrique, and was thus leading Bizet away from his true bent. It is full of pillage, rape, conspiracy, arson and the loftiest sentiments. Act IV sees a wedding, the cremation of the Kremlin, the condemnation of the heroine and her brother to instant execution and the collapse of the tsar in a fit so apoplectic that he is given up for dead. The music is very uneven and has all the faults that might be expected from Bizet's grappling with such a subject. The heroic parts tend to flatulence, and religion as usual proves the composer's downfall: the women's prayer to the Virgin in Act II is laughably like the hymn to Brahma in *Les Pêcheurs de perles*, with the harmony rendered more palatable to Christian ears by copious dominant thirteenths. The orchestration is formidable. The march in Act III —one of Bizet's worst lapses—employs a brass band on the stage composed of two cornets, two trumpets, three trombones and three saxhorns (soprano, bass and contrabass), an assembly calculated to gratify the eye rather than the ear. This is in addition to a very large orchestra in the normal place, including a heavy battery of percussion, bells and organ. The influence of both Verdi and Meyerbeer appears in the ensembles, which are frequent and elephantine. The shade of the prelude to Act III of *Lohengrin* strays momentarily across the finale of Act I. If Bizet did withdraw the opera because he found it impregnated with Verdi he had reason, though Verdi is only one of several strong influences. There is quite as much of the Gounod of the more uplifting scenes in *Faust*.

Nevertheless *Ivan le Terrible* has a good deal that is original and dramatically conceived, especially in the first and fourth acts, and it is possible that what looks stiff on paper might reveal greater vitality in the theatre. In style and aim it is much closer to *Les Pêcheurs de perles* than to *La Jolie Fille de Perth*. But signs of exotic colouring are few. The opening of Act III:

has a faintly Russian tinge, though the chorus that follows reverts sharply to the fashionable ballrooms of the Second Empire, and it is perhaps significant that the young Bulgarian's serenade, given in response to the tsar's request for a national song, is no other than the bolero from *Vasco de Gama* with the original words slightly modified. Essentially Bizet had only one type of local colour. Leading themes are used much as in the other operas, and one or two of them reveal a vivid sense of dramatic character. The motive of the double traitor Youloff, betrayer of his sovereign and his fellow conspirators, which appears first on violas and cellos when he is trying to ingratiate himself with the wronged Caucasians, is full of possibilities:

Ivan is characterized by a lively war-song in C minor, of which three complete versions survive. One of his airs in Act I uses the same chromatic *ostinato* figure as the prelude to *Les Pêcheurs de perles* and the dream in *Djamileh*. There are faint but arresting prognostications of the C minor *mélodrame* that accompanies Mère Renaud's entry in *L'Arlésienne*, nicely scored for the four woodwind soloists, and of José's 'Dût-il m'en coûter la vie.'

Bizet's self-borrowings here are curious and interesting. The duet in Act I for Marie and the young Bulgarian (who is both Ivan's secret agent and a vehicle for local colour) reappears as the flute theme at bar 28 of the prelude to *La Jolie Fille de Perth*, a transformation as successful as it is unexpected. The bolero from *Vasco de Gama* has already been mentioned. The opening scene of Act IV is a rehash (or prehash) of the posthumously published chorus *Le Golfe de Bahia*, again led by the young Bulgarian. Bars 5–8 of Marie's 'Ah! si ma voix encore' are identical with Zurga's 'Et nul ne doit la voir, nul ne doit l'approcher' in Act I of *Les Pêcheurs de perles*, and the duet for Marie and Igor in Act V is melodically almost the same as the original form of the duet 'O lumière sainte' in the same opera. This may be pure chance (if not, it is the only instance of Bizet re-using published material); but the appearance of the *Trompette et tambour* march from *Jeux d'enfants* of six years later at the beginning of Act V, in a solemn and serious context, throws a surprising light on his creative procedure. A number of passages were afterwards used in *Noé*.

It was reported in 1944 that the Germans, having 'rediscovered' the score, were supplying it with a new libretto, transferring the action to the Merovingian court of the sixth century; and according to a recent announcement the opera was performed in German (under its original title) at Mühringen Castle near Tübingen during 1946. But it is doubtful if any reconstruction could make *Ivan le Terrible* more than an interesting curiosity.

The development shown in *La Jolie Fille de Perth* is in some ways negative rather than positive: Bizet has eliminated many of the weaknesses of the two previous operas, but not pursued his advances, particularly in the harmonic sphere. It is a less arresting and a less uneven opera, and consequently has been generally underrated. For much of its apparent tameness the libretto is responsible. This extremely remote adaptation from Scott, by Saint-Georges and Adenis, is nothing but a receptacle for age-old operatic devices. The construction is poor, the characterization standardized, and the verse execrable. On the other hand there is no attempt at the monumental; the characters are, in intention at least, ordinary human beings. We are much closer to *opéra-comique*, and in this sense there is an advance: Bizet was now heading for the right goal along the right road, and needed only time in order to reach it. The weakest points in the music (which include most of Act IV) invariably correspond to those of the libretto.

The opening of Act I finds Smith in his workshop, lamenting the fact that Catherine Glover will not take her father's advice and consent to be his Valentine. He hears a noise familiar to operatic audiences: 'Je crois qu'on insulte une femme!' Mab, queen of the gypsies, rushes in and is given shelter, but has to be hurriedly hidden when Glover, Catherine and the apprentice Ralph appear, ready to celebrate the carnival with 'un peu de venaison, un superbe pâté, du vieux Wisky [*sic*] d'Écosse, un succulent pudding.' Smith gives the flirtatious Catherine a gold-enamelled flower, while Ralph growls out his jealousy. Presently a stranger, who turns out to be the Duke of Rothsay, comes in with a request to Smith to straighten his dagger; his real quarry of course is Catherine, who thinks a little flirtation with him in Smith's presence will do Smith good. Only the intervention of Mab prevents a fight between the two men, but her appearance from behind the arras gives rise to the usual recrimina-tions, and Catherine throws down Smith's flower, which is retrieved by Mab. The duke departs, having invited Catherine to a mid-night ball in his palace. In Act II amid the carnival revels the duke asks for Mab's assistance in abducting Catherine, who has refused him. Mab, herself a cast-off mistress of the duke, in revenge substi-tutes herself for Catherine and enters the palace. Ralph, the worse for drink, thinks he sees Catherine being abducted and rouses Smith, who has been vainly serenading her. As they rush off, the real Catherine appears at her window to answer Smith's serenade. In Act III the duke woos the veiled Mab while the courtiers dance a minuet off-stage, and in the process takes the gold flower. Presently Glover and the real Catherine appear, and to the astonishment of the duke and his courtiers ask for his consent to her marriage with Smith. Smith indignantly rejects her, and his resolution hardens when he sees the flower in the duke's hand; Catherine finds herself disbelieved by both parties. In Act IV Ralph has taken Catherine's part and is to fight a duel with Smith for her honour (on the banks of the Tweed—the librettists were weak at Scottish geography). She and Smith while away the time (as only a soprano and a tenor know how) by sentimentalizing over their past love. The fight is stopped at the last minute by the duke at Mab's instance, but mean-while Catherine has gone mad. She is cured by the odd method of being compelled to witness Smith serenading Mab at her (Catherine's) window, and all ends happily.

It is difficult to see how a worse libretto could be founded on Scott's novel. The story bristles with improbabilities that would be tolerated nowhere but in an opera-house, and the last act, in which the duke does not appear at all, is appallingly weak and undramatic. It seems to have been constructed solely for the purpose of intro‑ ducing a mad scene,[1] a device as popular then (witness Donizetti's *Lucia di Lammermoor*, Meyerbeer's *L'Étoile du Nord*[2] and Thomas's *Hamlet*) as is a display of tap‑dancing in a certain type of film to‑day. It is not surprising that Bizet could do little with the characters. Scott's mettlesome Smith becomes a typical asinine tenor, while his Duke of Rothsay, a memorable compound of vacillation, daring, charm and complete recklessness of other people's interests and his own, is turned into the traditional operatic seducer—and not a very efficient one at that. Catherine, a somewhat mawkish character in the original, is here the complete opposite—a frivolous coquette who deserves all that comes to her. Glover too is turned from a hard‑ boiled burgess into a *buffo* bass *manqué*. Mab, presumably based on the Glee‑maiden Louise, has flashes of genuine vitality, though her part is very much that of the conventional *seconda donna*. The one success is Ralph, though he bears not the remotest resemblance to Scott's Conachar, the disguised Highlander with a sharp tongue but a lamb's courage. Bizet makes him a real man; his drinking‑song in Act II with its fuddled accompaniment figure:

is a brilliant piece of characterization, piercing the comic façade of drunkenness to reveal the underlying tragedy. Nor does the libretto give the composer much chance to bring the background to life. The chorus of the Watch admirably sets the atmosphere for Act II, but the smiths at the anvil and the carnival (including the St. Valen‑ tine chorus) had long been stock devices of French and Italian opera. The complete absence of local colour may be due to Bizet's inability to find a musical equivalent for Scotland; but even if he

[1] There is no justification for this in Scott, whose heroine remains almost too level‑headed.

[2] In this opera (1854) the heroine, also called Catherine, is likewise restored to sanity by the re‑enactment of a scene from the past.

had one, it is difficult to see how he could have made use of it. The one opportunity for exploiting the exotic is seized with both hands. This is the justly famous Bohemian Dance, which remains significantly the best thing in the opera. It is no doubt due to the lack of such opportunities that the harmonic style of *La Jolie Fille de Perth* seems comparatively tame after *Les Pêcheurs de perles*.

These deficiencies in the libretto are particularly to be regretted, for Bizet does show signs of an increasing mastery of the dramatic style. His use of leading themes is less frequent than in *Les Pêcheurs de perles*, but far more effective. Glover's fussy little motive:[1]

which occurs in several related forms, nicely portrays that worthy as Bizet saw him. Smith's serenade (from *Don Procopio*) is put to a genuinely dramatic purpose in the finales of Acts II and IV. But best of all is Bizet's use of the theme that accompanies the duke's wooing of Catherine:

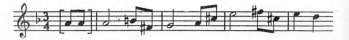

It comes three times in the trio 'De ce beau seigneur' (where the duke first approaches Catherine in Act I), in the orchestra in D major and G major, and then sung by the duke in C major to the words 'Que vous êtes jolie, quelle grâce accomplie.' Its later appearances are all in the orchestra: when the duke enlists Mab to assist his designs, very effectively (in the minor) in the finale of Act II when the majordomo takes off the supposed Catherine in a litter to the palace, and twice in Act III, at the approach of the litter and (in 6–8 time) when the duke announces that his victim has fled at the approach of dawn. On each occasion it serves to bind the action together in a striking and economical manner. The finale of Act II, with this smooth tune accompanying the abduction of the wrong

[1] Compare the very similar motive for Haroun's friends in *Djamileh*.

woman (its suave irony recalls the cello theme in the duet for Rigoletto and Sparafucile in Act I Scene ii of Verdi's opera—a scene Bizet much admired), with its echoes of Ralph's drunken song and the real Catherine's appearance at her window singing Smith's serenade now for the first time in the major key, is the finest piece of dramatic writing that Bizet had yet achieved.

Almost equally good from the musico-dramatic point of view is the minuet (familiar from Guiraud's arrangement in the second *Arlésienne* suite) that accompanies the duke's wooing of the false Catherine in Act III.[1] Again dramatic irony adds vastly to the success of a charming piece of music. The trio 'De ce beau seigneur,' where Smith tries to drown the duke's whispered advances to Catherine by his blows on the anvil, is effective in a more conventional way; so is the first finale, where Glover's tipsy song (he has been at the 'vieux Wisky d'Écosse') is ingeniously combined with the arguments of the other characters about the relative innocence of Mab and Smith. A sterner test is presented by the finale of Act III, the most substantial number in the opera; and Bizet comes out of it fairly well. It is perhaps a little stiff, in the manner of early Verdi, but we need only glance at the contemporary operas of Gounod and Thomas, not to mention Meyerbeer and Halévy, to notice at once an advance in dramatic power. The contrasts are well managed and the characters differentiated with skill. Particularly fine is Catherine's protestation of innocence, 'Il veut vous le cacher,' a long *crescendo* over a dominant pedal with the accompanying chords first halved in value and then halved again.[2] There is one dramatic failure: the duke's remarks in the opening chorus of Act III, and also a passage in the ensuing cavatina, 'Comme un rayon charmant,' are marked 'avec fatuité,' and there is little doubt that Bizet intended the music to portray the triviality of the duke's character. Unfortunately the music is not a dramatic presentation of triviality; it is trivial itself. Bizet tried the same thing again, this time triumphantly,

[1] An operatic seduction seems to have been traditionally accompanied by a minuet, as in *Don Giovanni* and *Rigoletto*. Guiraud used a synthesis of the vocal parts as a counterpart to the main theme at its return.

[2] pp. 168–9 of current Choudens vocal score; the passage is too long to quote.

with Escamillo, who is directed to sing the refrain of his famous song 'avec fatuité.'

The copious ornamentation of Catherine's part, which brought down the wrath of generations of French critics, may also have been intended to depict the frivolity of her character, as well as to serve as a show-piece for Christine Nilsson. Certainly her vocal polonaise 'Vive l'hiver,' with its likeness to the polonaise from *Mignon* and also to one of Bizet's own *Variations chromatiques*, is feeble enough, and the mad scene *à la* Donizetti raises a critical blush; but they represent a marking of time rather than a backsliding. Gounod's *Roméo et Juliette*, produced the same year, contains equally absurd concessions to convention. But the love music as a whole lacks distinction. Indeed all through his life Bizet found difficulty in giving individual expression to the more conventional forms of love; it was here that Gounod's influence struck deepest. He was to startle the world with a novel and unrivalled depiction of consuming passion, but in every one of his dramatic works, including *L'Arlésienne* and *Carmen*, the straightforward love music, though seldom poor and often charming and dramatically appropriate, tends to be less original than the rest of the score. But if Catherine and Smith remain typical figures of their period, there are the makings of more serious stuff in Mab. Mr. Martin Cooper aptly quotes a few bars of melodic recitative that throw the mind forward to a later and more vital gypsy, while the relationship of the Bohemian Dance to the *chanson bohème* in Act II of *Carmen* is too striking to need comment. Mab's *couplets* in Act I, 'Catherine est coquette,' inexplicably omitted from the current Choudens vocal score,[1] are pure Bizet:

[1] This score, presumably a cut version made for a revival, is unsatisfactory in other particulars. It tends to cut the best items, including the admirable opening chorus of Act II. It omits the F major section of Smith's serenade

The little figure (*a*) almost amounts to a Bizet fingerprint: it occurs prominently in the Glover motive quoted above, the scherzo of *Roma*, the *chanson bohème* and card scene in *Carmen* and many other places.

In *La Jolie Fille de Perth* Bizet has rid himself almost entirely of Meyerbeer's influence. There are still signs of Weber, notably in the first chorus with its echo of Ännchen's arietta in Act II of *Der Freischütz*; and of course Gounod. But there is much less of the rhythmic smugness (the duet with chorus that opens Act IV, especially Ralph's 'Moi, Ralph, simple artisan,' is a painful exception), and more of the lyrical charm of *Mireille*, which left its mark on the attractive St. Valentine chorus. Mab's 'Les seigneurs de la cour' in Act II also clearly derives from Sganarelle's *couplets* 'Qu'ils sont doux' in *Le Médecin malgré lui*. More significant is the influence of Verdi, apparent not only in the style but in the dramatic treatment: the duke again and again reminds us of his more virile counterpart in *Rigoletto,* Mab is not unlike Maddalena, and a similarity in treatment to the Rigoletto-Sparafucile duet has already been noted. Stylistic resemblances are scattered through the opera, especially in the ensembles, whose compound of stiffness and energy is very much that of early-middle Verdi. Bizet was a great admirer of *Rigoletto*, and Verdi's influence was no bad thing for him; his flexible melodies and vivid sense of drama, added to Bizet's native ability in those respects, helped to counterbalance the sugary seductions of Gounod.

There is much good music in *La Jolie Fille de Perth*, even if less strenuousness seems to have gone to its composition than into *Les Pêcheurs de perles* (a deceptive sign, especially with French music). The Bohemian Dance is a subtle miniature that repays close attention and analysis. The variations in rhythm, the alternation of minor and major key, the gradations of pace (from *andantino molto* to *presto*) and dynamics (from *ppp* to *fff con furia*) are managed with the greatest skill; the sudden check (*fpp*) when the minor key returns at the beginning of the 6-8 section serves brilliantly to redouble the excitement. Together with the Watch chorus 'Bons citoyens,' itself

(the Aubade of the Beecham suite) and inserts the minuet as an Entr'acte before Act III. It also miscalls the work an *opéra-comique*. The published full score is a mixture of this version and the original score of 1868.

an admirably vivid and dramatic scene possessing the rare ingredient of humour,[1] the Bohemian Dance illustrates one of Bizet's charac-teristic procedures. This is the melodic variation; each scene being built up like a mosaic from constant repetitions of a single short theme, simply varied in rhythm, harmony, scoring or dynamics. The device is old as the hills, but Bizet's application of it to dramatic purposes is his own. The opening of the Watch chorus on the bassoons is prophetic of the entr'acte before Act II of *Carmen*, while one of its cadence figures:

reappears most effectively at the end of Act III of the same opera.

In orchestration too a marked advance is apparent. The second act in particular is beautifully scored, as Bizet himself noted. He ranges farther afield in his choice of colours and shows a greater sureness and subtlety in their application. The scoring of the duke's love theme (p. 150) on its several appearances is particularly happy. When the duke is enlisting Mab's support it appears on two solo violas, then on two violins, then on a single clarinet. In the ironical litter scene we hear it on two violas, two cellos and one clarinet very low down, with the harmony supplied by three more solo cellos and two basses. It dies away on the violas and clarinet alone, echoed by a single horn. The solo clarinet is more prominent than in *Les Pêcheurs de perles*, with a certain emphasis on the chalumeau register; and the flute already receives that affectionate treatment that dis-tinguishes the score of *Carmen*. The prelude shows the delicacy of Bizet's scoring and the clarity of his part-writing at their best. Its fine web of woodwind solos looks forward to the entr'acte before

[1] The cut in the current vocal score spoils the effect of this.

Act III of *Carmen*. In the Bohemian Dance, opening with the favourite combination of flute and harp, he obtains a most exhilarating effect by simply ringing the changes on the groups of instruments that play the tune. The sparing but most effective use of the percussion should be noted here. The serenade, which introduces the hitherto silent English horn, is scored with a nice blend of richness and restraint, plucked strings now taking the place of the guitar. In happy contrast the accompaniment to Ralph's drunken song employs the lowest notes of violins and clarinets (often in thirds), with bassoons, cellos and horns prominent in staccato interjections. The scene ends on a *pppp* chord for three trombones. The closing scene of the act, with all the strings divided (the cellos in five parts), is a rich and dramatic piece of atmosphere-painting. In the first half of Act III he uses a second orchestra behind the scenes, consisting of first flute, second oboe, two solo violins, two cornets, third trombone, harp and triangle. It is this group that plays the minuet during the seduction scene. This too begins with flute and harp alone, but the flute is joined, one by one and in unison, by the two violins and the oboe.

Much the most interesting of the unfinished operas of which fragments have survived is *La Coupe du Roi de Thule* (1868; libretto by Gallet and Blau). It is a matter for real regret that Bizet went no farther with this, and still more so that some sheets of the manuscript have clearly been lost since he handled them; for it represents an important stage in his development.[1] The story concerns a young fisherman, Yorick, who falls under the spell of Myrrha, a woman of the Arlésienne-Carmen type. The old King of Thule too is dying of love for her, but she has become the mistress of Angus, his favourite and presumed successor. Only the royal jester Paddock remains, beneath his professional veneer of irony, devoted to his master. Angus and the court are waiting impatiently for the king to die, but Myrrha reminds them of the legend of the golden cup, given to the first King of Thule by the siren Claribel, queen of the sea. This is the emblem of royalty, and each king on his death-bed summons his successor to bestow it on him. But the dying monarch,

[1] For a full account of this work and the circumstances of its composition, see *Music & Letters*, vol. xxviii, No. 4, October 1947.

who has no heir, summons not Angus but Paddock, who throws the cup into the sea. Myrrha offers her love to whosoever will bring it back, and Yorick, ignoring all appeals, plunges after it. In Act II we see Claribel in her turn possessed by vain love for Yorick; she offers him immortality, but he asks only for the cup and remains unshaken even by a vision of Myrrha in Angus's arms. So he brings back the cup to Myrrha, who thanks him politely and bestows herself and the throne on Angus. Then at last Yorick calls the siren to his aid; the sea rises, and the guilty couple and corrupt court are overwhelmed.

Given the romantic convention, the libretto is a good one, refreshingly free from the inflated sentiments and grand renunciations customary at the Opéra. The attraction for Bizet obviously lay in the Myrrha-Yorick relationship. We have already seen how, in his letters to Galabert, he emphasized the fatal fascination of Myrrha. The music amply reflects this interest. Two portions of it [1] have been published, both in misleading circumstances: the prelude, under the inaccurate and confusing title of *Marche funèbre*, and the song *La Sirène*, first of the posthumous *Seize Mélodies*, to which new words were fitted by Catulle Mendès. The prelude, which has remained quite unknown, is a splendid piece, powerful and well constructed. It opens with an arresting phrase on full orchestra:

---

[1] Further investigation has discovered at least two more (see additional note on p. 163). Bizet certainly wrote much more of *La Coupe du Roi de Thule* than remains at the Conservatoire. Unfortunately the manuscripts of the extracts which Guiraud made from the unfinished operas for posthumous publication (see p. 125) have disappeared.

The sombre main theme follows on bassoons and cellos and is twice
repeated, each time an octave higher. Perhaps 'repeat' is the wrong
word, for only the opening bars are the same; the continuation
develops an expanding vitality till it reaches a big climax that very
strikingly foreshadows, in melody, rhythm and accompaniment, the
Frédéri theme in *L'Arlésienne*:

This is something more than coincidence; clearly this type of phrase
came to symbolize for Bizet the emotional state of a young man in
the grip of a passion he cannot shake off or control. There are
affinities too with phrases in José's flower song. After the climax

the opening unexpectedly returns, this time modulating to E flat, the key of the central section. This begins with a melody for flute and English horn in octaves with harp accompaniment and a long inner pedal on the horn, and contains another foreshadowing of the Frédéri music, though not of the same phrase. A shortened version of the main theme returns, followed by a coda in which the second half of the E flat section bursts out *fff* in B major. A sinister chromatic passage with clashing major sevenths leads to a gloomy end: Bizet had the vision to close with the more genuine and tragic Myrrha element instead of the conventional happiness of Yorick's union with Claribel. The latter is presented in the E flat section, which is identical with the song *La Sirène*, sung by her in vain appeal to Yorick in the second act. The final cadence of the song, which does not appear in the prelude, has a beautiful touch of poetry:

Bizet set portions of all three acts in full score; the manuscript is written with great care, and the frequent stage directions reflect his search for dramatic truth. Unfortunately there are numerous lacunae. An air for Paddock in Act I is characteristic and expressive, and nicely depicts the sincere love for his master that underlies the jester's nature. Myrrha's entry is carefully treated, with a violin solo that Bizet might have used later as a leading motive. The Legend, in which Myrrha tells the story of the cup, is complete except for fifteen bars (one sheet) in the middle. It contains some fine music, from the stirring first phrase based on the initial bars of the prelude to the splendid B major climax where the singer is joined by the chorus:

PAGE FROM THE MANUSCRIPT OF 'LA COUPE DU ROI DE THULE'
(ACT I, FINALE)

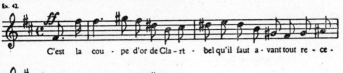

C'est la cou - pe d'or de Cla - rt - bel qu'il faut a - vant tout re - ce -
voir, la cou - pe d'or!

The finale of Act I arrests attention for a different reason. Yorick, holding Myrrha to her vow, thus announces his departure in search of the cup:

Myr-rha____ la brise est for - te et le flot__ é-cu-

mant__ Si_ la mer me rap-por - te gar-de-moi ton ser-

ment,__ Si_ la mer me rap-por te gar-de-moi ton ser—ment

This, with only slight differences, is the melody of José's 'Dût-il m'en coûter la vie,' the great climax in Act III of *Carmen*. What is more, after a stormy interlude in which Paddock begs Yorick not to go, there follows, as in *Carmen*, a repetition of the whole passage a semitone higher—this time as a duet for Myrrha and Yorick.[1] In *Carmen* Bizet improved both the vocal line and the accompaniment, but the dramatic parallel is most illuminating. In both operas the victim leaves his betrayer on the climax of the finale, and the audience, on the stage and in the hall, know what she will do the moment his back is turned; in both operas, ignoring the advice of the spectators, he emphasizes his resolution by repeating his outburst a semitone higher; but whereas in *La Coupe* it is his departure that he proclaims, in *Carmen* it is his refusal to depart—overborne as this is by weightier considerations a moment or two later. The dramatic gain in the later opera, with José cornered between Carmen, Escamillo and Micaela, is enormous, but the seeds of that great scene lie in this unregarded manuscript of six years earlier. Surely only a sudden flash of insight could have revealed to Bizet the new use he could make of this old theme.

The fragments of Acts II and III are fewer and briefer, but the last two bars of all, after Yorick has fallen into Claribel's arms, intro-duce the motive in 12–8 time later used to characterize Djamileh. This is sung to the words 'Vagues murmurantes,' and is almost cer-tainly a reminiscence of the siren music in Act II. It is also fairly clear that Bizet would have brought back the music of 'Myrrha, la brise est forte' in Act III. The orchestration of the opera is very rich, but much more subtle than that of any earlier work. Two English horns appear in the Legend, and the whole score uses three flutes (sometimes two piccolos), trumpets as well as cornets and four each of bassoons and trombones, including a contrabass trombone which appears elsewhere only in *Noé*. In the prelude the timpani play chords with the trombones, a device no doubt derived from Berlioz.

There are very few lapses in the music, which is quite free from the

[1] Myrrha of course sings 'Je tiendrai mon serment.' This was an addition by Bizet, who rightly thought that the librettists had not tied Myrrha sufficiently to her oath.

mistaken grandiosity of *Ivan le Terrible*. When he was writing it Bizet felt that a radical change was taking place within him; he spoke of changing his skin both as man and artist. The results appear, not in any technical feature of his style, but in a great emotional and dramatic advance: *La Coupe du Roi de Thule* gives the first unmistakable sign of a genuine tragic power that was to culminate in *L'Arlésienne* and *Carmen*. From now on his progress to maturity was rapid; and its acceleration should be dated, not from his marriage or his experiences in the war of 1870, but from the spiritual crisis which he underwent while composing *La Coupe du Roi de Thule*.[1]

Bizet's completion of Halévy's *Noé* presents a problem. He wrote to Lacombe (about October 1869): 'Halévy left three acts nearly finished; but I've had to score it all—pretty well guess it all—and I have to compose a fourth act that is short enough.' It has always been assumed that this fourth act (actually the second scene of Act III) was the extent of his original contribution. An examination of the score shows this to be far from the case. The final scene as printed in 1885 consists of only two numbers, an orchestral Intermezzo (*L'Arc-en-ciel*) based on somewhat nondescript music that has occurred earlier in the opera, and a final 'Hymne à Dieu' that proves (most inappropriately) to be an arrangement of the solo song *Chant d'amour*. Bizet was not responsible for this: a note states that the finale and ballet music were lost and their places supplied by the publisher from other works by Bizet (the ballet music is an arrangement of excerpts from *Djamileh* and the song *La Coccinelle*). If Bizet wrote any music for this scene, it does not survive. On the other hand, his pen is recognizable in many other parts of the score. The posthumous volume of *Seize Mélodies*, edited by Guiraud (who presumably knew exactly what was Bizet's work), contains two excerpts from *Noé*, 'Pourquoi pleurer?' from Act I and 'Qui donc t'aimera mieux?' from Act III, Scene i. Each of these episodes forms the middle section of a duet; in each case the remainder, in a more old-fashioned style, can be assigned with fair confidence to Halévy. Phrases from 'Pourquoi pleurer?' are used as a leading motive

[1] It may be added that the opera with which Eugène Diaz won the prize offered for a setting of this libretto has a dreary insipidity difficult to parallel even in the annals of mid-nineteenth-century France.

throughout the first two acts. Internal evidence proves that practically the whole of the long duet for Sarai and Ituriel in Act II is Bizet's work; it is a compound of several passages from *Ivan le Terrible*, the last of them, at Sarai's 'Ah! c'est par trop d'outrage' (p. 138 of vocal score), having a very characteristic melody. The entr'acte before Act II must also have been put together by Bizet. Of its four themes the first stylistically suggests Bizet rather than Halévy, the second is taken from the preceding finale, the third from 'Pourquoi pleurer?'; while the fourth is no other than the opening of *Vasco de Gama*, written ten years earlier but not yet published. The curtain at once goes up to reveal 'an oasis in the desert,' and the same phrase from *Vasco de Gama* is again quoted later when the desert is mentioned in the text.

There is no doubt that Bizet's work on *Noé* was greater than is commonly supposed and is inextricably mingled with Halévy's [1]; it is difficult to say more, especially as in finishing another man's work he would presumably try to adapt his style and would certainly not feel himself free to experiment. But certain other passages strongly suggest his hand rather than Halévy's. Among them are the last ten bars of p. 149, a typical Bizet coda (compare the end of the first chorus of *Les Pêcheurs de perles*, the departure of Escamillo in Act II and of the smugglers in Act III of *Carmen*); Sem's 'Reviens à toi' (p. 161) with its strong lyrical impulse (never one of Halévy's strong points) and particularly the sudden modulation from D flat to C major; and the really fine first finale based on a tune that at once suggests Bizet:

Not that it is fair to ascribe only the best music to Bizet; a lot of the smug religious stuff is only too much within his compass.

The whole question is perhaps academic, for *Noé* is unlikely to be revived. Apart from the uneven quality of the music, the libretto

---

[1] Attempts to disentangle it proved vain owing to the disappearance (since 1938) of Halévy's original manuscript.

is among Saint-Georges's more fantastic efforts. The story, concerned with the sexual digressions of Noah's family and the fallen angel Ituriel (who loses his wings on the stage to an orgy of diminished sevenths), reads like a mixture of *Paradise Lost* and *The Country Wife* couched in the most inflated language of Scribe. The behaviour of the characters and the landscape is unpredictable in the extreme, and it is not clear who survives the flood which terminates the first scene of Act III. It is, however, unlikely that the loss of the final scene deprived us of the chance of judging Bizet's powers of animal characterization.

Additional Note on 'La Coupe du Roi de Thule'

Further research on this most interesting opera has revealed some striking facts, in particular a scheme of leading motives more elaborate than in any of Bizet's other operas. Only a fraction (perhaps a sixth) of the opera survives, yet at least seven and probably ten distinct motives reappear on one or more occasions, some of them in subtle transformations (though there is no resemblance to Wagner's symphonic texture). For instance Yorick's love for Myrrha and Claribel's love for Yorick are expressed by variants of what must be a basic Yorick motive, of which one form is quoted on p. 157. Other themes appear to denote the legend of the cup, the efficacy of the cup, the characters of Myrrha and Paddock, and Claribel's pitying view of Yorick's love for Myrrha (this was later used in *Djamileh*, at the words 'L'amour était ma vie' in the final duet). The fine song *N'oublions pas!* (see p. 125) is Yorick's first air in Act I; two of its motives occur elsewhere in the opera. The duet *Les Nymphes des bois* (p. 126) is the chorus of sirens that opens Act II. It is likely that several other posthumous pieces, including the duet *Rêvons*, the song *L'Abandonnée* and even perhaps *Le Gascon* come from this opera. But most important is the sheer quality of the music; not only the Legend, but Paddock's air 'Quand la nuit te couvre' and the *mélodrame* for Myrrha's entry (all unpublished) are jewels worthy to be set beside the best of *L'Arlésienne* and *Carmen*.

THE libretto of *Djamileh* is based on *Namouna* by Alfred de Musset, a reflectively amorous poem after the manner of Byron's *Don Juan*; and this at once explains its dramatic weakness. There is very little story, and what there is has little of the dramatic. Haroun, a dis-illusioned voluptuary who proclaims his love for nothing except love itself, changes his mistress once a month: the old one is pensioned off with a gift of jewellery while a new candidate is bought by his servant Splendiano in the slave-market. The reigning mistress, Djamileh (she is a Spaniard in Musset's poem), has the misfortune to fall in love with Haroun, and when the day of dismissal arrives she makes a bargain with Splendiano: he is to admit her disguised as her successor, and if this proof of devotion fails to win Haroun, he can have her for himself. Splendiano thinks he is on a certainty, but Haroun's heart after a struggle capitulates to Djamileh.

There seems little chance for a dramatic composer here. Haroun is a hopeless hero, being no more than an abstraction; there is almost no action, and one of the few incidents—Djamileh's bargain with Splendiano—takes place in spoken dialogue; and with only one real character little dramatic conflict is possible. Yet such is Bizet's advance as a musical dramatist that *Djamileh*, his first *opéra-comique* proper, is not far short of a masterpiece. He seizes his chances with unusual skill and contrives not only to cover up many of the defects of the libretto but to create a work of art that stands firmly on its own feet. His power of evoking an atmosphere in which the characters move and have their being is at its highest; from the opening chorus of off-stage voices acclaiming the sunset on the Nile, accompanied

only by quiet chords and a persistent rhythm ♪ 𝄾 ♪ ♪ ♪ ♪ ♪ on the tambourine—a maturer version of the initial chorus of Act II of *Les Pêcheurs de perles*—the dramatic illusion is complete. Here Bizet triumphantly achieves what he attempted with only partial success in *Les Pêcheurs de perles*—an exotic background that is interesting in itself and in complete harmony with the foreground. In charac-terization too he does wonders. Nothing could vitalize Haroun, but his moods at least are musically portrayed. Splendiano is a clever study of the type immortalized in Mozart's Osmin; his *couplets*, 'Il faut pour éteindre ma fièvre,' are turned with admirable wit. Haroun's gaming friends, with their fussy motive so reminiscent of Simon Glover and their brilliant little unaccompanied chorus behind the scenes, are surprisingly alive. But the great achievement is the character of Djamileh herself. In this portrait of a young girl in love Bizet far surpasses anything in the earlier operas. This is no conventional soprano quavering the same old sentiment in the same old manner, but a vital and original creation. The theme in the orchestra in 12–8 that heralds her silent appearance in the opening scene, though dramatically effective, has no exceptional merit (it came from *La Coupe du Roi de Thule*, as did one passage in the final duet of *Djamileh*[1]), but the first music she sings, when she tells Haroun her alarming dream, reveals that combination of strength and tenderness that characterizes her throughout. This fine passage [2] is based on the same chromatic *ostinato* figure on the dominant as the prelude to *Les Pêcheurs de perles*, and provides another link with that opera. The Ghazel of Nour-Eddin, King of Lahore, the song of a girl's unrequited love, which she sings at Haroun's supper-table, has a moving pathos and an extraordinarily subtle melodic and harmonic charm. The irregular rise and fall of the vocal line, the varied phrase lengths, the monotonous rhythm of the accompaniment figure, the long pedals, above all the exquisite harmony, combine to give the piece a most individual and compelling atmosphere. We are nearer Ravel's world than Gounod's here. The harmony of the refrain:

[1] See note, p. 163.

[2] Note the Puccini octaves, as usual reserved for a special dramatic effect as in Jose's 'Et moi, Carmen, je t'aime encore.' The heavily charged atmosphere too foreshadows Carmen's fatal reading of the cards.

was altogether too much for the critics of 1872, and half a century later the shifting tonality defeated Landormy's attempts at textbook analysis and reduced that schoolmasterly critic to puzzled mortification. Equally remarkable, both musically and in psychological understanding, is Djamileh's lament, when she has made her compact with Splendiano but is fearful of the outcome. Here again the harmony upset contemporaries, as well it might. Some writers have detected in the opening bars:

an echo of *Tristan*, which Bizet almost certainly did not know. The Phrygian mode tonality with the ending on the dominant and some remarkable chords towards the end with their curious hints of Scarlatti or Falla:

suggest that fate was already pointing Bizet's steps towards the Iberian peninsula. He seems to have divined by some instinct the Moorish link between North Africa and Spain. Djamileh's dance (*Almée*), where the English horn makes its sole and striking appearance in the opera, is rhythmically reminiscent of the Bohemian Dance in *La Jolie Fille de Perth*; it is in the same melodic variation form, but the exotic colouring is much more pronounced. Its sinuous melody, half in the major key, half in the minor, winding its way through many combinations of voices and instruments accompanied by a syncopated rhythm that produces characteristic pedal clashes, gives that effect of drowsiness and seductive languor that David no doubt intended in his corresponding dance in *Le Désert*:

Only at the very end does Bizet let down his heroine and his opera, and significantly this is the weakest moment of the libretto. We cannot believe in Haroun's conversion to true love and feel that Djamileh's fate is only postponed. In a final plea she sings the third stanza of the Ghazel, in which the love-sick maiden dies of her despair; this is a beautiful dramatic stroke, but the final duet sinks to the conventional level of any Gounod opera. It is as if something in Bizet's creative personality instinctively felt the falseness of the dramatic situation.

Musically *Djamileh* is his first really mature work. Gounod's influence is still perceptible, but not predominant: significantly it is strongest in the music of the undramatic Haroun, who could not have stirred Bizet deeply. His *couplets* in praise of love, 'Tu veux savoir,' are conventional and derivative but not out of place; the equally derivative final duet, because it involves a previously individual character in Djamileh, does strike a false note. Bizet handles

the exotic element with entire success. It is never unpleasantly
obtrusive, never mere titillation of the ear, as in David or for that
matter many 'nationalist' composers of any age or land; it is always
subservient to the dramatic purpose and never an end in itself. The
music is as new and fresh to-day as in 1872. The *mélodrames* too are
excellent. They are not quite so finely chiselled as those in *L'Arlésienne*, but they concentrate a wealth of dramatic suggestion in a small
space. The chorus of Haroun's friends behind the scenes, a mere
matter of twenty-two bars, has the pith and shapeliness of the minia-
tures in *Jeux d'enfants*, which Bizet was composing about the same
time. There is a wealth of subtle detail in the scoring, especially of
the exotic numbers. The strings, often divided, find rich employ-
ment; one of the *mélodrames* (No. 8b) has seven string soloists. A
piano is introduced in the opening chorus, the only other instruments
being the tambourine and the oboes, which double the languorous
soprano melody. *Djamileh* is alone among Bizet's operas in having
an extended overture, which however does not quite live up to its
splendid opening. The main theme with its bold appoggiaturas:

and its nice suggestion of the barbaric is used in the opera as a march for the slave-dealer and his wares. It dominates the overture, suitably enough, but the two episodes are less interesting, and the second overbalances the whole by its disproportionate length. Bizet might have tightened up the work by introducing here the theme in 12–8 time that characterizes Djamileh herself.

Djamileh contains some of the most striking music that Bizet wrote. In criticizing the libretto we should remember that it did call forth such music: as with *L'Arlésienne*, he was obviously inspired by the lyrical intensity of his text, and created something which it is impossible to conceive as having come into existence without it. He is known to have been attracted by Musset's *Namouna*, especially the sufferings [1] of the heroine, before he ever saw Gallet's libretto or set about revolutionizing *opéra-comique*. It is perhaps not fanciful to suppose that his eye fell upon the words printed at the head of the first canto: 'Une femme est comme votre ombre: courez après, elle vous fuit; fuyez-la, elle court après vous.' Not long afterwards he was to come across this in the mouth of Mérimée's (and Meilhac and Halévy's) Don José: 'Suivant l'usage des femmes et des chats, qui ne viennent pas quand on les appelle et qui viennent quand on ne les appelle pas. . . .' It was this element in woman, and its effect on her victim, that Bizet has interpreted with greater dramatic truth and vividness than any other musician.

The music to Daudet's play *L'Arlésienne* has become so popular in concert form that a mental effort is required to appreciate its original purpose. It is never easy to write incidental music for a straight play. The composer is not only restricted to small forms; he must play second fiddle to the dramatist, to whom he is not a partner but a servant, a kind of extra effects man. He may be allowed a modified fling in the way of an overture and a few entr'actes (through which the audience is sure to talk), but when the curtain is up he is usually confined to what the French call *mélodrames* (i.e. background music to the dialogue) with perhaps a chorus or a dance here and there. He is thus largely at the mercy of both

[1] He must have imagined them, for Musset, after endless Byronic reflections of his own, polishes her off with a few stanzas not untouched by irony at the end.

audience and stage characters. If he is too reticent, he will not have scope to express himself and his music will not survive or bring him credit; if he is too bold, he will be at odds with the dramatist and his subtleties will probably not be heard. The most he can do is to put the audience in the right humour for each act and underline the dramatic situation as best he can, while adding such musical elabora-tions as he chooses for the few able to appreciate them.

Bizet's answer to this problem is notable. He had proved himself a miniaturist in the *Jeux d'enfants* of a year before; he now transferred this new talent to the stage and strengthened it with his fully matured dramatic powers. He composed twenty-seven numbers, none of them extended in form and many consisting only of short *mélodrames* less than twenty bars long. Not a single one is musically or drama-tically negligible. Except for a few short choruses all the music is instrumental. When the play was first produced Daudet's friends were afraid that the music would kill it. Something like the oppo-site in fact occurred: the play survives only through the music, and it is impossible to appreciate the latter fully (so wonderfully is it inte-grated with the dramatic situation) without going to the trouble of reviving the former. In one sense the music is too good: it exposes with painful vividness the drawbacks of the *mélodrame*. For nobody can listen with full attention to music and dialogue at once, and when the lovely *Adagietto*, for instance, is accompanied throughout by spoken dialogue, the intelligent listener may applaud the psycho-logical aptness of the music, but he damns the convention that necessitates its ruin in performance. A play with incidental music is a far more misshapen hybrid than an opera, for its com-ponents cannot be evenly balanced. We thus reach the paradox that the only place where we can listen to the *Adagietto* in comfort is the concert-hall.

In one respect Bizet was fortunate. Daudet's play is a far better piece of work than any of the composer's earlier libretti. It tells the story of two peasant brothers, Frédéri, the elder, who is bewitched by a girl from the neighbouring town of Arles, and Janet, always known as 'L'Innocent' because of his arrested development. Frédéri dis-covers that his Arlésienne (whom the audience never sees) is the mistress of a shady character called Mitifio, and the shock nearly unsettles his reason; however, through his mother's influence he becomes engaged to Vivette, a girl from his own environment who has long loved him. A chance meeting with Mitifio on his wedding-eve brings back all his passion, and unable to withstand it he throws himself to his death. At this point 'L'Innocent,' who in an obscure manner has understood his brother's sufferings, regains his wits, and so the mother, by the same blow that deprives her of one son, gains another. Two things are notable about this story. It is a drama of real life, and peasant life at that; and it depends for its power not on any specifically dramatic quality, but on its lyrical intensity, especially its depiction of the Provençal background. There is something inexorable in the landscape that reflects the lives of Daudet's peasants, with their mixture of drabness and colour, of protest and resignation. The human tragedy is one with the environment in which it is set, and both are presented in a strong, clear light, with a notable absence of sentimentality. All this is re-created in Bizet's music with extraordinary subtlety. There is nothing manufactured about his local colour [1]; it *is* the Provence of Daudet's play (the qualification is important, for the standard must be artistic and not topographical).[2] But it is quite wrong to ascribe this to the use of traditional themes (a new feature in Bizet's work), or even to the fact that he had visited Provence whereas he never set foot in Ceylon, Scotland or Spain. It is unquestionably due to the combination of an evocative text with his newly found creative maturity. In fact the original music, especially the *Carillon*, *Pastorale* and the wordless female chorus that opens Act II, is quite as picturesque and apposite as that based on traditional tunes. There are three of these [3]: the *Marcho dei Rei*,[4] on which

[1] To a northern Frenchman like Bizet, Provence would appear almost as much a foreign country as Egypt or Spain.

[2] If *L'Arlésienne* is more genuinely Provençal than *Carmen* is Spanish, as is commonly admitted, this is no artistic reflection on the music; it is only a comment, more or less relevant, on the insight into local conditions of Daudet on the one hand and Meilhac and Halévy on the other.

[3] He found the themes in a collection published in 1864 by the *tambourin* (Provençal tabor) player Vidal of Aix.

[4] This tune, known in the eighteenth century as the *Marche de Turenne*, was probably not of Provençal origin at all, but a military march by a

the first section of the prelude and two choruses in the last scene are based, the *Danse dei Chivau-Frus*, familiar as the *Farandole* in Act III, and the very beautiful *Er dou Guet*, which makes a solitary appearance when 'L'Innocent' is trying sleepily to console his love-sick brother with a fairy story. The tunes are wholly assimilated to Bizet's style and treated throughout in the manner of composed music: the *Marcho dei Rei* is made the theme for a set of variations, and is later worked in canon and contrapuntally combined with the *Farandole*.

But the rarest qualities of the score are dramatic, and are of course lost when it is played in the concert-hall. The advance even on *Djamileh* is considerable. The characters are distilled in music that is all the more pregnant through being expressed of necessity in concentrated form. The themes of the two brothers, on which the second and third sections of the prelude are based, are beautiful and appropriate in themselves and admirably contrasted. 'L'Innocent's' theme, heard in its complete form on the unusual but strangely effective colouring of the saxophone (one of that instrument's few reputable appearances) suggests both the fuddled brain and the hidden serenity of spirit:

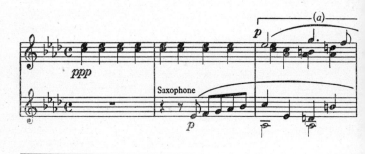

composer of the Lully school which one of the Avignon *noëlistes* adapted to the Three Kings story. The music was first printed in 1759, but the words are found in a manuscript of 1742 with the indication 'sur l'air de la Marche de Turenne.' See J. Clamon, 'Bizet et le folklore provençal' in *Revue de Musicologie*, November 1938.

The little four-note clarinet figure (*a*)[1] is repeated eight times above the tune in unaltered form, persisting like an obsession throughout the changing harmonies beneath it. This theme undergoes a number of later transformations (with or without figure *a*), mostly of a harmonic nature, before reappearing in its complete form in the last entr'acte and in the moving *mélodrame* (No. 25) when 'L'Innocent,' as the old shepherd Balthazar had always prophesied, wakes up to his full mental stature. The harmonic turns which Bizet gives to the incomplete melody are very telling in their dramatic effect: the suspense of the dominant and diminished sevenths in No. 2, the diatonic hopefulness of No. 4, when Balthazar detects an awakening in 'L'Innocent's' brain like the stirring of a silkworm in its cocoon, and the agitated modulations of Nos. 8 and 9. The transformation in No. 8 indeed is sufficiently subtle to persuade Mr. Cooper that he is hearing a totally new melody.

Frédéri's theme by contrast is wild and passionate. Both the dramatic situation and the music are prophetic of a later character torn by a similar passion—Don José. We see the simple countryman carried away, made desperately jealous and finally destroyed by his love for a worthless woman he cannot bring himself to forget; and in both stories contrast is supplied by the homely but rather colourless girl who loves him and who is characterized (most appropriately) by music in the traditional style of Gounodesque sentiment. If the girl from Arles had appeared, her music would surely have

[1] Meyerbeer had made much of this phrase in the big duet for Valentine and Raoul in Act IV of *Les Huguenots*—needless to say in a much less subtle manner.

shown some foreknowledge of Carmen. The *mélodrames* based on Frédéri's theme are even more remarkable than those based on 'L'Innocent's.' The chromaticism of No. 10, when Frédéri is lying miserably in the barn, trying to get away from his mother and Vivette, has a flavour of Franck:

while at the end of No. 26 occur a few bars that illustrate with

FIRST PAGE OF A LETTER FROM BIZET TO LACOMBE (DEC. 1868)

incomparable vividness Bizet's dramatic economy, here achieved, as so often, by a chromatic scale on a pedal bass. On the last chord Frédéri appears for the last time, to throw himself to his death:

Vivette's music is the least original part of the score, but (like Micaela's in *Carmen*) it is in character and valuable as contrast. Only when the E flat entr'acte (the *Intermezzo* of the second suite) is played out of its context does it approach banality; in the play this movement occurs immediately before the scene in which Frédéri consents to marry Vivette. The later appearances of the tune call for little comment; but the version on tremolo strings in No. 16 recalls the similar treatment of a similar theme in *Les Pêcheurs de perles*. The music associated with Mitifio is of very different calibre. In the whole work he is given less than twenty bars, mostly in bare octaves, yet the effect is unforgettable. Seldom can so much have been suggested by so few notes; and once more we find the chromatic scale pedal gambit employed with striking effect:

A third type of love-music, happily contrasted with Vivette's and Frédéri's and perhaps rarer and finer than either, is that provided for Balthazar and Mère Renaud, who loved and parted in youth and now meet again after fifty years. The stage knows many a jealous tenor and simple soprano, but to portray such a love as this without lapsing into the sentimental or trivial is no mean feat. The *Adagietto* for muted strings in four-part harmony (it is marked simply *adagio* in the original score) is so simple and so perfect that it defies criticism. Here is the apotheosis of the Gounod element in Bizet, purged of all weakness and infused with a breadth and a serenity that were altogether beyond Gounod. The melody is beautifully extended and the harmony is full of quiet touches that strike home by just avoiding the commonplace, such as the exquisitely unexpected chord [1] (*x*) in the final cadence:

---

[1] This chord is bowdlerized in the current (though not the original) piano score, B flat appearing for the A in the viola part.

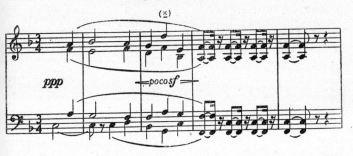

This economy of effort extends to movements of more complex structure. The finale of Act I is a miracle of compression: it comprises Mitifio's exit (five bars), an ironical echo of the drinking-chorus in the orchestra, while Frédéri bids Francet and Balthazar drink to his Arlésienne and they tell him to throw away his glass for the wine will poison him (six bars), four bars of accompaniment while Frédéri reads the fatal letters, the return of the drinking-chorus (nine bars) and a passionate restatement of the Frédéri theme in the orchestra as the curtain falls (seven bars). Every facet of the scene is presented with incomparable vividness in thirty-one bars. Musically these vignettes are often equally striking. The wordless chorus that opens Act II, after thrumming out its distinctive rhythm for some time on the simplest harmonic basis of repeated chords, plunges into a series of wild modulations towards the end and gets back to its key only just in time. This is a characteristic trick of Bizet's, and its almost unfailing success is a sufficient comment on his mastery of form and balance. The trio of the *Intermezzo* (the *Minuet* of the first Suite [1]) illustrates the consummate ease with which he handled the difficult art of two-part counterpoint. Neither of the themes is in itself very distinguished, and the saxophone and clarinet tune recalls the trio of the *Roma* scherzo; but its effortless combination with the flowing violin melody (on a tonic and dominant pedal) and the exquisite felicity and economy of the scoring lift the movement on to an altogether higher plane. Towards the end of this trio a phrase on the oboe:

---

[1] In Bizet's autograph it is entitled *Valse-Menuet*.

looks back to the tune on the same instrument in the *adagio* of
the early Symphony.

The orchestration is a remarkable *tour de force*. Owing to Carvalho's
limited funds Bizet was allowed only twenty-six players, who were
disposed on the following odd plan: 2 flutes, 1 oboe (taking English
horn), 1 clarinet, 2 bassoons, 1 saxophone in E flat, 2 horns, timpani
and tambourine (1 player), 7 violins, 1 viola, 5 cellos, 2 basses and
a piano, besides a harmonium behind the scenes to accompany the
choruses. In the published full score the items used in the suites
appear in their final form; we thus do not have the original scoring.
But the *mélodrames* show how Bizet went to work. Every one of them
repays close attention. The limitation, so far from hampering him,
drew forth new subtleties, this time in a manner approaching that
of chamber music. Several pieces are for solo string quartet, muted
in the *Er dou Gouet* (No. 13) and *Adagietto*. Mère Renaud's entry
(No. 19) employs two flutes, two violins and viola with enchanting
effect. The solitary viola—an instrument accustomed to bewail its
neglect by composers—has a most grateful part; twice it takes charge
of 'L'Innocent's' theme—in No. 4 with the obsessional counterpoint
(Ex. 50, *a*) on the English horn and the repeated thirds low on the
flutes, and in No. 25 with (*a*) on one flute and the thirds on two
violins. The saxophone adds a very distinctive colouring; it is
tempting to suppose that Bizet chose it for the exotic and mournful
timbre it gives to 'L'Innocent's' theme in the prelude. Numerous
alterations and corrections in the manuscript, especially in the
Pastorale, attest the trouble that Bizet took before he was satisfied
with the lay-out.

The first Suite, put together by Bizet himself for a Pasdeloup concert a month after the performance of the play, consists of the *Prelude*,
Intermezzo (with its title changed to *Minuet*), *Adagietto* and *Carillon*.
The *Prelude* (except for the scoring) and *Adagietto* are unchanged;
the latter of course gains by its separation from the spoken dialogue;

but the former, owing to its loose form, is unsatisfactory away from the theatre. To the *Intermezzo* Bizet added six bars of coda, a little duologue for strings and wind ending *pppp*, a neat touch that has escaped comment. As a middle section to the *Carillon* he used the exquisite *mélodrame* that accompanies the entrance of Mère Renaud, with its plaintive flute melody and remarkable discords, transposed up a semitone to C sharp minor, and followed it with a new and striking passage leading back to the opening: while flutes and strings persist with the 6–8 melody, two of the horns suddenly break in with their original *ostinato* and gradually drag the music back to 3–4 time. Bizet rescored this Suite for full orchestra, adding a second oboe, second clarinet, third and fourth horns, two trumpets, two cornets, three trombones and side-drum, as well as a full complement of strings. With these resources he was able greatly to extend the dynamic range. For instance, Frédéri's theme in the *Prelude* is introduced by the first two desks of the strings only, the others entering gradually, till the complete theme appears on the full orchestra. This would have been impossible on the original orchestra with its few violins and solitary viola. Similarly in the string passage that ends the trio of the *Minuet* the desks drop out one by one at intervals of a bar, till the opening theme reappears *aussi pp que possible*.

The second Suite, arranged by Guiraud after Bizet's death, makes a less satisfactory whole. Guiraud improved the balance of the E flat entr'acte (now confusingly entitled *Intermezzo*) with twelve additional bars of recapitulation, and treated the *Pastorale* and ensuing chorus in the same way as Bizet had treated the *Carillon* (though much less individually); but the entr'acte sounds weak when divorced from its stage context, and the so-called second *Minuet*, imported for the occasion from *La Jolie Fille de Perth*, is not happy in this company. Guiraud's version of the *Farandole*, a free arrangement of Bizet's material from Nos. 22–24, including the *Marcho dei Rei* in canon and the two tunes in contrapuntal combination, though effective, involves too much repetition. The transference of the choral parts to the orchestra brings a loss of contrast and rather damps the exhilaration of the climax. In his rescoring Guiraud used the same forces as Bizet in the first Suite, with additional percussion in the *Farandole*, but the effect is considerably more blatant, especially in the *Pastorale* and *Farandole*.

The unfinished *Don Rodrigue* of 1873 demands a few words. The manuscript in the Conservatoire library has the vocal parts complete, but little else, the accompaniment being indicated by occasional pencil sketches, though it is clear that Bizet had a very large orchestra in mind. It is of course quite impossible to judge an opera on these remains, but the themes have less character than we should expect from a work written at the same time as *Carmen*. The cause no doubt is the libretto, by Gallet and Blau, which belongs to the monumental five-act school established by Scribe for Meyerbeer; for *Don Rodrigue* was intended for that imposing mortuary, the Opéra. It is the story of a family feud, the hero and heroine springing of course from the rival clans, varied by external war and a strong religious element. The music bears no sign of Spanish colour, but only too much of the style of *Patrie*. Indeed, the main theme of that overture appears in Act V as an orchestral march, immediately followed by the dreadful march from *Ivan le Terrible* in all its saxophonic splendour (this is the one number Bizet wrote out in full). One other item is resurrected from *Ivan le Terrible*: Temrouk's aria in Act I reappears, slightly altered, in the first finale. The religious element, as we might expect, brings out all that is squarest and most sequential in Bizet's melodic invention: the movement that produced *Hymns Ancient and Modern* was not a purely English phenomenon. Some of the fragments suggest better things, such as a female chorus in the finale of Act II and the following expressive tune accompanying an aria of Chimène, the much-loved and long-suffering heroine, in Act I:

The vocal ensembles, especially two trios in Act II, are richer than usual in counterpoint and overlapping phrases, a feature which would soften the squareness of the themes. But this was not the right material for Bizet, and Guiraud and others were certainly wrong in thinking the world has lost a masterpiece. It was in fact a thoroughly retrograde step over which no tears need be shed. Legendary heroes were beyond Bizet's grasp; besides, he was already at work on a portrait of real men and women that was to go a long way towards killing the whole school to which *Don Rodrigue* belonged.

CHAPTER IX

'CARMEN'

THE libretto of *Carmen* has in its time been criticized for diametrically opposite reasons. To most contemporaries it was so shocking that it ought never to have been staged; later writers have damned it as a timid watering down of Mérimée's novel. Both criticisms fail for precisely the same reason: they neglect the angle that most matters— the dramatic. Considered thus, *Carmen* has one of the half-dozen best libretti in operatic history. The story is so familiar as not to need summarizing here; more revealing is an examination of the alterations—nearly every one a dramatic improvement—made by Meilhac and Halévy to Mérimée's original.

The adaptation of a novel to the stage is at best a risky and difficult undertaking; the two forms demand wholly different treatment. With a masterpiece like Mérimée's *Carmen*, which depends very largely on style, the task is even harder. In order to gain the fullest effect from his tale of fascination and crime Mérimée brings it into close contact with everyday life; he uses two principal means for this purpose, the novelist's device of putting the whole story into the mouth of one of the characters (José, who tells it to Mérimée himself on the eve of his execution) [1] and the low tone and classical detachment of his descriptions. Both methods were closed to the librettists (though something like the second can be and is supplied by the composer); they have to find other means of striking the balance. Therefore they drew Micaela as a foil to Carmen, acting on a hint of Mérimée's, and developed Escamillo (Lucas in the novel, a shadowy figure who never speaks) as a foil to José. If the full passion and horror of the Carmen-José situation is to be brought home to a theatre audience, it is essential for some such character as Micaela to be shown on the stage: as Ellen Terry once observed, before you can

[1] Just as Des Grieux tells the story of *Manon Lescaut*, another work in which (as Ernest Newman has pointed out) the hero is really the centre of interest though the title is that of the heroine.

be eccentric you must know where the circle is. The novelist has many ways of appealing to his audience; the dramatist only one—by showing on the stage what he wants his hearers to grasp; and he can point a contrast only by showing both sides. The essence of Mérimée's *Carmen* is the transformation of José from the simple high-principled soldier to the murderous brigand; in order to appreciate this in the theatre we must see the former as well as the latter. Hence Micaela is (*a*) a contrast by which to measure Carmen, (*b*) a symbol of José's character and psychological environment before he met Carmen.[1] So far from being a sin against Mérimée, she is an ally.

The necessary concentration of the events related by Mérimée is carried out with remarkable skill. The librettists' second act is a brilliant synthesis of several incidents in the novel, in which neither Lucas nor the smugglers appear till later and the duel with Zuniga[2] takes place on a different occasion. Very skilful also is the dramatic means used to convey Mérimée's conception of the characters. The habanera, which concentrates in a few lines a great deal of Mérimée's Carmen; the seguidilla, which develops the character of both José and Carmen and at the same time carries the action forward; the flower song; the card scene; the superbly dramatic finale of Act III; the little scene just before the catastrophe when Frasquita and Mercedes warn Carmen that José is lurking in the crowd: all these were the invention of Meilhac, Halévy and Bizet. The final duet is little altered, much of the original dialogue being preserved—except in one particular; in the novel it occurs (most movingly) in a lonely spot in the mountains and ends with José's burying Carmen's body in a wood in accordance with her expressed wish, before riding to Seville to give himself up. The change of scene to the bullring, with Escamillo's audible triumph coinciding with José's final desperate appeal and the murder, was a masterly dramatic touch.

The libretto has been further criticized for diluting Mérimée's

---

[1] This point is carried rather far in a Russian adaptation by Lipskerov, *Carmencita and the Soldier*, in which the part of Micaela is taken by three singers representing the voice of true love in José's heart!

[2] Not so called by Mérimée. The librettists took the name from an authority cited in a footnote.

characters, particularly José. There is a grain of truth in this. José's intense Basque pride is largely lost (Mérimée described him as looking like Milton's Satan), but all the essentials of his moral disintegration are there. In Mérimée he commits at least three murders, killing not only Carmen but her husband García le Borgne (one of the vilest scoundrels in literature) and the lieutenant (in the scene corresponding to the duel in Act II). The omission of these horrors is a gain to the ópera. Mérimée, depicting the gradual collapse of an honest nature, carries the story over a period of many months between José's release from prison and the final catastrophe. The librettists had a far shorter space in which to show the same process. Having of necessity worked the duel with Zuniga into Act II, they could not allow José to kill him without making his deterioration in this act much too rapid and at the same time weakening a great deal that follows, including the final murder. The inclusion of the inessential García could only have made Act III unnecessarily episodic, and the gradual decline of José from connivance at Carmen's escape, through desertion, armed resistance to an officer and smuggling to murder is far more effective than any sequence of duels and homicides. The softening down of Carmen, too, is more apparent than real. In Mérimée she is a thief and a perpetual liar; in the opera we have little of this, but those sides of her character that are essential to the tragedy—her unscrupulousness, her courage, her passionate love of freedom and of course her endless fascination —are preserved and nourished to the full. Mérimée's novel has virtually only two characters. The librettists not only presented the central conflict at full strength (breaking conventions right and left in the process [1]), but set it in a background of characters whom they either invented or greatly developed, thus displaying it to the best possible dramatic advantage.

Let it be interposed here that if any one wanted to soften down Mérimée, it was not Bizet but Meilhac and Halévy. It was Bizet —following a principle he had evolved in his Rome days, that a composer should find his subjects for himself—who sent them to the novel in the first place; and when, fearful of the public reaction, they

[1] Gauthier-Villars's attempt to deny this reveals an astonishing ignorance of the history of *opéra-comique*.

suggested modifying the original, he 'ferociously'[1] resisted them. There is extant, by a happy chance, the manuscript of the words of the habanera,[2] which prove to have been the work of Bizet himself. Halévy's suggested verses, also preserved, are much milder in tone and much farther from Mérimée, and a note in his writing states that his first inclination was to supply even 'tenderer' verses for Carmen's first song. The form in which Bizet wrote his words makes it almost certain that he already had Yradier's tune in mind: i.e. the words were fitted to the music instead of vice versa. The Yradier habanera was not the original version, which was in 6–8 time and was actually rehearsed[3]; it seems then that the words as well as the music were originally different.

If Bizet was responsible for this most crucial scene, how much else that is dramatically vital in the libretto may we not owe to him? In fact the manuscript score does give us a glimpse of the dramatic composer at work. One consequence of the new habanera was the exquisite chromatic nine-bar passage in its distinctive rhythm immediately before Carmen trips José at the end of Act I. This replaced the following bald original:

---

[1] This is the librettists' word: Soubies and Malherbe, *Histoire de l'Opéra-Comique*, vol. ii.

[2] Reproduced opposite. Edgar Istel, to whom we owe by far the fullest, most accurate and most sympathetic study of the opera, was the first to grasp its full significance, thought it was known to Weissmann and Landormy.

[3] According to Guiraud Bizet rewrote the piece thirteen times before Galli-Marié was satisfied with it; perhaps this should be taken with a pinch of salt. Bizet certainly did rewrite passages at the request of singers; Laparra quotes an example from the seguidilla, altered at the request of Lhérie, the original José. Lhérie said that Bizet showed a touching compliance in such matters.

Bizet also modified the words of the seguidilla, changing the calamitous first line 'J'irai dimanche en voiture,' for which the rhyme was
'Manger une friture,' to 'Près des ramparts de Séville.' Still more
interesting changes were made in the finales of Acts III and IV.
In the former as originally written Escamillo sang his refrain behind
the scenes twice in full—the first time with a chromatic accompaniment for solo cello which it would have been difficult to bring off.
The second refrain was interrupted by José twice crying 'Micaela,
partons!' The removal of this psychological absurdity (if anything
it should be Micaela crying 'José, partons!') and the far greater conciseness of the final version are evidence of Bizet's dramatic understanding. In Act IV José was directed to stab Carmen on the
words 'Eh bien! damnée!' This was followed by a return of the
fanfare and chorus 'Victoire!' of a moment before over a descending
chromatic scale, during which Carmen 'tombe appuyée sur son bras
gauche.' At this point later patching has obliterated the original.
The cut, with the *fortissimo* triumph of 'Toréador, en garde!' coming
right on top of 'damnée!' was a brilliant improvement, but it has
left posterity in several minds as to the exact moment of the murder.
Bizet (perhaps through oversight) did not cancel the direction to José
to stab Carmen at 'damnée!' which is preserved in the orchestral
but not in the vocal score. Evidently his original idea was that she
should be stabbed at 'damnée!' and not die at once, but the desire
for concentration at all costs made him change his mind and insert
the direction 'Il s'élance vers Carmen,' etc. Did he originally mean
to convey something of that wonderful sentence of Mérimée's: 'Je
crois voir encore son grand œil noir me regarder fixement; puis il
devint trouble et se ferma'—especially as the chorus is singing at that
very moment, with savage irony, the Toreador's refrain, 'Et songe bien
en combattant qu'un œil noir te regarde'? Both these finales, and
several other scenes, underwent numerous small cuts, all clearly
designed to secure the immediacy of dramatic contrast. Some
further last-minute modifications are mentioned below.

One quite fortuitous element has interfered with the appreciation
of the libretto and the opera as a whole. Outside France *Carmen* has
hardly ever been performed as Bizet wrote it; consequently it has
repeatedly been misjudged, not only by the general public but by

persons who ought to know better,[1] on a version that is not authentic. The recitatives with which it is always performed in this country are not Bizet's work at all; they were written by Guiraud after Bizet's death, at the request of Jauner, the director of the Vienna Opera, for the production of October 1875. Their inclusion in the printed score, even in France, adds further confusion. Guiraud, sometimes using Bizet's themes, committed no stylistic solecisms; but in converting Carmen from *opéra-comique* to grand opera he very considerably distorted it. The original spoken dialogue, which was much longer, not only introduced a good deal of Mérimée, but in many places eased the dramatic action and helped in the evolution of character. For instance, the appearance of both Micaela and Escamillo in Act III, which in the current version seems a typical piece of operatic coincidence, is well motivated in the original, Micaela having paid a large sum to an unwilling guide to take her to the smugglers' haunt and Escamillo being busy collecting wild bulls for his next fight. The suppression of the dialogue in Act I not only deprives us of a typical piece of Carmen mendacity (the only one in the opera), but makes nonsense of Zuniga's request to José for information about the cigar factory, the point of which is that he has held his post in Seville for only two days. The scene leading up to the seguidilla, very subtly managed in the dialogue, is sadly mutilated in the recitative; and the same applies to several scenes in Act II, especially that immediately following José's entry, which is pure Mérimée. Lack of space forbids mention of the details, but the general effect of the substituted recitative is to make the dramatic action proceed in a series of jerks instead of by smooth transitions, and to take the stuffing out of many minor characters, especially Zuniga, Lillas Pastia and the smugglers, all of whom are nicely differentiated. Guiraud also spoiled an excellent *mélodrame* in Act I—the scene in which Carmen defies Zuniga—by adding extraneous recitatives: only Carmen should sing here. These may appear small points, but their cumulative effect is considerable: an opera that depends so

[1] One French critic, Gaudier, damns Bizet heartily for the recitative before Micaela's air in Act III. This is the one Guiraud interpolation done at the Opéra-Comique, which otherwise uses a condensed version of the spoken dialogue.

much on correctness of dramatic expression cannot afford an alien load of stiff and conventional recitative—a load which, in view of his known attitude, it is very doubtful if Bizet would have sanctioned. *Carmen* should never be performed without the original spoken dialogue.

For it is above all a great work for the stage, and must be considered from the dramatic as well as the musical point of view. Not that it has much to fear from musical judgment alone; but when the two elements reinforce one another to the extent that they do in *Carmen*, the result is far greater than a sum of the parts. For one thing, individual items lose considerably by subtraction from their contexts. Thus Escamillo's *couplets,* the habanera and José's flower song, though they keep their freshness to a remarkable degree, are apt to be judged—and even condemned—without reference to their context, when perhaps the most striking feature of all three is their musical revelation of character. Escamillo's music, especially the famous *couplets* [1] and the duet in Act IV, 'Si tu m'aimes,' has been damned as trite; but the triteness lies not in the music, but in the character. Escamillo is flashy and superficial, the successful sportsman whom neither bull nor woman can resist (and how well he knows it!); his *couplets* would perhaps be less abused if every singer obeyed Bizet's instructions and sang the refrain *piano avec fatuité,* ending *pianissimo.* Micaela is mild and conventional, and her rather Gounodesque music—the greatest possible contrast to Carmen's—though certainly the least original part of the score, is wholly appropriate. The supreme vindication of the music of both these characters comes in the finale of Act III, where it is worked convincingly with the business-like gusto of the smugglers, the scorn of Carmen and José's

[1] Bizet is said to have remarked after composing this piece: 'Well, they asked for ordure, and they've got it.' The critic who takes this as a serious self-criticism must be very hard up for ammunition. 'Ordure' was Bizet's usual term for any noisy or pretentious music. It has been stated that the *couplets* were inserted during rehearsal at the request of either Halévy or du Locle. The manuscript proves this to be untrue. If Halévy was responsible for their inclusion, as he claimed, it must have been at an earlier stage. Incidentally Halévy implies that here again words as well as music were written by Bizet.

jealous passion into one of the finest dramatic ensembles in any opera. The ten-bar orchestral epilogue in which, as Istel well remarks, the conflicting emotions of each character are somehow revealed, is almost without a rival for pregnancy of dramatic statement. Similarly in Act IV, when the bullfighting music from within proclaiming Escamillo's hollow triumph over an animal breaks in on the personal tragedy played out by Carmen and José on the stage, the effect is overwhelming: not because the bullfighting music is great in itself, but because it contributes to a great dramatic situation. *Carmen* is rich in dramatic irony, a quality never so potent as when expressed through the suggestive powers of music; on page after page of the score we are struck by the extraordinary appropriateness of the musical detail both to the unfolding of each character and to the progress of events on the stage. Nor is the situation ever static; the tension is very subtly relaxed or tightened by turns. What appear to be set numbers in the old style, like the admirable quintet in Act II, are quite as effective in carrying on the action as original conceptions like the seguidilla, whose combination of song, dance, *mélodrame* and recitative (typical of Spanish folk-music) was something quite new in *opéra-comique*. Even pieces which seem at first glance to be altogether out of touch with their surroundings—the entr'acte to Act III [1] or Micaela's air 'Je dis que rien ne m'épouvante'—are seen as essential points of repose before a renewed quickening of the drama.

Bizet's insight into dramatic truth is not confined to giving each character music that would be nonsensical in the mouth of any other. In José he has created a hero [2] whose very far-reaching development

[1] Landormy's attack on this beautiful piece is one of the quaintest eccentricities of French criticism. The possibility (resting on Pigot's unsupported statement) that it was originally composed for *L'Arlésienne* has no relevance whatever. Two other items said to have been taken over from other works are the chorus 'Quant au douanier' (also from *L'Arlésienne*, where it began 'Pour récolter le vermillon') and Micaela's 'Je dis que rien ne m'épouvante' (from *Grisélidis*).

[2] Shaliapin is reported to have said that once only in his life he regretted that he was not a tenor—after his first reading of *Carmen*, 'a score in which the whole of life seems to vibrate.'

can be illustrated from the music alone—an achievement as notable as it is rare. In Act I he is the simple countryman, albeit in dragoon's uniform: he and his music are in tune with Micaela:

Ma mè - re je la vois! Oui, je re - vois___ mon vil - lage!_

Perhaps the hidden turning-point is marked by the passionate tune in A major just after Carmen has thrown the flower—a rhythmic cousin of the duke's wooing theme in *La Jolie Fille de Perth*—which returns in a wonderful *diminuendo* when José leads her, a defiant prisoner, out of the factory after the stabbing scene. The entr'acte before Act II, an anticipation of his first utterance after his release from prison, already shows the difference that experience has made: there is a touch of bravado, of a self-confidence more bumptious than balanced. It is his method of compensating for the overwhelming disturbance that Carmen has created in his heart. In the famous flower song we see how much more profound is this passion than his love of Micaela ever was; and the significance of the modulation [1] in the last bars that so startled Bizet's contemporaries surely lies in José's intuitive knowledge that his passion has grown beyond his control; it is an appeal, at once desperate and pathetic, to Carmen's pity. In Act III he is already a vagabond: a smuggler with a conscience, without the rude vigour of the rest of the gang, a man in the grip of a woman he knows he cannot trust but whom he cannot bring himself to leave. He is like an animal in a cage, and a cage of his own making; for when she opens the door to drive him out he refuses to go. Maddened by a mixture of jealousy, conscience and despair, with Micaela begging him to return to his dying mother and the flashy Escamillo vaunting his power

---

[1] It is strictly not a modulation at all, but a bar and a half of remote and alien harmony at the approach of an apparently conventional cadence. Technically it anticipates a device common in Debussy.

over Carmen before his eyes, he bursts out in what is the emotional climax of the whole opera [1]:

Dût - il m'en coû-ter la vi - e, Non, Carmen, je ne parti - rai pas!

The repetition of this passage a few moments later in G instead of G flat is one of those electrifying strokes which only the certainty of genius would risk. In Act IV José is different again. He is still the slave of his feelings, but hysteria has given way to the desperation of the cornered animal, and the last pangs of conscience have been dispelled. He will make one more appeal; if Carmen still refuses, he knows what to do. His music has a grim quality, a hardness of heart quite alien to the simple dragoon of Act I but wholly convincing here, and Bizet reinforces it by anticipating the device so often used (and abused) by Puccini of writing for voice and bass in octaves:

Mais moi, Carmen, je t'aime en - co - re, Car - men, hélas! moi je t'a-do - re!

José is a character easily swayed. It is notable that whereas music associated with Carmen, Escamillo and even Micaela recurs later in the action, no phrase sung by José is ever repeated—except one: the music of his words to Carmen in the finale of Act III 'Tu me dis de la suivre!' is identical with that of 'Un baiser de ma mère' in Act I. This is probably a fortuitous or subconscious reminiscence,

---

[1] The fact that Bizet was here using material from *La Coupe du Roi de Thule* in no way invalidates this claim, though it throws interesting light on his creative procedure. Landormy's attitude to the passage is amusing and typical. He criticizes the harmony and the dramatic handling: José ought to shrug his shoulders at Carmen's infidelity with Escamillo, which is quite insufficient to provoke such jealousy.

but it is curiously moving and dramatically appropriate, for Carmen is telling him to go back to his mother.

José is really the central figure of *Carmen*. It is his fate rather than Carmen's that interests us. But she is not only a very vital character, but a totally new conception in opera. She is a new type of heroine, and she represents a new kind of love. Hitherto the heroines of opera—and still more of *opéra-comique*—had belonged, almost to a woman, to the spotless and suffering soprano school. The great majority were negative; they tended to suffer rather than act; despite (or because of) their scrupulous moral rectitude they were the football of men and fortune. They were a convention that had fallen behind the times and needed renewing; and much the same applied to the leading tenors. The 'villains,' on the other hand, both male and female, often initiated more of the action, attained a greater vitality and even stole the audience's sympathy. In *Carmen* the heroine and the villain are combined in one person. Villain heroes had been seen before—Don Juan, for instance—but this invasion of one of the tenderest illusions of the old *opéra-comique*, that the heroine at least must be spotless, was something new and shocking,[1] especially as the authors had rejected a perfectly suitable heroine (and a genuine soprano instead of a mezzo) in Micaela. Nor had a love like Carmen's been fully defined on the operatic stage. Violetta had been a prostitute, but at least we had not seen her exercising her trade. Carmen on the other hand not only seduced José, but set about it on the stage, and only too successfully: when the 'true' love of Micaela is thrown in the balance against her the scales sink down heavily on the wrong side. This of course is psychologically and dramatically right, but it was horribly shocking in 1875. The final murder, too, was unheard of in *opéra-comique*: indeed de Leuven, one of the directors, the same who had wanted a plate dropped to enliven *Djamileh*, is said to have resigned because he could not persuade Bizet to provide a happy ending. Carmen's love has the intensity

---

[1] Violetta had been shocking enough, but her portrait was considerably softened by Alfred's 'true' love (not to mention the moral homilies of Germont senior, before which she is made to bow), and she is given something like an apotheosis at the end. Nor of course was *La Traviata* an *opéra-comique*.

and capriciousness of flame, and for sheer infectiousness her music is unrivalled. Both musically and dramatically it is admirable. For she infected men like a plague: José, Zuniga, Escamillo, all go down with it. With José, the most innocent and therefore the most vulnerable, it proves mortal, and in listening to the music which Bizet puts in the mouth of both of them we know that the end is inevitable. There is nothing sordid about Carmen; the many imitations perpetrated later, especially by the Italian *verismo* school, have obscured Bizet's restraint here. He cannot be blamed if his successors exceeded the bounds imposed by art; the *verismo* of Carmen never crosses this frontier. Her character receives a complete musical representation; we see not only her effect on others, but her own qualities—fearlessness, gaiety, freedom, fatalism (in the superb passage when she reads the cards), and even an occasional glimpse of tenderness. One of Bizet's subtlest touches is the little phrase in the middle of the quintet:

Je suis a - mou - reu - - se!

which makes clear that Carmen's love for José is, if only for the moment, something very different from her later dalliance with Escamillo (compare 'Si tu m'aimes').

Bizet's great advance with *Carmen* was dramatic; musically he breaks less new ground. This is not to decry him; he greatly broadens and consolidates the advances made in *Djamileh* and *L'Arlésienne*, at the same time doing away with the weaknesses of his earlier operas. Even the Gounodesque elements are far more enterprising than Gounod ever was: there is more vitality in Micaela's music than in that of any Gounod heroine—a fact overlooked by those who wish Micaela to talk the same language as Carmen. The harmonic idiom of the exotic parts, especially the *chanson bohème* with its perpetual semitone clashes, is often very striking; and it is easy to imagine the shudders which passages like the following (from the opening chorus of Act III):

Allegretto moderato

Prends gar - de de faire un faux pas! Prends gar - de

de faire un faux pas!

sent down French spines in 1875. There are occasional lapses, of
course; the worst of them, the *allegro* 2–4 section of the duet for
Escamillo and José in Act III, is usually cut in performance. This
scene, incidentally, was even longer as Bizet wrote it: several pages
are omitted from all versions after the original vocal score of March
1875.[1] Their loss is not felt, nor is that of the scene for Morales and
chorus immediately before the changing of the guard in Act I.
This is pleasant and characteristic, but it holds up the action. Both
these scenes were cut by Bizet himself between March and June
1875 and not, as is generally supposed, by Carvalho in 1883. The
style of *Carmen* is essentially that of the two previous theatre works
on a greater scale and put to a much bigger dramatic purpose. But
its posthumous conversion to grand opera should not blind us to the
fact that it is *opéra-comique*. That does not mean comic opera; it is
the opera of everyday life, which includes both comic and tragic.
Bizet's renovation of the genre is discussed in Chapter X; let it be
noted here that though he seems to hold out one hand to Verdi and

[1] Delmas is wrong in supposing that this was a proof. There is a copy
in the British Museum. It is the only score that does not include Guiraud's
recitatives.

Puccini, the other still points back past Auber and Rossini to his first and greatest love, Mozart. The quintet in Act II is worthy to be set beside the great ensembles of *The Marriage of Figaro* and *The Barber of Seville* among the finest blossomings of the old *opera buffa* stock. Like the composers of those works Bizet had the not too common gift of musical humour; the scene of Zuniga's capture by the smugglers is exquisitely humorous, and the bassoon counterpoint with which it is embellished never topples into farce.

On the Spanish element much unnecessary ink has been spilt. One critic [1] has devoted a whole book to the question how much of *Carmen* is genuinely Spanish, and how much better the rest would be if it attained an equal level of Hispanicism. This is to misconceive Bizet's whole purpose. It is not the business of a composer whose scene is set in a foreign country to imitate the music of that country. This could only result in pastiche, for the native can obviously do it better than the foreigner. All Bizet had to do was to conjure up a Spanish background for French listeners: being a Frenchman he could not do better than write French music. He never went to Spain (when it was suggested he said it would be tiresome and unnecessary [2]); yet in one or two places he created, apparently by instinct, music so deeply imbued with the Spanish spirit that listeners have been misled into supposing that this was one of his principal aims and condemning the rest of the score accordingly. The facts of his borrowing from alien sources are as follows.

The habanera, as is well known, is an adaptation of a song called *El Arreglito ou la Promesse de mariage* by the Spanish-American composer Sebastián Yradier (1809–65), who wrote many pieces popular in the salons of the day. Apparently [3] Bizet had heard it sung as a folksong and based his habanera on what he remembered, ignorant of its true authorship; when this was pointed out he added the note in the vocal score 'Imitated from a Spanish song, the property of the

---

[1] Raoul Laparra, *Bizet et l'Espagne*. His conclusion is that *Carmen* would have been a better opera had Bizet lived among Spanish gypsies.

[2] Compare Debussy, who never went farther into Spain than San Sebastián; yet according to Falla he could be completely Andalusian in feeling.

[3] *Le Ménestrel*, 2nd January 1887.

publishers of *Le Ménestrel* '—i.e. Heugel, who had issued it in Yradier's
Fleurs d'Espagne (1864). This was not its first appearance; it is
advertised on the front page of *Le Ménestrel* for 11th January 1863.
Yradier was one of those composers whose adaptations of folksong
fall half way between the original and art music, but he is known
to have composed at least one Mexican 'folksong.' In any case the
provenance of the piece would not be Spain at all, but Cuba: the
habanera, akin to the tango, is a product of Negro music, and an
orgiastic dance, not a song. Its erotic connotations seem to have been
grasped intuitively by Bizet. The significant point, however, is the
manner in which he improved on his original. Although Yradier's
basic scheme—verse in D minor, refrain in D major—is the same,
and the melody of both is in some sort preserved, Bizet's deft alterations transformed it from a tame drawing-room piece into a dramatic
scene of real genius. Yradier's song is both long-winded and lop-
sided; it is full of weak ritornelli and has a rambling second half on
quite new material. Bizet did away with all this, improved the
melody by prolonging its chromaticism and adding the triplet in
the fourth bar, and above all by varying the threefold repetition in
the refrain; and he substituted a vital harmonic interest for Yradier's
stiff and awkward accompaniment. This is Yradier's version of the
melody and refrain:

The brilliant entr'acte before the last act tells a somewhat similar
story. It is based on a *polo* (a wild Andalusian song) from a *tonadilla*
or short dramatic dialogue called *El criado fingido* by Manuel García,
the father of a line of famous singers. García first sang this in
Madrid in 1804, when he was an unknown minstrel of obscure
(possibly gypsy) origin: his compositions bear about the same relation

to Spanish folksong as Yradier's to Spanish-American—that is to
say he took elements of genuine folk idiom and embroidered them
for his own purposes. His *polo* was printed in a volume called
Échos d'Espagne,[1] brought out in 1872 by Bizet's friend and pupil
Paul Lacombe. Thanks to the autograph-hunting propensities of
an employee of the Conservatoire library, a slip is preserved bearing
the words: 'I request a list of the Spanish songs in the possession of
the library.—BIZET.' According to Tiersot the only volume available was *Échos d'Espagne*; and it seems likely that this collection of
Spanish songs and dances (some genuine, some bogus) was the sole
documentary source for the Spanish elements in *Carmen*.[2] But for
García's *polo*, all the pieces are anonymous. Again Bizet transformed his original from a rambling recitation to a taut masterpiece
packed with vitality and drama. García's two main themes are
as follows:

Bizet follows him in emphasizing and concluding on the dominant:
this is a characteristic of *cante jondo* (literally 'deep song'), the folk
melody of southern Spain that reflects the centuries of Moorish
domination.[3] The influence of the guitar, an instrument introduced
by the Moors and always used for the accompaniment of *cante jondo*,
is apparent not only here but in other parts of the opera, such as the
chanson bohème of Act II, where Bizet is not using Spanish material

[1] Where however it is wrongly attributed to another *tonadilla*, *El poeta
calculista*, written a year later. This contains a similar *polo*; it is possible
that both had the same folk origin. See Julien Tiersot's article in *The
Musical Quarterly*, October 1927.

[2] Bizet's widow stated that Bizet had only Yradier's *Fleurs d'Espagne*.
This is almost certainly a slip for *Échos d'Espagne*.

[3] Compare the lament in *Djamileh*.

but working independently within the framework of its idiom. This is a real creative process, not an imitation, and it produces music that is far more vital than many a pious resuscitation of folk material. Other features redolent of *cante flamenco* (Spanish gypsy music, a later derivative of *cante jondo*) are the treatment of the accompaniment to the *chanson bohème* in successive fifths, the irregular descending scale in the bass of the introduction to the same piece and the augmented seconds of the Carmen theme.

Istel has shown that Bizet used one more Spanish tune in *Carmen*. This is the snatch of melody sung by Carmen when she defies Zuniga in Act I. The words ('Coupe-moi, brûle-moi,' etc.) are taken from a translation by Mérimée of a work by Pushkin, *Les Bohémiens* [1]; the tune:

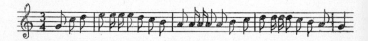

a satirical song on female hair styles, comes from Ciudad Real, south of Madrid. The change of rhythm from 3–4 to 6–8 is typical of Bizet's neat modification. This may be the tune which Sarasate, a colleague of Bizet's at the Conservatoire, is supposed to have contributed to *Carmen*. But although these alien elements, whether they be Spanish, South American, Moorish or gypsy, do help to give the music that extraordinarily vivid and evocative atmosphere which no amount of repetition seems to stale, they form a very small ingredient in the whole. This is a French, not a Spanish opera, as any Spaniard will confirm; and Laparra goes much too far in calling García's *polo* the egg from which the whole of *Carmen* sprang [2]. The chief significance of the alien elements lies in the complete transformation they undergo in their passage through Bizet's creative imagination: they emerge as much his own as the rest of the score.

The use of the leading theme calls for a certain amount of comment, as it has been misunderstood. Bizet is not 'toying with the

[1] A variant is quoted by Liszt, *Des Bohémiens et de leur musique en Hongrie*.
[2] He even tries to show that the leading motive is thematically derived from it.

Leitmotiv' [1]; his practice has nothing to do with Wagner's. Wagner used the leading theme for two purposes, one dramatic, the other symphonic, to bind together the strands of his music-drama into a coherent musical whole. Bizet made no attempt at a symphonic structure: his purpose was purely dramatic, and there is no reason why his leading theme should be a veritable Proteus, since its main purpose is as a bearer of dramatic irony.[2] Its various forms must be relatively simple, and it must have sufficient musical character to survive repetition. In *Carmen* the leading motive occurs in two forms (*a*) and (*b*):

It will be seen that the prelude form is quoted second, for there can be no doubt that Istel is right in maintaining that (*a*) is, as it were, the root position. The prelude was almost certainly composed after the rest of the opera, and it is manifestly designed to conjure up the atmosphere of Act IV rather than Act I. Thus (*a*) represents Carmen herself, fickle, laughing, elusive, while (*b*) stands for her

[1] Gerald Abraham, *A Hundred Years of Music.*

[2] Operas which try to graft a symphonic treatment of themes on to a conventional operatic structure, such as Smetana's *Dalibor,* suffer from an irreconcilable duality. There was of course nothing original in Bizet's method; it had been used by many composers, notably Meyerbeer.

fatal influence on José. In Act I (*a*) predominates; it occurs on four different occasions to (*b*)'s solitary appearance when Carmen throws the flower in José's face. In Act II (*a*) does not appear, but (*b*) is used very effectively on the English horn just before the flower song. In Act III we hear (*a*) when Carmen foretells her own fate in the cards and (*b*) at the climax of the finale, when José leaves her and her new lover with the threat of his return. In Act IV we have (*a*) muttered by the violins at José's entrance (not (*b*) because it is Carmen's fate that is foreshadowed here; we are meant to recall the card scene) and (*b*) at the climax of the duet and when José gives himself up after the murder. Bizet's theme in its two forms is admirably suited to fulfil its dramatic purpose and is never run to death: he had learned restraint since *Les Pêcheurs de perles*. And if variety were needed, it is supplied by the scoring. There is a world of suggestive difference between (*a*) on the flute and on the cellos and basses (before and after Carmen reads the cards), and (*b*) on the English horn (Act II) and the full orchestra (Act IV).

The variety of aspects under which Bizet will present a theme without subjecting it to symphonic treatment in the Wagnerian manner is astonishing. The delightful tune of the duet 'Là-bas, là-bas dans la montagne' in Act II is made to evoke anything from wistful nostalgia to a rousing paean in honour of 'la chose enivrante, la liberté!' Even such clear-cut melodies as the habanera and the refrain of Escamillo's *couplets* undergo such transformations, the former generating profound suspense in D flat over sustained chords on the strings just before Carmen's escape in Act I,[1] and the latter (in the same key) with its clinging organ-like harmonies painting a vivid picture of the coolly self-satisfied Escamillo leaving the smugglers' den. The amount of contrapuntal ingenuity to which this bold-as-brass tune is subjected almost redeems it for the most refined ears. One of the great moments of the opera is the orchestral counter-theme added to it during the murder of Carmen: crude and naïve on paper, this is extraordinarily effective as a dramatic stroke. Another such felicity is the combination of the recall theme (two cornets)

[1] The suspense here is purely musical. We know exactly what is going to happen (even if we do not know the story, Carmen has just told us), yet the moment never loses its thrill.

with Carmen's dance in Act II; it is so simple and so fluent as almost to escape attention: [1]

Indeed Bizet's counterpoint is never forced and usually serves a manifest dramatic purpose. The fugue that accompanies the bustle of Carmen's escape in Act I stands as an action piece beside the battle fugue in Verdi's *Macbeth*. Nor did Bizet the miniaturist die with *L'Arlésienne*: the twenty bars for solo clarinet and bassoon in the entr'acte to Act II are effortlessly exquisite, and the finely drawn lines of the next entr'acte rise to the height of lyrical intensity. With this we may couple his almost Schubertian skill and unexpectedness in modulation. He needed less space in which to take the remotest tonal corners than almost any composer before him. Often—as in the seguidilla—his modulations seem on paper so reckless as to disintegrate the fabric of the music, yet in performance he always triumphs. It is the same with his transitions. With all his apparent impetuosity

[1] Bound up with the manuscript is a faint pencil sketch in which the themes are tried out in combination.

he had an impeccable and very French sense of style in the finish of a piece or its junction with its successor.[1] It is this combination of emotional passion with artistic restraint that gives the opera its chief musical distinction.

It would be easy (and in another place not unprofitable) to expend a whole chapter on the scoring of *Carmen*, which sets the crown on Bizet's claim as one of the supreme masters of the orchestra. He was far in advance of his French contemporaries. It is interesting to compare his method with Wagner's. Both composers used the orchestra, not in the traditional stage manner as a skeleton to support the voice (for long Verdi's only resource), but to create a world of sound in which the characters have their being. But whereas Wagner, with a different purpose in view, often produces an impression of inner stress and turmoil in which the voices have to struggle to be heard, Bizet's aim was always clarity and co-operation. Wagner's orchestra might be likened to the elements against which the voices strive; Bizet's supplies the air they breathe. His scoring has something of the sharp outline and virility of Berlioz (whose famous treatise he admired and recommended to his pupils), combined with the grace and economy of Mozart. It is remarkably supple; its specific gravity varies with the dramatic situation, from the brilliant blatancy of the bullfighting music, where everything is laid on in a blaze of colour, to the mountain air and flute-coloured serenity of the entr'acte to Act III, from the rustling of the muted strings in the cigarette girls' chorus, which Nietzsche likened to a breath from the garden of Epicurus, to the electric expectancy of the last entr'acte. Although the extremes of noise and delicacy are both employed, the listener is seldom conscious of any overloading or undue thinning of the texture: problems of balance seem to have been solved almost before they were posed. What could be subtler as a piece of atmosphere-painting than the short passage in Act IV when Frasquita and Mercedes warn Carmen that José is in the crowd? The simple tune for the flutes in thirds with the bassoons in contrary motion against it has a Mozartian charm that might seem absurdly

[1] See for instance the departure of Escamillo in Act II and the smugglers in Act III, or the link between the flower song and 'Là-bas, là-bas dans la montagne,' always ruined in performance by applause.

out of place: yet in conjunction with a single cornet,[1] which has but two notes throughout the scene (thirty-one bars), it suggests incomparably the hidden danger, the sign as yet no larger than a man's hand that Carmen's basking in Escamillo's triumph is to be short-lived. Played on the piano the passage sounds almost commonplace. All through the opera Bizet uses the wind instruments with great subtlety, variety and sureness of effect. The shrill chorus of the street urchins marching behind the soldiers as they change the guard is vividly introduced by two piccolos, cornet and plucked strings. A single low D on solo clarinet (p. 287 of Peters full score) paints Carmen's amazed anger when José says he must answer the recall to barracks. As Carmen foretells her death in the cards, the gradual piling up of the heavy brass seems to suggest the full weight of destiny poised to destroy a single human life. (This passage is followed by one of Bizet's most breath-taking transitions, a little phrase of six quavers on second violins and cellos in octaves leading straight back to the cheerful ditty in which Frasquita and Mercedes began to foretell their own happy futures.) The colouring of the entr'acte to Act IV is unique, with its blend of the picturesque and the sinister in the sinuous tune for solo piccolo and clarinet two octaves apart. But of all the wind instruments it is the flute on which the most care is lavished. Its low notes, so remote and often so ineffective, are exploited as well as the more familiar upper register. In the seguidilla, besides leading off with the main theme,[2] the first flute, beginning on its bottom D, indulges in a grotesque little canon with Carmen herself as she shamelessly plays the harlot with José. A few moments earlier, again at the very bottom of its compass, it has been echoing her contemptuous laughter at her captors. At the end of the duet 'Là-bas, là-bas, dans la montagne' it lingers nostalgically in the distance (*ppp*) over a quiet sustained chord (*pppp*) on four horns—to be followed by another lovely transition passage for violins in four parts and violas (p. 315). It is difficult not to

[1] In the Peters full score, the only one generally available, the cornets are, quite without authority, replaced by trumpets.

[2] These eight introductory bars, as well as the two opening bars of the duet 'Je vais danser' in Act II, also for flute, were afterthoughts added in the margin of the manuscript.

mention once more that masterpiece of rich yet delicate scoring, the
entr'acte to Act III, in which all the woodwind soloists, including
the English horn (which only makes two other appearances in the
opera), combine with the harp and some very attractive string writing
to weave a spell of rare magic. Bizet gives comparatively few opportunities to solo strings, but the ironic little commentary by the solo
violin in the duet 'Je suis Escamillo,' when that worthy is telling José
(who does not know him) that Carmen's affections have already left
her soldier-friend, should not escape notice. Another solo string
passage was cut out by Bizet himself. Between the arrival and
departure of the guard in Act I, in the place now occupied by
Guiraud's recitative 'Une jeune fille charmante,' the manuscript has
a *mélodrame* for solo violin and cello with string accompaniment.
This is in the form of a canon at the octave beginning as follows:

The suppression of this deft little piece, whose lay-out recalls Bizet's
orchestral version of *Petit Mari, petite femme*, is much to be regretted.

Carmen is one of the comparatively few operas that are both a
treasure for musicians [1] and a sure success with the general public
that loves a good tune. Yet at the risk of repetition it must be
emphasized again that the rarest quality of *Carmen* is neither its
melodic fertility nor its wealth of musical subtlety, but lies in Bizet's
approach to the dramatic problem. Just as his musicianship ensured

---

[1] The list of its admirers among other composers is unusually compre-
hensive, including such opposites as Brahms and Wagner, Gounod and
Wolf, Tchaikovsky and Busoni, Debussy and Saint-Saëns, Puccini and
Stravinsky, Stanford and Delius. See John W. Klein, *Bizet's Admirers
and Detractors*, in *Music & Letters*, October 1938.

a stylistic balance between *élan* and finish, so in his handling of the drama he was able to give full expression to the passions of the characters (and in *Carmen* they tear at the very roots of human nature) and at the same time to stand aside and allow their fate to move us. He writes as it were from inside and outside at the same time; he does not distort or load the dice; he makes no extraneous assault on the emotions, as Puccini does. He thus conveys the same overwhelming impression as Mérimée of reality heightened by art, of a perilous proximity to everyday life [1] combined with a timeless detachment from it. It was this freedom from moral preoccupation (so unlike Wagner, and so rare in the nineteenth century) that impressed Nietzsche, the maligned author of some of the most sensible criticism of *Carmen*, when he was seeking a personal antidote to Wagner. His opposition of Bizet [2] to Wagner is by no means the nonsense it has been called, for the two stand at opposite poles: in Wagner's music-dramas the one interesting character is always Wagner himself, whereas Bizet's object was to present his characters in the round and withdraw his own personality into the background (he did this so successfully that he has been accused of having no personality at all). Wagner wrote symphonic music in dramatic form, but the symphonic interest always predominates. Bizet brought the more orthodox operatic tradition to a climax by making music and drama reinforce one another at every turn instead of standing in each other's light. All his manifold gifts in the purely musical sphere are subordinated to this end, and they enable him to achieve that satisfying synthesis of two wilful and not easily reconcilable arts to which all opera aspires but very seldom attains. Bizet may not rank with the greatest composers—though he might have reached this position had he lived—but in *Carmen* he achieved what is undeniably one of the finest musico-dramatic creations of any age.

[1] It is possible that Mérimée's story was based on a genuine experience of his own. A *soi-disant* descendant of Carmen even appeared in 1907. She claimed to be the child of Carmen's daughter and a British artilleryman at Gibraltar.

[2] He might equally have chosen Verdi, who stands with Bizet in this matter; but Verdi's two greatest operas were unwritten when Nietzsche wrote.

CHAPTER X

DEVELOPMENT AND MUSICAL PERSONALITY

BIZET's development as an artist presents a curious problem, on which his biographers so far have shed little light. Until the recent discovery of the Symphony it was generally held (despite other evidence to the contrary) that he developed very slowly, taking a good twelve years to free himself from the cramping influences around him. But the Symphony cannot be explained on this hypothesis. It bears alien influences, of course, but possesses a maturity astonishing in a boy of seventeen; above all, it is completely free from doubts and hesitations. It goes straight to the mark. How did it come about that a composer who wrote this at seventeen could fall so adrift in after years and only fulfil its promise in the last few years of his life? What caused the partial eclipse of the infectious spontaneity that marks his earliest and latest work?

The answer is to be found in the letters written from Rome in the winter of 1858–9. They supply two inter-related reasons, one mainly artistic, the other psychological. At the age of twenty Bizet began to be assailed by the doubts that afflict all young creative artists. Delmas prints an interesting letter to a fellow-artist written in December 1858:

Like you I am afraid, and like you I begin many things with ardour and get discouraged the moment I finish them, when I see I have not done what I wanted to do. Yet I have taken a big step forward since leaving Paris: at the Conservatoire I was a good pupil; here I am beginning to think myself an artist, I go forward alone, but what howlers, what failures! Truly happy is he who avoids breaking his neck amid the obscurities of art. Yet I have a living light to guide me, I have a goal, I know what is good and what is beautiful; there are moments when I think I am getting there, and then a big cloud descends on me and I have to start groping again. . . . Happy the men who, like Raphael, Mozart, Correggio, Rossini, have received from heaven the artistic gift in all its purity and perfection; happy also those who, like Michelangelo and Beethoven, have

206

by the power of their *reason* and their genius come to discover the last word in greatness and beauty. It would really be wonderful to put one's name even in the margin of the golden book of intelligence! Quiet! If any one heard us they wouldn't understand, they would take our ambition for conceited folly; let us await the future in silence and say only this: whatever happens, we shall always be among the privileged, for we love and understand beauty. Yes, I certainly thank God every day for having made me like this. . . . I see many who don't think as I do. They haven't my artistic worries and doubts, but they haven't my joys either, and I pity them.

On the last day of the year he developed this in a letter to his mother:

There are two sorts of genius: natural genius and rational genius. While immensely admiring the second, I shall not conceal from you that the first has all my sympathies. Yes, I dare to prefer Raphael to Michelangelo, Mozart to Beethoven, and Rossini to Meyerbeer. . . . It is solely a matter of taste, one type of ideas has a greater attraction for me than the other. When I see the 'Last Judgment,' when I hear the Eroica Symphony or the fourth act of *Les Huguenots*, I am moved, surprised, I have not enough eyes, ears or intelligence to admire with. But when I see the 'School of Athens,' the 'Dispute of the Holy Sacrament,' the 'Virgin of Foligno,' when I hear the *Marriage of Figaro* or the second act of *William Tell,* I am completely happy. I experience a sense of perfect well-being and satisfaction, I forget everything. Oh, how lucky one is to be thus favoured!

He was always trying to find an underlying correspondence between the arts.

All the arts touch, or rather there is only one art. Whether one expresses one's ideas on canvas, in marble or in the theatre is of little importance: the idea is always the same. I am more than ever convinced that Mozart and Rossini are the two greatest musicians. While admiring Beethoven and Meyerbeer with all my faculties, I feel my nature brings me to love art that is pure and fluent rather than dramatic passion. It is the same in painting—Raphael is the same man as Mozart; Meyerbeer feels as Michelangelo felt.

We may smile at Bizet's examples (nearly every one at that date overrated Meyerbeer), but the broad distinction between the two types of genius is familiar to all students of the arts, especially of music; and there is no doubt that Bizet was right in feeling that his true place was with Mozart and Rossini. This was the Bizet of the Symphony and *Don Procopio*, and of *L'Arlésienne* and *Carmen*, the Bizet who so often finds as if by instinct the felicitous touch that redeems some old formula from the commonplace and gives it a new bloom. But it was not the only Bizet: about the same time he began to feel that he was letting his music come too easily. 'Happily I have made great progress,' he wrote in October:

I can *rewrite*, and I am profiting by it. You know that in Paris, when I composed anything, I could never begin it again; here, on the contrary, I am delighted to do so. Another sign of progress: it seems to me that all my facility and musical *triture* is no longer any use to me; I can do nothing without an idea. . . . I have enormous trouble in composing.

Another letter in much the same terms has been quoted in Chapter II. This greater self-realization has always been taken as a sign of advance; but in a composer of Bizet's type this by no means follows. For him the supreme danger is self-consciousness. If any ulterior aim interposes itself between his response to a creative stimulus and its realization, the result is apt to be spoiled. Like Carmen's love, natural genius will not be tamed; it must be always free. Even Mozart, the prince of instinctive composers, found his muse constrained when he had to accommodate it to the King of Prussia's cello. With Bizet the results were far more serious. In his middle works, beginning with *Vasco de Gama*—the very next thing he wrote after that winter—though much is gained, the vital freshness is partly lost. We are conscious of effort, of a forcing of the inspiration into channels for which nature never intended it, in particular of an attempt to achieve the grandiose and heroic. He proposed in 1859 to write 'something tragic and purely German,' and this remained his ambition for many years. In March 1867 he was ashamed to confess to Lacombe his natural susceptibility to Italian music:

I am German by conviction, heart and soul, but I sometimes get lost in artistic houses of ill fame. And I confess to you under my breath, I find infinite pleasure there. I love Italian music as one loves a courtesan. . . . Like you, I put Beethoven at the head of the greatest and most excellent. The choral Symphony is for me the culminating point of our art. Dante,

Michelangelo, Shakespeare, Homer, Beethoven, Moses! Neither Mozart with his heavenly form, nor Weber with his powerful and colossal originality, nor Meyerbeer with his mighty dramatic genius, can in my opinion dispute the palm with the Titan, the Prometheus of music.

Beethoven has ousted Mozart, Raphael has yielded to Michelangelo. At the same time comes a renewed emphasis on absolute music: he advises Lacombe not to write for the stage till he knows what he wants to do, but 'one must write symphonies.' He is suspicious of music that sounds like improvisation: only Chopin succeeded in that, and he is a bad model. Rational genius is now supreme; natural genius, it seems, is an illicit love. But who is Bizet's example in the cult of German music? Not a German at all, but Charles Gounod; and a less suitable model he could not have found. For Gounod was not only a much less original composer than the Germans (Weber, Mendelssohn, Schumann) who also influenced Bizet at this period, but he had taken the same wrong turning as Bizet. It was a case of the blind leading the blind. Instead of developing his charming lyrical gift, he had in *Faust* tackled a subject far too big for him and in *La Reine de Saba* set himself to outdo Meyerbeer; and his attempts to write heroic and religious music were calamitous. Bizet imitated him with distressing faithfulness, especially in *Ivan le Terrible*. He did work through this cult of the monumental, which swamped the less vital Gounod, but not till the end of the sixties; even later it occasionally reared its head, as in *Patrie* and *Don Rodrigue,* and we may perhaps be thankful that *Geneviève de Paris* never saw the light. The whole process began in Rome when Bizet discovered the need for an 'idea' and first set out to compose German music.

The second reason for his decline explains why he succumbed so easily to the first. He lacked the self-knowledge to understand, and the strength of character to correct, his deviations from the course marked out for him by nature. This was not due to any lack of creative vitality, or to want of trying, still less to deliberate stifling of his gifts. The letters show very clearly where the fault lay. Somewhere deep within him, in regions which it is now impossible to explore (it may or may not be connected with too easy success in childhood), there lay a basic lack of self-confidence which was for ever inhibiting surrender to his creative impulses. 'You accuse me of having too little stability in my ideas,' he wrote to his parents, 'and appearances support you.' His continual vacillation between one operatic project and another might be set down to youth's propensity for false starts, did it not persist throughout his life. Bizet in less than twenty years must have left more operas unfinished than almost any composer who ever lived. What appeared a splendid idea one day was condemned as hopeless the next. The symptom of the trouble was fear. 'I am afraid of my return,' he wrote in the letter of October 1858 quoted above,

I am afraid of contact with the directors and the makers of stage pieces, whom I do not dignify with the name of poets. I am afraid of the singers; I am afraid, in a word, of that silent ill-will which says nothing disagreeable to your face but obstinately prevents your going ahead.

The only way he could see of killing this fear was to prove to himself that he was a success. We have seen how this need for self-esteem (and hence for the esteem of others) not only led him to pursue false gods and deprive the world of much that it had a right to expect, but brought him very little material reward. A letter of March 1859 in which he discusses the recent failures of French operatic composers is very revealing. He finds Massé deficient in style and breadth of conception and sees a want of experience in Félicien David, but the chief lack is

the sole means a composer has of making himself understood by the public to-day: the *motif*, wrongly called the idea. One can be a great artist without having the *motif*—it is then necessary to renounce money and popular success—but one can also be a superior artist and possess this precious gift, witness Rossini. Rossini is the greatest of all [*sc.* contemporaries] because like Mozart he has all the qualities: loftiness, style and last of all —the *motif*.

Bizet goes on to claim that he has found the *motif* in comic opera (in *Don Procopio*); next year he will look for it in grand opera, which is much more difficult. He couples this with one of those asseverations which seem designed to encourage himself as much as his mother. 'I know what I am doing and what I am worth, and when I say "I have arrived" there will be many other people of the same opinion.' Whatever Bizet meant by the *motif*, he was clearly running a risk in the emphasis he laid on the need for being understood by the public. The composer with something to say must train his public (difficult as this was in nineteenth-century France), not follow it; and if a large measure of incomprehensibility has attained a certain snob-value in recent years, it remains a fault on the right side.

However grave this defect in Bizet's moral make-up, it is very far from being the cynical betrayal of his art that certain critics have denounced. Works like *L'Arlésienne* and *Carmen* are not written by mistake, as Landormy naïvely seems to suppose. Cynicism that is more than surface-deep is impossible to a nature like Bizet's, though it can deceive itself to the extent of believing that its concessions and retreats are genuine advances. It is neither profitable nor becoming for the essentially barren race of critics to take up a lofty moral tone towards creative artists. Bizet needed sympathy, and if we are to understand him his memory still needs it. He was sadly ill-equipped to deal with failure. 'In order to succeed to-day you have to be either dead or German,' he wrote to Gallet; and to Galabert: 'To be a musician to-day you must have an assured independent income or else a real talent in diplomacy.' Bizet had none of these assets, and although death did give a sudden boost to his reputation, this was followed by an extreme reaction which has not yet been corrected.

What, then, is his true position in the history of music? It has been said that he 'contributed little to the progress of his art.' [1] Even on the narrowest view this can be justified only if opera is excluded from the art of music. Bizet's contributions to the progress of opera were very considerable, but they have been obscured by two facts: they are clearest in the dramatic rather than the musical sphere, and they have not been followed up. In 1869 he set himself to revolutionize *opéra-comique*. At this date the form had become nearly as fossilized as grand opera. Originally a reaction from the inflated heroics of the larger institution, it had gradually ceased to represent real-life characters and descended to the reproduction of types.

[1] Gerald Abraham, *A Hundred Years of Music.*

With the possible exception of *Mignon,* no French *opéra-comique* between *Fra Diavolo* (1830) and *Carmen* has kept the stage. By giving the form a blood transfusion from real life, including its tragic as well as its comic elements, Bizet killed the stale *buffo* and senti-mental types. He went some way towards finishing off the old grand opera as well: for one of the clearest results of *Carmen* was that the two kinds of opera suddenly ceased to diverge. Henceforward they began to yield to a single form lying half way between the two. In the operas of Massenet the old distinctions, including that of spoken dialogue, lost their validity. At the same time Bizet helped to break the tyranny of the singer, which by the suppression of dramatic unity was threatening—as it had done a century earlier till Gluck came to the rescue—to kill opera as an art (especially in Italy and France) and turn it into a concert in fancy dress. He thus brought the con-test between drama and music which is the history of opera to a fresh climax. The balance he struck between them remains one of the most satisfying in its history. Then, all too soon, he died. He founded no school, and none of his successors had the creative power to carry on where he left off. In Italy Puccini developed the *verismo* side of *Carmen* till it became threadbare. In France the slender talent of Massenet inclined more and more to Gounod rather than Bizet, and the one composer with the vitality and individuality required to extend the genre, Emmanuel Chabrier, allowed his senses to be seduced by the odour of Bayreuth. For in the years following Bizet's death France went Wagner-mad. *Carmen,* damned as Wag-nerian in 1875, passed suddenly from the spearpoint of advance into the cul-de-sac of reaction, and was condemned for the lack of those very qualities which had been found so dangerous ten years before. Doubtless Bizet would have advanced beyond *Carmen* by that time, especially in the harmonic sphere; but he was no longer alive to hold his position in the race. After the Wagner furore the last chance of a Bizet school of opera had vanished.

One result of this reaction was that French critics, judging *Carmen* by Wagnerian standards which did not apply, found it tame and tentative. But though Bizet was not a European revolutionary like Wagner or Liszt, he was an innovator in his own way, which was the typical French method of beginning from the inside and working

CARMEN

Opéra-Comique en quatre actes.

H. MEILHAC et L. HALÉVY MUSIQUE de GEORGES BIZET

POSTER FOR THE 1875 PRODUCTION OF 'CARMEN'

outwards. He used old devices in a new way to open up new dramatic and musical possibilities; and it is possible to consider this a more progressive process than the use of new devices to say what has often been said before—the operatic method of Richard Strauss. Bizet's innovations were just sufficient to be of use to his own purposes; and it would be churlish to demand more. The composers who lay up a stock of technical material for their successors, like Liszt, are seldom gifted with first-rate creative power: perhaps it is their method of compensating for their defect. The artist with something to say is generally too busy to experiment in a vacuum.

Bizet was not entirely without influence on his successors. Chabrier certainly and Ravel probably owed him something. But he influenced most clearly a composer of a very different temperament—Tchaikovsky. What may be called the Frédéri-José element, which we have seen was implicit in Bizet as early as the unpublished *Romance sans paroles* and first became explicit in *La Coupe du Roi de Thule*, exercized a growing influence on Tchaikovsky towards the end of his life. Perhaps he saw in the passion-torn José something of himself; at any rate his later work, especially the first movement of the B minor Symphony, is full of echoes of Bizet's tragic heroes. Compare the melody, texture and harmony of its second subject with this from José's flower song:

- raî - - - - - tre, Qu'à je

ter un re- gard sur moi

There is no space to add to what has been said on the musical
development of Bizet's style and his mastery of the orchestra. But
his wonderful melodic gift has sometimes received less than justice.
It was indeed related to Gounod through what may be termed the
female line, but there was far more to it than that. Gounod's melody
at its best, as in the opening theme of the *Mireille* overture, is charming,
but it is subject to the same limitations as Mendelssohn's, being apt
when lively to fall into an amiable jogtrot, when tender into sentimentality. Bizet's has far greater energy, variety and flexibility. The
length and the compass of many of his tunes are alike remarkable. The
main melody of the entr'acte to Act III of *Carmen* and 'L'Innocent's' theme from *L'Arlésienne* both have a range of two octaves and
extend for ten and a half and sixteen bars respectively of unbroken
melody in slow time; they are beautifully balanced and nicely extended to escape a too regular symmetry. He had an easy command

of the two extremes of movement, by steps and wide leaps, and often the two are very happily combined; in Carmen's seguidilla, where there is also great freedom of modulation, the effect is extraordinarily individual. He was a master of the melodic paragraph, and by judicious control over rhythm and the rise and fall of the melody produced whole numbers which seem to spring forth effortlessly complete from the first bar to the last. From the earliest days he had shown a happy skill in extending a melody a little longer than the ear expects, and his approach to a cadence often has an originality and beauty of its own. When he combined these various qualities in a single piece, as in José's flower song or the *Arlésienne* Adagietto, he produced gems of a singular perfection—and this quite apart from their dramatic connotations. Rhythmically the influence of Gounod was far more dangerous, but even at the worst period it was never exclusive. Some credit should probably go to Félicien David for the quasi-oriental rhythms which, though monotonous in themselves, helped to liberate Bizet from the four-squareness of Gounod. They enabled him to give continuity to a piece by treating them rather in the manner of an elementary passacaglia. This process reached its climax in the Ghazel and Almée of *Djamileh*. But the chief counter-agent to Gounod was probably Verdi, whose rhythmic energy (in his early work) seemed to be concentrated on the propulsion of the melody, leaving a very subordinate function to the accompaniment. With Gounod the fault was all the other way, a weak melody often reposing on a rich accompaniment; and Bizet did need some thrust to overcome the paralytic grip of the four-bar sequence, which was especially cramping in the Gounodesque heroic parts of his middle-period operas. Later in his career he could write square melodies, such as the tenors' welcome to the cigarette girls ('La cloche a sonné') in Act I of *Carmen*, which retain their life and freshness. The much-abused refrain of Escamillo's *couplets* need only be compared with the thrice-repeated rhythm of the soldiers' chorus in *Faust* for the saving grace of its rhythmic variety to be appreciated. French music has not on the whole been fertile in melodic invention, having contented itself in great degree with only two or three types of tune. Bizet ranks with the still more individual Berlioz among its few outstanding melodists.

His work at all periods bears certain well-marked fingerprints. His very personal use of chromatic harmony over a pedal (which he by no means reserved for the conventional suggestion of the bucolic) has already been noted. There is a close family resemblance, rhythmic and melodic, between the bolero in *Vasco de Gama*, the opening chorus of *Djamileh* and one of the themes of the F sharp minor chorus in *L'Arlésienne,* all designed to evoke an exotic atmosphere. José's 'Dût-il m'en coûter la vie' is several times foreshadowed, for instance in the song *N'oublions pas* and in an air from *Ivan le Terrible*, as well as being directly anticipated in *La Coupe du Roi de Thule*. The opening phrase of the *Roma* scherzo is prominent in the first finale of *Don Procopio*, the Glover motive and Mab's *couplets* (Act I) in *La Jolie Fille de Perth*, the gaming chorus in *Djamileh* and the card scene in *Carmen*; in each context except the last it suggests a cheerful bustling. The most prominent of all the melodic fingerprints derives from a phrase in the slow movement of Mozart's clarinet Quintet:

MOZART

This struck many an echo from Bizet (as it did from Mendelssohn, e.g. in the slow movement of the D minor piano Concerto). It is prominent in the duet for Leila and Zurga in *Les Pêcheurs de perles*, *Le Golfe de Bahia,* the song *Vieille Chanson*, the *Sérénade* for piano, the trio that precedes the Ghazel in *Djamileh* and most of all at Escamillo's 'Si tu m'aimes' in Act IV of *Carmen*. The resemblances are of course all fortuitous and only serve to reveal certain grooves along which Bizet's mind worked in the process of creation. There is often a link of another kind between his works. Like Bach, Handel, Berlioz and others, he had a habit of re-using earlier material. There are at least twenty-three instances of this process, which has little significance in itself; but it is notable that nearly always the old matter fails to adorn its new surroundings. The four alien passages in *Les Pêcheurs de perles* are among the weakest in the opera, and some charming things in *Don Procopio* are quite ruined by translation elsewhere. Only twice—in *Trompette et tambour* and José's 'Dût-il m'en coûter la vie'—did Bizet markedly improve on his earlier versions; though it is only fair to add that we do not possess the originals of the other insertions in *Carmen*. In his earlier work he seems to have taken up old material uncritically as it came to hand instead of passing it anew through his imagination.

He wrote his best work very rapidly. The early Symphony was finished in a month, *L'Arlésienne* in not more than two, and probably less; whereas the laboured *Roma* took him years. His method of composition was to immerse himself in his subject, allow the essentials to penetrate his imagination and write down little or nothing till the music was nearly complete in his head. With a composer of his instinctive type the success of this method depends a good deal on the quality of the original stimulus: a libretto that was inadequate, especially in its dramatic construction and presentation of character (like *La Jolie Fille de Perth*), would tend to produce an uneven response. Not that he accepted his libretti without criticism: in every instance of which we have any information he made considerable modifications in the text,[1] sometimes rewriting whole scenes himself. But he lacked the extreme fertility of purely musical invention that could turn a triviality like the book of *Così fan tutte* into a masterpiece. Nor was he open to a great range of stimuli. Religion drew from him the sorry *Te Deum*; patriotism had no better result. But he was intensely susceptible to the dramatic conflict engendered by certain emotions, especially sexual passion and jealousy. If his imagination was profoundly stirred he interpreted the clash of character with an intensity and objectivity of vision rare in any age and almost unknown among his contemporaries with the sole exception of Verdi. Here indeed is the compensation for his lack of a strong directive personality or moral preoccupation. For he could sink himself in his characters. To very few is it given to enter into the natures of such diverse human beings as it was to Bizet. In his best work the characters never shout and thump a tub; whenever this happens, it is Bizet ventriloquizing and trying to supply at a conscious level what his libretto failed to stir in the unseen depths of his personality. Bizet had it in him to be the greatest musical dramatist of his age. Where

[1] See in particular his correspondence with Galabert about *La Coupe du Roi de Thule* and with Gallet about *Don Rodrigue*.

Wagner's characters were legendary, Meyerbeer's historical, Gounod's classical and Verdi's at first those of romantic melodrama, Bizet's in his two greatest works were of his own century and of the common people. He steered a course equally remote from the disguised symphonist Wagner and the meretricious eclectic Meyerbeer. There are two kinds of effect in the theatre—effect for effect's sake and effect to heighten dramatic tension. The former, which was Meyerbeer's method, calls attention only to itself; the latter, which was Bizet's, is willing even to conceal itself if it assists or elucidates the dramatic situation. Meyerbeer, who introduced a ballet of bathing belles in *Les Huguenots*, would hardly have been content with less than a Highland Rally, complete with a caber-tossing demonstration by Henry Smith, in *La Jolie Fille de Perth*. It is Verdi to whom Bizet stands closest—Verdi who was thirty-nine when he uttered the irresistible crudities of *Il Trovatore* and well over seventy before he reached the height of his powers. It is well to remember that had Verdi died at thirty-six, as Bizet did, we should hardly have known his name.

However often Bizet proclaimed that his heart was Italian or German, however remote from France his operatic travels (not a single one of his operas, finished or unfinished—with the sole exception of the Provençal *Calendal*—has its scene in France), he remains essentially French, the supreme musical realization, as Romain Rolland says, of one pole of the French genius. He is the counter-weight, perhaps the complement, of Debussy, the clear sunshine of the Mediterranean as opposed to the twilight and the moonlight, exuberance and enthusiasm against delicate understatement. Perhaps there is less difference between the two extremes than is apparent to an outsider; perhaps every Frenchman has something of both. Certainly Debussy and Fauré, who had little superficially in common with Bizet, both ranked his genius at its true value. And they would have endorsed as wholly French the advice Bizet gave to his pupil Galabert: 'Without form, no style; without style, no art.'

APPENDIX A

CALENDAR

(Figures in brackets denote the age reached by the person mentioned during the year in question.)

Year	Age	Life	Contemporary Musicians
1838		Georges Bizet (registered Alexandre César Léopold) born, Oct. 25, in Paris, son of Adolphe Armand Bizet (28), a music-teacher.	Bruch born, Jan. 6; Castillon born, Dec. 13. Adam aged 35; Alkan 25; Auber 56; Balakirev 2; Balfe 30; Benedict 34; Berlioz 35; Borodin 4; Brahms 5; Bruckner 15; Cherubini 78; Chopin 28; Cornelius 15; Cui 3; David (Félicien) 28; Dargomizhsky 25; Delibes 2; Donizetti 41; Flotow 26; Franck 16; Gade 21; Gevaert 10; Glinka 35; Gounod 20; Guilmant 1; Halévy 47; Heller 23; Liszt 27; Lortzing 35; Mendelssohn 29; Mercadante 43; Meyerbeer 47; Nicolai 28; Offenbach 19; Reyer 15; Rossini 46; Rubinstein 8; Saint-Saëns 3; Schumann 28; Smetana 14; Spohr 54; Spontini 64; Strauss (J. ii) 13; Thomas (A.) 27; Verdi 25; Wagner 25.
1839	1		Mussorgsky born, March 21; Paer (68) dies, May 3.
1840	2	Baptized (Georges) at church of Notre-Dame-de-Lorette, March 16.	Götz born, Dec. 17; Svendsen born, Sept. 3; Tchaikovsky born, May 7.
1841	3		Chabrier born, Jan. 18; Dvořák born, Sept. 8; Pedrell born, Feb. 19.

Year	Age	Life	Contemporary Musicians
1842	4	Learns his notes from his mother at the same time as his letters.	Boito born, Feb. 24; Cherubini (82) dies, March 15; Massenet born, May 12; Sullivan born, May 13.
1843	5		Grieg born, June 15; Sgambati born, May 28.
1844	6		Rimsky-Korsakov born, March 18.
1845	7		Fauré born, May 12; Widor born, Feb. 22.
1846	8	Shows signs of remarkable aural memory. Receives elementary musical instruction from his father (36).	
1847	9	Interviewed by Meifred (56) with a view to entering the Conservatoire though under age. Sent to Marmontel's (31) piano class through the influence of his uncle Delsarte (36).	Mackenzie born, Aug. 22; Mendelssohn (38) dies, Nov. 4.
1848	10	Admitted to Conservatoire, Oct. 9.	Donizetti (51) dies, April 8; Duparc born, Jan. 21; Parry born, Feb. 27.
1849	11	Wins first prize for solfeggio. Joins Zimmerman's (64) fugue and counterpoint class, sometimes taken by Gounod (31).	Chopin (39) dies, Oct. 17; Nicolai (39) dies, May 11.
1850	12	Earliest known compositions, 2 Vocalises, Feb.	
1851	13	Wins second prize for piano at first attempt.	d'Indy born, March 27; Lortzing (48) dies, Jan. 21; Spontini (77) dies, Jan. 14.
1852	14	Shares first prize for piano with Savary. Joins Benoist's (58) organ class.	Stanford born, Sept. 30.
1853	15	On Zimmerman's (68) death joins Halévy's (54) composition class.	Messager born, Dec. 30.

Year	Age	Life	Contemporary Musicians
1854	16	Wins second prizes for organ and fugue. Composes *Grande Valse de Concert* and 1st *Nocturne* for piano, Sept. First published work (2 songs) issued, together with a song by his father (44).	Humperdinck born, Sept. 1; Janáček born, July 3.
1855	17	Wins first prizes for organ and fugue. Recommended by Halévy to director of Opéra-Comique as 'young composer, pianist and accompanist,' Sept. Composes Symphony in C major (begun Oct. 29, finished Nov.).	Chausson born, Jan. 21; Liadov born, May 11.
1856	18	Awarded second Prix de Rome for cantata *David*.	Martucci born, Jan. 6; Schumann (46) dies, July 29; Sinding born, Jan. 11; Taneiev born, Nov. 25.
1857	19	Ties with Lecocq (25) for prize offered by Offenbach for setting of one-act operetta *Le Docteur Miracle*. Bizet's operetta produced at Bouffes-Parisiens, April 9. Awarded first Prix de Rome for cantata *Clovis et Clotilde*, performed at Institut with great success, Oct. Leaves for Rome with fellow-pensioners, Dec. 21.	Bruneau born, March 1; Elgar born, June 2; Glinka (54) dies, Feb. 15.
1858	20	After leisurely journey and much sight-seeing reaches Florence, Jan. 12, where he hears Verdi's *I Lombardi*. Arrives in Rome, Jan. 28, and achieves immediate success as pianist. Composes *Te Deum* for Rodrigues prize, Feb.– May. Makes friends with	Hüe born, May 6; Leoncavallo born, March 8; Puccini born, June 22; Smyth (Ethel) born, April 23.

Year	Age	Life	Contemporary Musicians

writer Edmond About (30). Fortnight's holiday in Alban Hills, May – June. *Don Procopio* begun, summer.

1859   21   *Don Procopio* finished, March. Prolonged holiday, May 11– late Oct., during which he visits Cape Circe, Terracina, Naples and Pompeii and plans many compositions never finished. Serious attack of throat trouble at Naples. Begins a second Symphony, Oct., but abandons it and destroys MS., Dec. Receives permission to spend extra year in Rome instead of Germany. Begins Ode Symphony *Vasco de Gama*, Dec.

Chevillard born, Oct. 14; Spohr (75) dies, Oct. 22.

1860   22   *Vasco de Gama* finished, March. Begins and abandons *opéra-comique L'Amour peintre* and cantata *Carmen saeculare*, Jan.– April. Joined by his friend Ernest Guiraud (23). Short tour in mountains, June. Portrait painted by Giacometti, July. Leaves Rome with Guiraud, late July. Plans symphony *Roma*. On reaching Venice hears of his mother's (46) serious illness and hurries home, Sept.

Albéniz born, May 28; Charpentier born, June 25; Mahler born, July 7; Wolf born, March 13.

1861   23   His piano-playing impresses Liszt, May 26. Composes (or finishes) *Scherzo et Marche funèbre* for orchestra and overture *La Chasse d'Ossian*. His mother (47) dies, late summer.

Bréville born, Feb. 21; Chaminade born, Aug. 8; Loeffler born, Jan. 30; MacDowell born, Dec. 18.

Year	Age	Life	Contemporary Musicians
		Begins opera *La Guzla de l'Émir*, completed early in following year.	
1862	24	Withdraws *La Guzla de l'Émir* from rehearsal at Opéra-Comique on being offered libretto of *Les Pêcheurs de perles*. Assists Gounod (44) with production of *La Reine de Saba*, Feb. Visits Baden for music festival with Berlioz (59), Reyer (39) and Gounod, Aug.	Debussy born, Aug. 22; Delius born, Jan. 29; Halévy (63) dies, March 17.
1863	25	Scherzo performed by Pasdeloup at Cirque Napoléon, Jan. 11; repeated on 18th. *Vasco de Gama* performed by Société Nationale des Beaux-Arts. *Les Pêcheurs de perles* completed early in year; first performed at Théâtre-Lyrique, Sept. 30, and meets with mixed reception. B.'s father (53) buys land for summer residence at Le Vésinet, Oct. 3.	Mascagni born, Dec. 7; Pierné born, Aug. 16.
1864	26	Does much hack work for publishers and theatre directors, which probably undermines his health.	Meyerbeer (73) dies, May 2; Ropartz born, June 15; Strauss (R.) born, June 11.
1865	27	*Ivan le Terrible* composed and offered without success to Théâtre-Lyrique and Opéra. *Chants du Rhin* and probably other piano works written. Meets Edmond Galabert, who becomes his pupil, and Comtesse de Chabrillan (Céleste Mogador) (41).	Dukas born, Oct. 1; Glazunov born, Aug. 10; Magnard born, June 9; Sibelius born, Dec. 8.
1866	28	Working on *Roma*, June–July. *La Jolie Fille de Perth* begun	Busoni born, April 1; Satie born, May 17.

Year	Age	Life	Contemporary Musicians
		July, finished Dec. Also composes many songs and makes innumerable arrangements of dance-music and operas for publishers; complains of overwork.	
1867	29	Paul Lacombe (30) becomes his pupil (by correspondence). Hears and severely criticizes Verdi's (54) *Don Carlos*, March. Visit to Bordeaux, March. Writes cantata and hymn for competitions in connection with Grand Exhibition, *c.* May. Publishes critical article in *La Revue Nationale et Étrangère*, Aug. 3, but withdraws a second article when editor wishes to tamper with it. Becomes engaged to Geneviève Halévy, Oct., but engagement apparently broken off in same month. Contributes an act to composite operetta *Malbrough s'en va-t-en guerre*, produced Athénée, Dec. 13. *La Jolie Fille de Perth* produced at Théâtre-Lyrique after long delays, Dec. 26.	Granados born, July 29; Koechlin born, Nov. 27.
1868	30	Visits Brussels for performance there of *La Jolie Fille de Perth*, April. Makes first attempt to complete Halévy's *Noé*, finishes *Roma*, Aug., and composes songs and piano music, including *Variations chromatiques*, July. Serious attacks of angina, July and Aug., accom-	Bantock born, Aug. 7; Rossini (76) dies, Nov. 13.

Year	Age	Life	Contemporary Musicians
		panied by spiritual crisis, during which he begins to set *La Coupe du Roi de Thule* for Opéra competition, Aug.–Oct.	
1869	31	Abandons *La Coupe du Roi de Thule* on being invited by Du Locle to change the genre of *opéra-comique*. *Roma* performed by Pasdeloup (without scherzo) under title *Fantaisie symphonique, Souvenirs de Rome*, Feb. 28. Marries Geneviève Halévy, June 3. Completes *Noé* at second attempt, Nov.	Berlioz (66) dies, March 8; Dargomizhsky (56) dies, Jan. 17; Pfitzner born, May 5; Roussel born, April 5.
1870	32	Working at *Clarissa Harlowe* and *Grisélidis*. Holiday at Barbizon interrupted by outbreak of Franco-Prussian War, July 15. B. joins National Guard and remains in Paris throughout siege.	Balfe (62) dies, Oct. 20; Mercadante (75) dies, Dec. 17; Novák born, Dec. 5; Schmitt born, Sept. 28.
1871	33	Visit to Bordeaux, Feb. Leaves Paris for Le Vésinet after insurrection of Commune, March 18. Resumes work on *Clarissa Harlowe* and *Grisélidis*, but latter rejected by Opéra-Comique on ground of expense. *Djamileh* offered instead; music composed late summer. *Roma* revised (?) and *Jeux d'enfants* written, Sept.	Auber (89) dies, May 12.
1872	34	*Djamileh* produced at Opéra-Comique, May 22; a failure. B.'s son Jacques born, July 10. Incidental music to	Skriabin born, Jan. 4; Vaughan Williams born, Oct. 12.

Year	Age	Life	Contemporary Musicians
		L'Arlésienne composed rapidly during summer and produced at Vaudeville, Oct. 1. Another failure, but orchestral suite performed with immediate success by Pasdeloup (53), Nov. 10.	
1873	35	B. acts for Gounod (55), then abroad, in revival of *Roméo et Juliette* at Opéra-Comique, Jan. 20. *Petite Suite d'orchestre* from *Jeux d'enfants* performed at first Colonne concert, March 2. *Carmen* begun (spring), but dropped owing to difficulties with Opéra-Comique. *Don Rodrigue* composed during summer, but abandoned when Opéra burned down, Oct. 28.	Rakhmaninov born, April 1; Reger born, March 19; Séverac born, July 20.
1874	36	Overture *Patrie* performed by Pasdeloup (55), Feb. 15. After renewed and severe attack of angina B. goes to Bougival for summer and completes *Carmen*. Rehearsals begun, Dec. During winter B. attends Franck's (52) organ class at Conservatoire.	Cornelius (50) dies, Oct. 26; Holst born, Sept. 21; Schoenberg born, Sept. 13; Suk born, Jan. 4.
1875	37	B. decorated with Legion of Honour. *Carmen* produced at Opéra-Comique, March 3, and causes consternation in press. Du Locle commissions a new opera from same collaborators, but B. is taken seriously ill, late March. Slow recovery leads to relapse, May,	Coleridge-Taylor born, Aug. 15; Ravel born, March 7; Roger-Ducasse born, April 18. Albéniz aged 15; d'Albert 11; Alkan 62; Arensky 14; Balakirev 39; Bantock 8; Boito 33; Bordes 12; Borodin 41; Bossi 14; Brahms 42; Bréville 14; Bruckner

Year	Age	Life	Contemporary Musicians
		though he plans oratorio *Geneviève de Paris*. Bizet dies at Bougival nr. Paris, June 3.	51; Bruneau 18; Busoni 9; Chabrier 34; Charpentier 15; Chausson 20; Cui 40; Delibes 30; Dukas 10; Duparc 27; Dvořák 34; Elgar 18; Fauré 30; Franck 53; Gade 58; Glazunov 10; Goldmark 45; Gounod 57; Granados 8; Grieg 32; Heller 60; Holst 1; Humperdinck 21; d'Indy 24; Lalo 52; Leoncavallo 17; Liadov 20; Liszt 72; Loeffler 14; MacDowell 14; Mahler 15; Martucci 19; Mascagni 12; Massenet 33; Mussorgsky 36; Novák 5; Offenbach 56; Parry 27; Pedrell 34; Pfitzner 6; Pierné 12; Ponchielli 41; Puccini 17; Raff 53; Rakhmaninov 2; Reger 2; Rimsky-Korsakov 31; Ropartz 11; Roussel 6; Rubinstein 45; Saint-Saëns 40; Satie 9; Schmitt 5; Schoenberg 1; Séverac 2; Sgambati 32; Sibelius 10; Skriabin 3; Smetana 51; Smyth 17; Stanford 23; Strauss (J. ii) 50; Strauss (R.) 11; Suk 1; Sullivan 33; Taneiev 19; Tchaikovsky 35; Thomas (A.) 64; Vaughan Williams 3; Verdi 62; Wagner 62; Wolf 15.

	Title	Author of Words	Date Compos
1.	Opéra-comique, 'La Maison du docteur' (1 act)	Henry Boitteaux	Very e
2.	Operetta, 'Le Docteur Miracle' (1 act)	Léon Battu and Ludo-vic Halévy	1856 or
3.	Opera, 'Parisina'	Felice Romani	185
4.	Opéra-comique (1 act) [title unknown]	Edmond About	185
5.	Opera buffa, 'Don Procopio' (2 acts)	Carlo Cambiaggio	1858
6.	Opera, 'Esmeralda'	Victor Hugo	185
7.	Opera, 'Le Tonnelier de Nurem-berg' (3 acts)	E. T. A. Hoffmann (based on)	185
8.	Opera, 'Don Quichotte'	Cervantes (based on)	185
9.	Opéra-comique, 'L'Amour peintre'	Bizet, based on Molière	186
10.	Opéra-comique, 'La Guzla de l'Émir' (1 act)	Jules Barbier and Michel Carré	1861
11.	Opera, 'Les Pêcheurs de perles' (3 acts)	Michel Carré and E. Cormon	1862
12.	Opera, 'Ivan le Terrible' (5 acts)	Arthur Leroy and Henri Trianon	186
13.	Opera, 'Nicolas Flamel'	Ernest Dubreuil	? 186
14.	Opera, 'La Jolie Fille de Perth' (4 acts)	J. H. Vernoy de Saint-Georges and Jules Adenis	186
15.	Operetta, 'Malbrough s'en va-t-en guerre' (4 acts)	Paul Siraudin and William Busnach	186
16.	Opera [title unknown]	Arthur Leroy and Thomas Sauvage	186

known ormance	First Publication	Remarks
None	None	MS. at Conservatoire (vocal score only)
or. 1857	None	MS. at Conservatoire
None	None	Projected; perhaps not begun
None	None	Projected; probably not begun
ar. 1906	Choudens 1905 (vocal score only)	MS. full score at Conservatoire, differing in essentials from published vocal score
None	None	Projected; probably not begun
None	None	Projected; probably not begun
None	None	Projected; probably not begun
None	None	Unfinished; probably destroyed
None	None	Probably destroyed
ept. 1863	Choudens 1863 (vocal score only; full score much later)	1863 score differs in essentials from all later scores
1946	None	MS. at Conservatoire; Act V unfinished
None	None	Projected; partly sketched at piano
Dec. 1867	Choudens 1868 (vocal score only; full score much later)	1868 score differs in essentials from all later scores
Dec. 1867	None	Act I only by Bizet; probably destroyed
None	None	Projected

I. DRAMA

	Title	Author of Words	Date of Composition
17.	Opera, 'La Coupe du Roi de Thule' (3 acts)	Louis Gallet and Édouard Blau	1868
18.	Opera, 'Les Templiers' (5 acts)	Léon Halévy	? 186
19.	Opera, 'Noé' (3 acts)	J. H. Vernoy de Saint-Georges	1868-
20.	Opera, 'Vercingétorix'	?	?
21.	Opéra-comique, 'Calendal' (3 acts)	Paul Ferrier	1870
22.	Opéra-comique, 'Clarissa Harlowe' (3 acts)	Philippe Gille	1870-
23.	Opéra-comique, 'Grisélidis' (3 acts)	Victorien Sardou	1870-
24.	Opéra-comique, 'Djamileh' (1 act)	Louis Gallet	1871
25.	Incidental music, 'L'Arlésienne'	Alphonse Daudet	1872
26.	Operetta, 'Sol-si-ré-pif-pan' (1 act)	William Busnach	1872
27.	Opera, 'Don Rodrigue' (5 acts)	Louis Gallet and Édouard Blau	1873
28.	Opéra-comique, 'Carmen' (4 acts)	Henri Meilhac and Ludovic Halévy	1873-

NOTE. Conservatoire MSS. 453 and 466 (sketch

II. ORCH

29.	Overture in A minor–major	...	c. 185
30.	Symphony in C major	...	1855
31.	Symphony	...	1859
32.	Scherzo and 'Marche funèbre' (F minor)	...	1860-

¹ See Nos. 35, 78,

tinued

st known rformance	*First Publication*	*Remarks*
None[1]	None[1]	Fragmentary MS. at Conservatoire.
None	None	Unfinished; ? not begun
pr. 1885	Choudens 1885 (vocal score only)	Completion of F. Halévy's opera
None	None	Projected
None	None	Projected; perhaps not begun
None	None	MS. sketches at Conservatoire
None	None	Unfinished
May 1872	Choudens 1872 (vocal score) 1892 (full score)	
Oct. 1872	Choudens 1872 (vocal score; full score later)	See also No. 37
Nov. 1872	None	Probably destroyed. See p. 58
None	None	Unfinished. MS. at Conservatoire
Mar. 1875	Choudens 1875 (vocal score) ? 1880 (full score)	1875 vocal score contains passages omitted in all later scores

n unknown *mélodrame*) are spurious.

None	None	MS. at Conservatoire
Feb. 1935	Universal 1935	
None	None	Two versions begun; destroyed Dec. 1859
ov. 1861	None	Scherzo used in No. 34. MS. of Marche at Conservatoire

4, 95, 98, 125, 126.

II. ORCHESTR.

	Title	Author of Words	Date of Compositi.
33.	Overture, 'La Chasse d'Ossian'	...	1861
34.	Symphony in C major ('Roma')	...	1860–8
35.	'Marche funèbre' (B minor)	...	1868
36.	Petite Suite	...	1871
37.	Suite, 'L'Arlésienne'	...	1872
38.	Overture, 'Patrie'	...	1873

III. KE

39.	Four Preludes (C major, A minor, G major, E minor)	...	Very earl
40.	Valse in C major	...	Very earl
41.	'Thème brillant' in C major	...	Very earl
42.	First 'Caprice original' in C sharp minor	...	Very earl
43.	'Romance sans paroles' in C major	...	Very earl
44.	Second 'Caprice original' in C major	...	Very earl
45.	Grande Valse de concert in E flat major	...	1854
46.	'Nocturne' in F major	...	1854
47.	'Chasse fantastique'	...	? 1865
48.	'Chants du Rhin' (6 pieces)	Based on poems by Méry	1865
49.	'Trois Esquisses musicales' (piano or harmonium)	...	? 1866
50.	'Marine'	...	? 1868
51.	'Variations chromatiques de concert'	...	1868
52.	'Nocturne' in D major	...	1868
53.	'Jeux d'enfants' (12 pieces for piano duet)	...	1871

Also a great many arrangements, includi

ntinued

First known performance	*First Publication*	*Remarks*
? None	None	Lost
Feb. 1869	Choudens 1880	Includes Scherzo from No. 32, also No. 79. ? again revised 1871
Dec. 1880	Choudens 1881	Originally Prelude to No. 17
Mar. 1873	Durand 1882	Arrangement of 5 pieces from No. 53
Nov. 1872	Choudens ? 1876	Arrangement of 4 pieces from No. 25. Second Suite by Guiraud
Feb. 1874	Choudens 1874	

RD

...	None	MS. at Conservatoire
...	None	MS. at Conservatoire
...	None	MS. at Conservatoire
Oct. 1938	None	MS. at Conservatoire
...	None	MS. at Conservatoire
...	None	MS. at Conservatoire
Oct. 1938	None	MS. at Conservatoire
Oct. 1938	None	MS. at Conservatoire
...	Heugel 1865	
...	Heugel 1865	
...	Heugel 1866	
...	Hartmann 1868	Originally entitled 'La Chanson du matelot, souvenir d'Ischia'
...	Hartmann 1868	
...	Hartmann 1868	
...	Durand 1872	See No. 36

e of his own songs and dramatic pieces.

IV. Miscellaneou

	Title	Author of Words	Date of Composit
54.	Various fugues and exercises	...	1850–?
55.	Fugue in 4 parts	...	1854
56.	Fugue in 4 parts	...	1855
57.	Fugue in 2 parts	...	1866
58.	'L'âme humaine est pareille au doux ciel'	Lamartine	Very ea
59.	'Petite Marguerite'	Olivier Rolland	? 1854
60.	'La Rose et l'abeille'	Olivier Rolland	? 1854
61.	'Vieille Chanson'	Millevoye	? 1865
62.	'Adieux de l'hôtesse arabe'	Victor Hugo	1866
63.	'Après l'Hiver'	Victor Hugo	1866
64.	'Douce Mer'	Lamartine	1866
65.	'Chanson d'avril'	Louis Bouilhet	? 1866
66.	'À une Fleur'	Alfred de Musset	1866
67.	'Adieux à Suzon'	Alfred de Musset	1866
68.	'Sonnet'	Ronsard	1866
69.	'Guitare'	Victor Hugo	1866
70.	'Rose d'amour'	Millevoye	1866
71.	'Le Grillon'	Lamartine	1866
72.	'Pastorale'	Regnard	1868
73.	'Rêve de la bien-aimée'	Louis de Courmont	1868
74.	'Ma vie a son secret'	Félix Arvers	1868
75.	'Berceuse'	Mme Desbordes-Valmore	1868
76.	'La Chanson du fou'	Victor Hugo	1868
77.	'La Coccinelle'	Victor Hugo	1868
78.	'La Sirène'	Catulle Mendès	1868
79.	'Le Doute'	Paul Ferrier	by 186
80.	'L'Esprit Saint'	?	?
81.	'Absence'	Théophile Gautier	?
82.	'Chant d'amour'	Lamartine	?
83.	'Tarantelle'	Édouard Pailleron	?
84.	'Vous ne priez pas'	Casimir Delavigne	?

STRUMENTAL WORKS

First known Performance	First Publication	Remarks
None	None	MSS. at Conservatoire
None	None	2nd Prize, 1854. MS. at Conservatoire
None	None	1st Prize, 1855. ? Lost
None	None	Written for Galabert. ? Lost

NGS

Oct. 1938	None	MS. at Conservatoire
...	Cendrier 1854	Reissued by Choudens in 1888 as 'Rive d'amour' and 'En Avril,' with new words by Armand Silvestre
...	Cendrier 1854	
...	Choudens 1865	
...	Choudens 1867	
...	Choudens 1867	
...	Choudens 1867	
...	Choudens 1867	
...	Heugel 1866	
...	Heugel 1866	
...	Heugel 1866	Published together as 'Feuilles d'album'
...	Heugel 1866	
...	Heugel 1866	
...	Heugel 1866	
...	Hartmann 1868	
...	Hartmann 1868	
...	Hartmann 1868	
...	Hartmann 1868	
...	Hartmann 1868	
...	Hartmann 1868	
...	Choudens 1886	Dramatic fragment from No. 17
...	Choudens 1886	? Dramatic fragment. Used in No. 34
...	Choudens 1869	
...	Choudens 1872	
...	Choudens 1872	
...	Choudens 1872	
...	Choudens 1873	

V. Son

	Title	Author of Words	Date of Compositi
85.	'Le Colibri'	Alexandre Glan	*c.* 1868–?
86.	Serenade, 'Oh, quand je dors'	Victor Hugo	?
87.	'Vœu'	Victor Hugo	?
88.	'Voyage'	Philippe Gille	?
89.	'Aubade'	Paul Ferrier	?
90.	'La Nuit'	Paul Ferrier	1868
91.	'Conte'	Paul Ferrier	?
92.	'Aimons, rêvons!'	Paul Ferrier	? 1868
93.	'La Chanson de la rose'	Jules Barbier	?
94.	'Le Gascon'	Catulle Mendès	? 1868
95.	'N'oublions pas!'	Jules Barbier	1868
96.	'Si vous aimez!'	Philippe Gille	?
97.	'Pastel'	Philippe Gille	?
98.	'L'Abandonnée'	Catulle Mendès	? 1868

Excerpts from the published drama

VI. Miscellaneo

99.	Vocalise for soprano in C major	...	1850
100.	Vocalise for two sopranos in F major	...	1850
101.	'Chœar d'étudiants,' male chorus and orchestra	Scribe	Early
102.	Valse in G major, mixed chorus and orchestra	?	1855
103.	Cantata, 'L'Ange et Tobie'	Léon Halévy	*c.* 1855–
104.	Cantata, 'Héloïse de Montfort'	Émile Deschamps	*c.* 1855–
105.	Cantata, 'Le Chevalier enchanté'	Marquis de Pastoret	*c.* 1855–
106.	Cantata, 'Herminie'	Vinaty	*c.* 1855–
107.	Cantata, 'Le Retour de Virginie'	Rollet	*c.* 1855–

tinued

st known *rformance*	*First Publication*	*Remarks*		
Oct. 1938	None	Rejected from 'Vingt Mélodies,' 1873. MS. at Conservatoire		
...	None	MS. at Conservatoire		
Oct. 1938	None	MS. at Conservatoire		
...	Choudens 1886	Used in No. 124		
...	Choudens 1886			
...	Choudens 1886	Used in No. 126		
		From No. 17	Most, if not all, o	
...	Choudens 1886		these are excerpts	
...	Choudens 1886	Used in No. 125	from unfinished	
		? From No. 17	dramatic works,	
...	Choudens 1886		fitted with fresh	
...	Choudens 1886	? From No. 17	words after Bizet's	
...	Choudens 1886	From No. 17	death	
...	Choudens 1886			
...	Choudens 1886			
...	Choudens 1886	? From No. 17		

ks are excluded from the above list.

CAL WORKS

...	None	MS. at Conservatoire	
...	None	MS. at Conservatoire	
...	None	MS. at Conservatoire	
...	None	MS. at Conservatoire	
None	None	Unfinished. MS. at Conservatoire	
None	None	Unfinished. MS. at Conservatoire	
None	None	Unfinished. MS. at Conservatoire	
None	None	Unfinished. MS. at Conservatoire	
None	None	MS. at Conservatoire	

	Title	Author of Words	Date o Composit
108.	Cantata, 'David'	Gaston d'Albano	1856
109.	Choruses for competitions	?	1856—
110.	Cantata, 'Clovis et Clotilde'	Amédée Burion	1857
111.	'Te Deum,' soli, chorus and orchestra	...	1858
112.	Ode Symphony, 'Ulysse et Circé'	Based on Homer	1859
113.	Ode Symphony, 'Vasco de Gama'	Louis Delâtre, altered by Bizet	1859—6
114.	Cantata, 'Carmen saeculare'	Horace	1860
115.	'Le Golfe de Bahia,' soprano or tenor, chorus and piano	Lamartine	by 186
116.	'Saint-Jean de Pathmos,' part-song for male voices	Victor Hugo	? 1866
117.	'Chants des Pyrénées'	Traditional	? 1867
118.	Cantata, 'Les Noces de Pro-méthée'	?	1867
119.	Hymn	?	1867
120.	Cantique, 'La mort s'avance,' mixed chorus and orchestra	Abbé Pellegrin	?
121.	'Ave Maria'	Charles Grandmougin	?
122.	Duo, 'La Fuite'	Théophile Gautier	?
123.	'La Chanson du rouet,' solo voice, chorus and piano	Édouard Blau	?
124.	Duo, 'Le Retour'	Jules Barbier	?
125.	Duo, 'Rêvons'	Jules Barbier	? 1868
126.	Duettino, 'Les Nymphes des bois'	Jules Barbier	1868
127.	Oratorio, 'Geneviève de Paris'	Louis Gallet	1874—5

The four so-called *Motets et Hymnes* are all arrangemen

The manuscripts of many of the publish

AL WORKS—*continued*

t known ormance	First Publication	Remarks
...	None	2nd Prix de Rome. ? Lost
None	None	MSS. at Conservatoire
ct. 1857	None	1st Prix de Rome. MS. at Conservatoire
None	None	MS. at Conservatoire
None	None	Projected; probably not begun
863	Choudens 1880	
None	None	Unfinished; ? destroyed
...	Choudens 1880	Used in No. 12. A version for piano solo also exists
...	Choudens	
...	Flaxland 1867	Accompaniments to 6 'Mélodies Populaires'
None	None	Written for competition. Lost
None	None	Written for competition. Lost
...	None	MS. at Conservatoire
...	None	? Lost
...	Choudens 1872	
...	Choudens 1880	
...	Choudens 1887	See No. 88
...	Choudens 1887	See No. 92. ? From No. 17
...	Choudens 1887	See No. 90. From No. 17
None	None	Projected; probably not begun

Posthumous dramatic fragments fitted with fresh words

(probably all) of which were not made by Bizet.

are also at the Conservatoire.

APPENDIX C

About, Edmond François Valentin (1828–85), French writer, born in Lorraine. Studied archaeology in Athens. Wrote novels and political pamphlets, one of which cost him a week's imprisonment from the Germans after the war of 1870.

Adam, Adolphe Charles (1803–56), French composer. Prolific writer of ballet and *opéra-comique*. Professor of composition at the Paris Conservatoire from 1849.

Aubryet, Xavier (1827–?), minor French music critic. Published a volume *Les Jugements nouveaux* in 1860.

Banville, Théodore de (1823–91), French lyric poet. Also a literary and musical critic.

Bellaigue, Camille (1858–1930), French music critic. A prolific author of musical biographies, including an early Life of Verdi. Attached to the *Revue des Deux Mondes* from 1885.

Benoist, François (1791–1878), French organist and composer, professor of organ at the Paris Conservatoire 1819–72. Prix de Rome 1815; composed operas, ballets and a mass.

Benoît, Camille (1851–1923), French composer, pupil of César Franck. Curator of the Louvre museum from 1895.

Béranger, Pierre Jean de (1780–1857), French poet. Wrote many popular songs, the satirical tone of which brought him government persecution and imprisonment.

Blaze de Bury, Baron Henri (1813–88), French writer on music, mostly under the name of F. de Lagenevais. Succeeded Scudo as music critic of the *Revue des Deux Mondes* 1864.

Bouhy, Jacques Joseph André (1848–1929), Belgian baritone singer. Studied at Liège and Paris, where he first appeared at the Opéra in 1872. The first Escamillo in *Carmen*. Director of the New York Conservatoire 1885–9.

Bülow, Hans Guido von (1830–94), German pianist and conductor, first husband of Cosima Wagner (*née* Liszt).

Calvé, Emma (real name *Rose Emma Calvet*) (1858–1942), French soprano singer. One of the most successful interpreters of Carmen.

Carafa. See note, p. 15.

Carvalho, Léon. See note, p. 38.

Çarvalho, Marie Caroline Félix (*née Miolan*) (1827–95), French soprano singer. Married the impresario Léon Carvalho in 1853. Created the heroines in most of Gounod's successful operas.

Castro, Guilhem da (1569–1631), Spanish dramatist. Corneille owed much to his play on the Cid.

Clapisson, Antoine Louis (1808–66), French composer and violinist. A successful composer of *opéra-comique*, he was elected to the Academy in preference to Berlioz.

Clément, Félix (1822–85), French composer and writer on music. Compiler of compendious encyclopaedias on church music and opera.

Colonne, Édouard (really *Judas*) (1838–1910), French conductor and violinist. Founder of Concerts Colonne 1873. The first to popularize Berlioz.

Combarieu, Jules Léon Jean (1859–1916), French musicologist. Founder of the *Revue Musicale* and author of an important history of music.

Comettant, Jean Pierre Oscar (1819–98), French pianist and music critic, for many years on the staff of *Le Siècle*.

Daudet, Alphonse (1840–97), French novelist and dramatist, renowned for his studies of Provençal peasant life.

David, Félicien César (1810–76), French composer. Travelled in the east and introduced mild orientalism to western music in his symphonic ode *Le Désert* (1844).

Delaborde, Élie Miriam (1839–1913), French pianist and composer, pupil of Alkan and Moscheles, professor at the Paris Conservatoire 1873. The war of 1870 drove him to London with his hundred and twenty-one parrots and cockatoos.

Delmas, Marc Marie Jean Baptiste (1885–1931), French composer and writer on music. Prix de Rome 1919.

Delsarte, François Alexandre Nicolas Chéri. See p. 2.

Dubois, François Clément Théodore (1837–1924), French composer. Prix de Rome 1861. Organist at the Madeleine 1877, director of Paris Conservatoire 1896–1905.

Escudier, Léon (1821–81), French music critic and publisher. With his brother Marie he wrote a *Dictionnaire de Musique* (1844) and published many of Verdi's works.

Faure, Jean Baptiste (1830–1911), French baritone singer. Leading baritone at the Paris Opéra for many years from 1861.

Galli-Marié, Marie Célestine Laurence (1840–1905), French mezzo-soprano singer. First appeared at Strasbourg in 1859. The original Carmen.

García, Manuel del Popolo Vicente (1775–1832), Spanish tenor singer and composer. Author of many rudimentary operas based on folksong, in which he himself appeared. His three children were all famous singers.

Gasperini, A. de (c. 1825–68), French music critic. Wrote for *Nation*, *Liberté* and *Figaro* (1861–7).

Gauthier-Villars, Henry (1859–1931), French author and music critic, advocate of Wagner in France. Published many of his books under the pseudonym Willy.

Gautier, Théophile (1811–72), French poet and novelist. For a time dramatic and musical critic of *La Presse* and *Le Moniteur Universel*.

Gouvy, Louis Théodore (1819–98), German-French composer. Of French parentage and education, he lived mostly in Germany, where he found himself more appreciated. Composer of seven symphonies.

Grisar, Albert (1808–69), Belgian composer. Abandoned a business career at Liverpool for successful light opera in Paris.

Guiraud, Ernest (1837–92), French composer, born at New Orleans. Prix de Rome 1859. Professor of composition at the Paris Conservatoire from 1876.

Habeneck, François Antoine (1781–1849), French violinist and conductor, of German descent. Founder of Société des Concerts du Conservatoire, conductor at the Paris Opéra 1824–47. The first conductor to cultivate Beethoven in France.

Halévy (really *Lévy*), *Jacques François Fromental Élie* (1799–1862), French composer of Jewish extraction. Prix de Rome 1819. Composed many operas in various styles. Professor at the Paris Conservatoire from 1827.

Halévy, Léon (1802–83), archaeologist and dramatist, brother of the above. Wrote librettos for his brother and others.

Halévy, Ludovic (1834–1908), dramatist, son of the above. Author (in collaboration with Henry Meilhac) of many librettos for Offenbach.

Heller, Stephen (1814–88), Hungarian pianist and composer, resident in Paris from 1838.

Hérold, Louis Joseph Ferdinand (1791–1833), French composer. Prix de Rome 1812. Wrote numerous light operas (many in collaboration) and died of consumption.

Heugel, Jacques Léopold (1815–83), French music publisher and founder of the musical periodical *Le Ménestrel* (1833).

Hoffman, Ernst Theodor Wilhelm (1776–1822), German novelist and amateur composer of operas. Changed his third name to Amadeus in homage to Mozart. The hero of Offenbach's *Contes d'Hoffmann*.

Imbert, Hugues (1842–1905), French writer on music. Attempted to popularize Brahms in France.

Isouard, Niccolo (1775–1818), Maltese composer. Abandoned the study of artillery for music and wrote numerous light operas in Paris.

Istel, Edgar (born 1880), German musicologist and composer. Has written on Spanish folksong and various aspects of opera, and now lives in U.S.A.

Jonas, Émile (1827–1905), French composer. Professor of solfège at the Paris Conservatoire 1847–65, bandmaster and copious composer of operettas.

Joncières, Victorin de (real name *Félix Ludger Rossignol*) (1839–1903), French composer and critic, originally a painter. Opera composer, an early French admirer of Wagner and music critic of *La Liberté* from 1871.

Jouvin, Benoît Jean Baptiste (known as *Bénédict*) (1820–?), French music critic. On staff of *Le Figaro* from 1856. Wrote books on Auber and Hérold.

Jullien, Jean Lucien Adolphe (1845–1932), French critic. A passionate champion of Wagner, Berlioz and other composers then regarded as modern. Music critic of the *Journal des Débats* for over fifty years.

Karg-Elert (really *Karg*), *Sigfrid* (1877–1933), German organist, pianist and composer.

Lacombe, Paul (1837–1927), French composer. Correspondence pupil of Bizet.

Lamoureux, Charles (1834–99), French violinist and conductor. His Concerts Lamoureux (1881) popularized Wagner with the French public.

Landormy, Paul Charles René (1869–1943), French critic. Author of many books on history of music.

Laparra, Raoul (1876–1943), French composer and writer on music. Wrote operas in a Spanish idiom.

Lecocq, Alexandre Charles (1832–1918), French composer. A prosperous composer of operettas in the Offenbach manner.

Legouvé, Ernest (1807–1903), French dramatist. Collaborated with Scribe in *Adrienne Lecouvreur* (1849).

Litolff, Henry Charles (1818–91), Anglo-Alsatian composer mostly resident in Paris. He owned a successful music-publishing business at Brunswick.

Malherbe, Charles Théodore (1853–1911), French musicologist. Librarian at the Opéra from 1898. A famous collector of musical autographs.

Mapleson, James Henry (1830–1901), English impresario. He sang opera in Italy, managed a number of London opera-houses, called himself a colonel and published a book of chatty reminiscences (*The Mapleson Memoirs* 1888).

Maréchal, Charles Henri (1842–1924), French composer. Prix de Rome 1870. Inspector of musical education 1896. Wrote mostly for the stage.

Marmontel, Antoine François (1816–98), French pianist and teacher. Professor of piano at the Paris Conservatoire from 1848.

Massé, Félix Marie (known as *Victor*) (1822–84), French composer. Prix de Rome 1844. Professor of composition at the Paris Conservatoire from 1866. A facile composer of operas and operettas.

Mendès, Catulle (1841–1909), French poet, journalist and dramatist, author of several opera librettos.

Mercadante, Giuseppe Saverio Raffaele (1795–1870), Italian composer, mostly of operas and masses. Director of the Naples Conservatoire from 1840.

Mérimée, Prosper (1803–70), French novelist and author of archaeological and historical dissertations.

Méry, Joseph (1798–1865), French poet.

Mistral, Frédéri (1830–1914), Provençal poet, author of several epics in the Provençal language. Nobel prize 1904.

Mogador, Céleste (real name *Vénard,* afterwards *Comtesse Moreton de Chabrillan*) (1824–1909), French actress, circus-rider, author and courtesan. Published plays, novels, poems and memoirs.

Mottl, Felix (1856–1911), Austrian conductor and composer, worked under Wagner and (1881–1903) at Carlsruhe, where he revived many unfamiliar works.

Nilsson, Christine (1843–1921), Swedish soprano singer. Appeared first in Paris 1864, London 1867.

Paer, Ferdinando (1771–1839), Italian composer. Wrote operas for Venice, Vienna and Dresden and finally settled in Paris.

Paladilhe, Émile (1844–1926), French composer. Prix de Rome 1860.

Pasdeloup, Jules Étienne (1819–87), French conductor. Founded the Société des Jeunes Artistes du Conservatoire (1851) and the Concerts Pasdeloup (1861), at which he introduced many unfamiliar works.

Perrin, Émile César Victor (1814–85), French impresario. Successful manager at various times of the Opéra-Comique, Opéra and Théâtre Français in Paris.

Pougin, François Auguste Arthur Eugène Paroisse- (1834–1921), French musicologist. A prolific author, biographer and contributor to periodicals.

Reber, Napoléon Henri (1807–80), French composer. Professor of harmony (1851) and composition (1862) at the Paris Conservatoire.

Reyer (originally *Rey), Louis Ernest Étienne* (1823–1909), French composer. Wrote operas on oriental and Nibelungian subjects and succeeded Berlioz as music critic of the *Journal des Débats*.

Roqueplan (really *Rocoplan), Louis Victor Nestor* (1804–70), French journalist and impresario. Director of the Paris Opéra (1847–54), Opéra-Comique (1857–60) and other theatres. Dramatic critic of *Le Constitutionnel*.

Roze, Marie Hippolyte (née *Ponsin*) (1846–1926), French soprano singer. Appeared first at the Opéra-Comique in 1865. For some years a member of the Carl Rosa Company in England.

Saint-Georges, Jules Henri Vernoy, Marquis de (1801–75), French novelist and librettist. Wrote a hundred and twenty librettos for Donizetti, Auber, Adam, Halévy, etc.

Saint-Victor, Paul de (1825–81), French literary and musical critic. A formalist of the old school.

Sarasate y Navascues, Pablo Martín Melitón (1844–1908), Spanish violinist and composer, studied at Paris Conservatoire.

Sarcey, Francisque (1827–99), French journalist and dramatic critic.

Sardou, Victorien (1831–1908), French dramatist. Many of his melo-dramatic plays were found suitable for conversion into opera librettos.

Scribe, Eugène (1791–1861), French dramatist and librettist. A prolific manufacturer of opera and *opéra-comique* librettos, especially for the school of Meyerbeer, Halévy, Auber, etc.

Scudo, Pierre (originally *Pietro*) (1806–64), Italian critic who lived in Paris and wrote in French. After failing as a singer he took to criticism and became music critic of the *Revue des Deux Mondes*.

Séré, Octave (pseudonym of *Jean Poueigh*) (born 1876), French critic and composer, pupil of Fauré and Lenepveu.

Soubies, Albert (1846–1918), French musicologist. Wrote many historical works, especially on opera.

Tarbé, Edmond, French critic, son of a female amateur composer. Some time music critic of *Le Figaro*. Founder and director (1869–77) of *Le Gaulois*.

Thalberg, Sigismond (1812–71), Austrian pianist and composer, natural son of a count and a baroness. Toured with great success as a salon virtuoso.

Tiersot, Jean Baptiste Élisée Julien (1857–1936), French musicologist and composer, pupil of Massenet and Franck. Librarian at the Paris Con-servatoire from 1910 and President of Société Française de Musicologie.

Vidal, François (1832–?), Provençal poet and author of a work on the tambourine and pipe (galoubet) of Provence.

Weber, Johannès (1818–1902), French critic. Secretary to Meyerbeer in Paris. Music critic of *Le Temps*, 1861–95.

Weissmann, Adolf (1873–1929), German music critic, author of many biographical studies and historical works.

Wilder, Jérôme Albert Victor (van) (1835–82), Belgian critic and poet. Made French translations of many great works, including *Messiah* and Wagner's later operas.

Yradier, Sebastián (1809–65), Spanish composer. Was singing-master to Empress Eugénie in Paris and lived for some years in Cuba. Wrote popular Spanish songs based on folk melodies.

Zimmerman, Pierre Joseph Guillaume (1785–1853), French pianist, teacher and composer. Professor of piano at the Paris Conservatoire from 1820. He was Gounod's father-in-law.

APPENDIX D

BIBLIOGRAPHY

(NOTE.—*Only a few of the most important periodical references are listed below. A great number of other books and periodicals have been used in the compilation of this book.*)

Bellaigue, Camille, 'Georges Bizet, sa vie et son œuvre.' (Paris, 1891.)

Berlioz, Hector, 'Les Musiciens et la musique.' (Paris, 1903.)

Berton, Pierre, 'Souvenirs de la vie de théâtre.' (Paris, 1913.)

Bizet, Georges, 'Lettres à un ami, 1865–72,' ed. Edmond Galabert. (Paris, 1909.)

—— 'Lettres. Impressions de Rome, 1857–60. La Commune, 1871,' ed. Louis Ganderax. (Paris, 1908.)

—— 'Exposition Georges Bizet au Théâtre National de l'Opéra,' illustrated catalogue. (Paris, 1938.)

—— 'Georges Bizet,' inauguration of monument. (Paris, privately, 1876.)

Burgess, Francis, 'Carmen.' (London, 1905.)

Chantavoine, Jean, 'Quelques Inédits de Georges Bizet,' in *Le Ménestrel*, 4th August–22nd September 1933.

Charlot, André and Jean, 'À propos de la Millième de Carmen,' in *L'Art du Théâtre*, January 1905.

Cooper, Martin, 'Georges Bizet.' (London, 1938.)

—— 'Carmen.' (London, 1947.)

Delmas, Marc, 'Georges Bizet.' (Paris, 1930.)

Galabert, Edmond, 'Georges Bizet. Souvenirs et Correspondance.' (Paris, 1877.)

Gallet, Louis, 'Notes d'un librettiste.' (Paris, 1891.)

Gatti, Guido M., 'Giorgio Bizet.' (Turin, 1914.)

Gaudier, Charles, 'Carmen de Bizet.' (Paris, 1922.)

Gauthier-Villars, Henry, 'Bizet.' (Paris, 1911.)

Grélinger, Charles, 'Bizet.' (Paris, n.d., *c.* 1915.)

Halévy, Ludovic, 'La Millième Représentation de Carmen,' in *Le Théâtre*, January 1905.

Hühne, Fritz, 'Die Oper Carmen als ein Typus musikalischer Poetik.' (Greifswald, 1915.)

Imbert, Hugues, 'Portraits et études. Lettres inédites de Georges Bizet.' (Paris, 1894.)

Imbert, Hugues, 'Georges Bizet.' (Paris, 1899.)

—— 'Médaillons contemporains.' (Paris, 1903.)

Imsan, Dora, 'Carmen, Charakter-Entwicklung für die Bühne.' (Darmstadt, 1917.)

Istel, Edgar, 'Bizet und Carmen.' (Stuttgart, 1927.)

Jullien, Adolphe, 'Musiciens d'aujourd'hui.' (Paris, 1892.)

Landormy, Paul, 'Bizet.' (Paris, 1924.)

Laparra, Raoul, 'Bizet et l'Espagne.' (Paris, 1935.)

Malherbe, Henry, 'Georges Bizet.' (Paris, 1921.)

Maréchal, Henri, 'Paris: Souvenirs d'un musicien.' (Paris, 1907.)

Marmontel, Antoine, 'Symphonistes et virtuoses.' (Paris, 1881.)

Mastrigli, Leopoldo, 'Giorgio Bizet: la sua vita e le sue opere.' (Rome, 1888.)

Moser, Françoise, 'Vie et aventures de Céleste Mogador.' (Paris, 1935.)

Musica, special Bizet number, June 1912.

Nietzsche, Friedrich, 'Randglossen zu Bizets Carmen,' ed. Hugo Daffner. (Ratisbon, 1912.)

Northcott, Richard, 'Bizet and Carmen.' (London, 1916.)

Parker, D. C., 'Georges Bizet, his Life and Works.' (London, 1926.)

Pigot, Charles, 'Georges Bizet et son œuvre.' (Paris, 1886; 2nd ed. with additions, 1911.)

Rabe, Julius, 'Georges Bizet.' (Stockholm, 1925.)

Revue de Musicologie, special Bizet number, November 1938.

Revue de Paris, 15th December 1899. (Gounod's correspondence with Bizet.)

Reyer, Ernest, 'Quarante Ans de musique.' (Paris, 1910.)

Saint-Saëns, Camille, 'Portraits et souvenirs.' (Paris, 1900.)

Séré, Octave, 'Musiciens français d'aujourd'hui. (Paris, 1915.)

Servières, Georges, 'Georges Bizet d'après les souvenirs de Pierre Berton,' in *Le Guide musical*, 8th–22nd March 1914.)

Soubies, Albert, 'Histoire du Théâtre-Lyrique, 1851–70.' (Paris, 1899.)

Soubies, Albert, and *Malherbe, Charles*, 'Histoire de l'Opéra-Comique.' (Paris, 1892.)

Tiersot, Julien, 'Un Demi-siècle de musique française, 1870–1917.' (Paris, 1918.)

—— 'Bizet and Spanish music,' in *The Musical Quarterly*, October 1925.

Voss, Paul, 'Georges Bizet.' (Leipzig, 1899.)

Weissmann, Adolf, 'Bizet.' (Berlin, 1907.)

Wilder, Victor, Obituary notice in *Le Ménestrel*, 4th–18th July 1875.

APPENDIX E

No doubt you have sometimes come across people, very intelligent and enlightened people at that, who seriously maintain the following somewhat paradoxical opinion: 'In order to give a sound estimate of a work of art, the first necessity is not to be an artist oneself.' There follow, in confirmation of this strange aphorism, a string of more or less specious reasons which may be roughly summed up as follows: 'Eclecticism, from which impartiality springs, is the critical virtue above all others; an artist with a strong personality cannot be eclectic; therefore art criticism should be confined to diplomats, doctors, financiers, writers—every honest citizen in fact who can read or write, provided he is not painter nor sculptor nor architect nor musician.' This ingenious system is of course not extended beyond the realm of art; its most ardent partisans would consider it ridiculous if you suggested a sculptor to look after their children's health or a musical composer to look after their business. I agree that every educated and enlightened man of feeling has the power, and therefore the right, to praise or blame any artistic production whatever; but that the creative artist, continually busy both with the highest ideas and the specialities of his art, should not be allowed to judge the work of his peers, under whatever pretext of propriety or good fellowship, seems to me completely illogical and supremely unjust. Holding this conviction, and following the example of Berlioz and Reyer, I have, though myself a composer, accepted the post of musical critic to the *Revue Nationale*, which has kindly been entrusted to my inexperience and good will.

Being a very modest amateur in all that concerns literature, I have never till to-day taken up the pen except to converse with my friends. This is my first 'copy,' my journalistic début. A timid and blushing schoolgirl in her white ballroom dress is less nervous at her first waltz than I am at the prospect of seeing myself printed alive. I come therefore bravely to ask the indulgence of the public—that public, kindly and terrible by turns, that is so severe on the hoarseness of Monsieur X, so indulgent towards the huskiness of Mademoiselle Z. So you realize, my dear reader, that you will find in my column not the powerful imagery of Paul de Saint-Victor, nor the sparkling wit of Nestor Roqueplan, nor the enchanting style of Théophile Gautier, nor the formal elegance and conciseness of B. Jouvin, nor the congenial ardour of Gasperini, nor the quick sensitivity of Xavier Aubryet, nor the caustic vigour of Ernest Reyer, nor . . . But some ill-natured fellow interrupts me and cries: 'Then what *shall* we find, you humbug?' You will find, sir, not the talents of the masters I have just mentioned, but two of their most essential qualities with which I hope you will be satisfied: (i) a profound study of the art of music and all that appertains to it, (ii) a good faith which neither my friendships nor my enmities will be able to weaken. I will tell the truth, nothing but the truth, and so far as possible the whole truth. I belong to no clique, and I have no comrades; I have only friends, and they will cease to be my friends the day they no longer respect my freedom of judgment and complete independence. Confining myself to the examination of purely artistic matters, I shall study the works themselves without bothering about the labels they bear. Respect and justice for all, that is my slogan. Neither incense nor insults, that is my line of conduct.

Since I have begun a profession of faith, I will go on and plunge straight into my subject. For some years now the cult of system has made disturbing progress in art and art criticism. From it springs that barren warfare, those arid discussions which bewilder, sap and consume the boldest, strongest and most fertile movements. From it also come those divisions, subdivisions, classifications, definitions, sometimes ambiguous and often quite wrong, but always valueless and dangerous. Quibbling takes the place of progress, wrangling supersedes creation. Composers are growing rare, while parties and sects multiply without limit. Art is reduced to abject poverty, while technology flourishes in abundance. Judge of it yourselves: we have French music, German music, Italian music, and by way of accessory Russian music, Hungarian music, Polish music and so on, without counting Arab music, Japanese music and Tunisian music, all three much in favour since the opening of the Universal Exhibition. We have also the music of the future, the music of the present and the music of the past; then there is philosophical and ideological music, recently discovered by a very talented journalist, to whom in passing I am happy to express my high esteem and lively sympathy. We have, too, melodic music, harmonic music, learned music (the most dangerous of all) and finally a state-patented brand of cannon music.[1] But I forget: to-morrow we shall have needle music and screw music, force-pump music and double force-pump music—this last above all! What balderdash it all is! For me there are only two kinds of music—good and bad.

---

[1] An allusion to Rossini's *Chants des Titans* for four bass voices and orchestra, performed at the 1867 Exhibition.

Béranger defined art like this: 'Art is art, and that's all there is to it.'
For those who have ears to hear, these few words contain a far more useful
lesson than the weightiest tomes on aesthetics. Must we run down Molière
in order to love Shakespeare? Is not genius of all countries and all times?
Are not the tragedies of Aeschylus more 'of the future' than those of
Racine? Beauty does not grow old. Truth does not die. A poet,
painter or musician devotes the utmost of his brain and soul to the conception and execution of a work; he thinks, doubts, grows enthusiastic,
despairs, rejoices and suffers in turn; and when, more anxious and afraid
than a criminal, he comes to us and says 'Look, and judge,' instead of
letting ourselves be moved we ask him for his passport, we ask ourselves
about his opinions, his relations and his artistic antecedents. That is not
the business of criticism; it is police work. The artist has neither name nor
nationality. He is inspired or he is not; he has genius or talent or he has
not. If he has, we must adopt him, cherish him, acclaim him; if he has
not, we must respect him, condole with him—and forget him. Mention
Rossini, Auber, Gounod, Wagner, Berlioz, Félicien David, Pitanchu—
whoever you like. Make me laugh or cry; show me love, hate, fanaticism,
crime; charm me, dazzle me, carry me away: I shall never do you the
stupid injustice of classifying and labelling you like an insect in a show-
case. Let us be unaffected and genuine, not demanding from a great
artist the qualities he lacks, but learning to appreciate those he possesses.
When a passionate, violent, even brutal personality like Verdi endows our
art with a work that is vigorously alive and compounded of gold, mud,
blood and gall, do not let us go up to him and say coldly: 'But my dear
sir, this lacks taste, it is not gentlemanly.' *Gentlemanly!* Are Michelangelo, Dante, Homer, Shakespeare, Beethoven, Cervantes and Rabelais
gentlemanly? Must genius be dressed up with rice-powder and almond
icing? Let us rather order our zouaves to storm the battlements in white
ties and silk breeches! Pardon my anger. But if you knew all I have
read and heard in the last five or six years, all the grief and misery I have
shared! Believe me, prejudiced criticism is a cruel, terrible, mortal weapon.
I was the pupil and friend of Halévy; more than once I had his confidences
on this subject. Neither his high position nor his incontestable reputation
could console him for the unjust and odious attacks of which he was the
victim. I do not want to doubt the good faith of Monsieur X. I believe
he was blinded and led astray by passion and prejudice, but I could never
forgive him the extreme pain he caused to the famous and revered master
whose memory I cherish. If the bitter critic wants to learn the art of being
at the same time severe and polite, friendly and sincere, let him study the

articles of Messieurs Tarbé des Sablons and Gaston de Saint-Valry. I recommend these models of courtesy and good taste; these gentlemen at least know the respect due from every critic to conscientious and sincere workers. But I fear my advice is too good to be listened to.

One further word. I have a horror of pedantry and false erudition. Certain critics of the third and fourth rank use and abuse a so-called technical jargon which is as unintelligible to themselves as to the public. I shall take care to avoid this absurd error. You will find here no information about octaves, fifths, tritones, false fifths, dissonances, consonances, preparations, resolutions, suspensions, inversions, cadences broken, interrupted or avoided, canons in cancrizans or other refinements. I will refer those who love this pleasing language to the learned articles of Monsieur de L——,[1] where they will learn, among other matters of earth-shaking interest, that Nicolo wrote *Les Rendezvous bourgeois* in non-invertible counterpoint; that we must listen to Mendelssohn's scoring with the most scrupulous attention, the composer of *A Midsummer Night's Dream* having treated the second bassoon part as melodically as that of the first violin. They will also discover there an admirable dissertation on Meyerbeer's celebrated unison, including a most curious parallel between the round from *Les Porcherons* and the introduction to the fifth act of *L'Africaine*; the minor tenth is there treated as a major tenth with charming confidence and adorable candour. Anxious to share his enlightenment not only with the public but also with composers (thus incidentally showing a fine upright character), Monsieur de L. is prodigal of advice as novel as it is ingenious on the use of brass instruments in general and the trombones in particular. I do not dare quote from memory, being afraid of spoiling certain felicities of style, but I strongly urge the reader to be assiduous in following Monsieur de L.'s courses. They are edifying, instructive—and fun.

The musical programme, so slow-moving in ordinary times, has been brought to a complete standstill by that millionaire-fairy known as the Universal Exhibition. The cashiers of our lyric theatres are asking for help: composers without work, please note! *Don Carlos* and *L'Africaine* at the Opéra; *Mignon* and *L'Étoile du Nord* at the Opéra-Comique; *Roméo et Juliette* and *Faust* at the Théâtre-Lyrique; *L'Oca del Cairo* at the Fantaisies-Parisiennes; *La Grande Duchesse de Gérolstein* at the Variétés—such is the musical balance-sheet at present. Meyerbeer, Mozart, Gounod, Ambroise

---

[1] Probably F. de Lagenevais, pseudonym of Henri Blaze de Bury, who succeeded Scudo as musical critic of the *Revue des Deux Mondes* in 1864. He was one of those most scandalized by *Carmen* in 1875.

Thomas, Verdi, Offenbach: two of them dead, two French and two foreigners—these are the lucky ones to-day. All things considered, the choice is excellent, and the art of music is worthily represented. Let us give our approval and applause.

[There follows a catalogue of stage works in production or preparation, including Bizet's own *Jolie Fille de Perth*. The announcement of a probable production of *Lohengrin* at the Théâtre-Lyrique is accompanied by three exclamation marks, and Bizet notes: 'M. de Leuven has at last commissioned a one-act piece from Monsieur Conte, winner of the Grand Prix de Rome in 1855! This date has a dreary eloquence!']

Before all these works are admitted to the honour of performance, there will be a deal of impatience, disappointment and despair. I tell you in all truth, composers are the pariahs and the martyrs of modern society. Like the gladiators of old, they cry as they fall: *Salve, popule! te morituri salutant!* [*sic*]. Music! What a splendid art, but a dreary profession! Still, let us wait in patience, and above all let us hope!

INDEX

INDEX

Index

Index

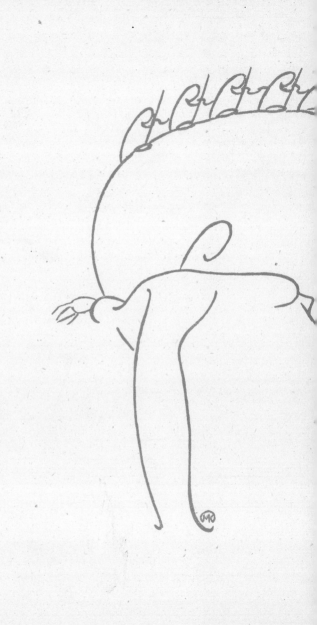